ROUTLEDGE LIBRARY EDITIONS:
ENVIRONMENTAL AND NATURAL
RESOURCE ECONOMICS

Volume 8

ECONOMICS AND LAND USE PLANNING

ECONOMICS AND LAND USE PLANNING

A.J. HARRISON

Routledge
Taylor & Francis Group
LONDON AND NEW YORK

First published in 1977 by Croom Helm Ltd

This edition first published in 2018
by Routledge
2 Park Square, Milton Park, Abingdon, Oxon OX14 4RN

and by Routledge
711 Third Avenue, New York, NY 10017

Routledge is an imprint of the Taylor & Francis Group, an informa business

British Library Cataloguing in Publication Data
A catalogue record for this book is available from the British Library

ISBN: 978-1-138-08283-0 (Set)
ISBN: 978-1-315-14775-8 (Set) (ebk)
ISBN: 978-1-138-08380-6 (Volume 8) (hbk)
ISBN: 978-1-138-08388-2 (Volume 8) (pbk)
ISBN: 978-1-315-11202-2 (Volume 8) (ebk)

ECONOMICS AND LAND USE PLANNING

A.J. HARRISON

CROOM HELM LONDON

Croom Helm Ltd
2-10 St. John's Road, London SW11

ISBN 0-85664-365-3 (hardback)
0-85664-470-6 (paperback)

Printed in Great Britain
by Redwood Burn Ltd, Trowbridge and Esher

CONTENTS

ACKNOWLEDGEMENTS

I would like to thank a number of former colleagues in the Department of the Environment for their comments and encouragement. They include Mike Gahagan, Sally Holtermann, Alan Robson, David Saunders, Laura Lyttelton and Mike Whitbread. In addition, I have been helped by papers written by other former colleagues, including Peter Carter (on uncertainty), Dick Dodwell (on shopping), Jeff Hollingworth (on offices) and Trevor Knight (on density control).

PART 1: BASIC ECONOMIC CONCEPTS

1 INTRODUCTION

1.1 Scope and Purpose of Book

The case for land-use planning is often taken for granted. Its purpose, in one recent text, is simply described as 'to produce the best use of land'. This definition might be taken to involve finding the best spatial arrangement of activities and the most suitable intensity of use for each parcel of land within the area being planned. The concerns of land-use planners in pursuit of these general objectives are familiar enough. Land-use planners think about such problems as where additional housing should be provided, where industrial sites should be allowed, how much redevelopment should take place on an inner-area site, how much shopping floor space should be provided. But why do these decisions fall to the public sector to make? Why are they not left to the individual household or firm?

There is no shortage of answers to these questions. Historically, one can point to nineteenth-century reformers horrified at the conditions which the unplanned growth of the great industrial cities produced or the later idealists such as Ebenezer Howard who, even after some of the worst evils had been tackled, pursued their various visions of the ideal balance between town and country, or to the major reports, Barlow, Scott and Uthwatt, which laid the foundations for much in British planning legislation. But partly because land-use planning has been used to redress obvious and agreed evils, the intellectual underpinnings have not been laid out and subject to analysis in the way, for example, that the case for central government management of the national economy has been examined, at both applied and theoretical level. In much of economics, the analysis or theory has preceded the application; in much of land-use planning the converse has been true.

Recently, however, land-use planning has come to attract critical analytic attention. It has become common to criticise those responsible for land-use plans for imposing their values on others, for ignoring the essentially political nature of their activities, for at one and the same time over- and underestimating the impact of their policies. For these reasons, such questions as 'why intervene?', 'when is intervention likely to be effective?' and 'what are the relative merits of different kinds of intervention?' are of current relevance. This book aims to answer these and similar questions using the concepts of modern micro-economics.

Economists and land-use planners have not in general got on too well together. But there are many signs now that the case for linking economic analysis to land-use planning is being recognised more widely. In part this is due to developments in economics. Traditionally economic analysis has centred on the workings of private markets and on the conditions under which free competition between firms produces a social optimum. In examining these problems it has tended to ignore the spatial dimension and to neglect the kind of problems with which land-use planners have been concerned, such as urban congestion and pollution. As a result, economics has appeared irrelevant to the day-to-day concerns of land-use planning.

But in recent years, in part stimulated by a growing awareness of the failures of private markets in the environmental field, economics has developed tools of analysis particularly relevant to the field of land-use planning. Chief among these are the concepts of externalities and public goods which describe basic weaknesses in the ability of unmodified market forces to meet social, as opposed to private, objectives. In addition, the body of work principally in urban and regional economics devoted to spatial issues has grown rapidly in recent years.

At the same time, experience with the implementation of land-use plans has brought out the need to come to terms with the economic processes within which planners must work. Developments in the theory and practice of planning have also contributed. The current economic climate has made both local and central governments pay particular attention to their spending plans, and in the process made many land-use plans, prepared in more optimistic times, look irrelevant. This has served to emphasise what was already a significant trend towards linking the development of land-use plans with the allocation of resources as a whole, not merely land itself. The central task of the land-use planner has come to be described as being to advise on the best allocation of resources. This is the central problem with which economic analysis is concerned.

The principal aim of this book is to provide a framework for the analysis and appraisal of policies towards the use of land by relating the techniques of economic analysis to the concerns of land-use planning. It does not aim to defend or justify any particular policy. It has two important limitations. First, while one aim of the book is to show the importance of the financial and economic mechanisms with which planners must deal, it is not concerned with forecasting the detailed workings of such mechanisms in particular circumstances, nor is it concerned with the national economic context and its impact on land markets. It does not aim to provide a detailed analysis of industrial and commercial activities in urban areas or of the detailed workings of labour or land markets, the traditional fields of urban economics. Many texts have appeared recently summarising or providing an introduction to this work.

Second, we acknowledge from the outset that we are providing only part of the story. There has been a tendency in recent years for the aims of land-use planning to extend, at the level of endeavour if not achievement, to the limits of social and economic policy, to include, for example, problems of urban poverty or social *malaise*. This book will not go far in this direction, but will confine itself entirely to the traditional concerns of land-use planning of the kind mentioned above. These concerns are sufficiently complex to justify analysis in their own right, even if, when policy decisions are to be taken, the analysis informing them must be set in a broader context and informed by disciplines other than economics.

While the understanding which urban economics can contribute is essential to effective policy analysis, our prime concern is with the general justification for intervention in urban land and property markets, the conditions for effective intervention in such markets, the role of the public sector within the urban economy, the principles to be followed for evaluating intervention by the public authorities, and finally the practical problems involved in putting these principles into effect.

Despite its importance and its close connection with land-use planning, housing policy will receive very little detailed attention. Housing examples are used on a number of occasions and a great deal of the book is relevant to a consideration of the way in which planning policies influence the circumstances within which solutions to housing problems have to be found. But it does not attempt a detailed examination of the aims of intervention in the housing sector itself, although such policies have been, in British cities at least, important determinants of the use of land.

1.2 Political Assumptions

Although this book is concerned with analysis and not directly with policies, it cannot claim to be completely neutral either with regard to the role of analysis and the advice of experts, professionals, administrators or officials in the political process or with regard to the general political framework with which the advice is given. We must therefore make some of our most important assumptions clear at the outset.

Others will become clear later on.

It is now common ground that land-use planning, with its associated policies, is an inherently political activity and the actual process of planning is increasingly politicised through community action, more elaborate public enquiries and direct attempts to involve people in decision-making through various measures aimed at increasing public participation. The role of analysis must be defended, because it may seem to be both possible and desirable to take all the relevant decisions in some direct political way.

Analysis and politics do not always sit very easily together. Analysis tends to assume that explicitness and clarity of reasoning are virtues always to be pursued. Politicians may find it pays to obscure issues in the interest of getting things done and stilling opposition. At the other end of the spectrum analysis tends to be associated with professionalised bureaucratic processes which pay scant regard to the interests of the individuals they plan for.

The implicit claim of a book of this kind must therefore be a modest one. It rests on four beliefs: first, that those responsible for making political decisions do at times wish for an assessment of various policy options and, if they do, they would prefer it well grounded rather than not. Second, that although analysis can in no way determine the outcome of the political process, it may form and influence it. To the extent that facts and logic are brought to bear and are the currency of political debate, it is desirable that they should be accurate. Third, despite the process of politicisation referred to, there will, simply because of the complexity of modern society and government, inevitably remain large areas where technocratic decision processes predominate. If this is so, it is important that the values and judgements underlying them should be made clear.

Fourth, while the political process does, rightly, predominate and often sets aside the results of analysis, we need not accept that the particular political institutions and the existing powers and duties resting with public authorities are necessarily the right ones. Accordingly, there is a case for attempting an analysis which abstracts from existing institutions and tries to analyse the problems with which they deal in isolation from them.

Further political assumptions will creep in by virtue of the subject matter. Much of the discussion in this book is concerned with the workings of private markets, the advantages of different kinds of intervention, and the advantages of markets in relation to certain kinds of public sector activity. The UK is, and has been for a long time, a mixed economy, partly in public and partly in private ownership and intervention with the freedom of the individual household and the individual firm is commonplace. But much political discussion still focuses on the issues of public and private ownership and of the virtues of free enterprise or collective action.

The aim of this book is not to put one political case or another or to advocate the extension of public action in a blanket sense or its restriction in a similar way. The fundamental value judgement which underlies the analysis is that a mixed economy is desirable and that decisions to extend or limit the role of government should be taken with regard to the facts of the individual case. Thus one of the aims of the book is to enable anyone interested in these issues in the field of physical planning to understand better the nature of the arguments on either side. Inevitably this must mean, in certain sections, setting out the 'virtues' and the 'defects' of the free market system and other sections considering the advantages and disadvantages of public control.

Particular difficulty centres round the analysis of the price system and the uses of pricing within the public sector. A decision on how to price raises issues of equity and the distribution of welfare and is therefore political. If the merits of pricing policies seem overstressed, this is because much planning literature assumes the role and possible usefulness of the price system to be negligible and in doing so the functions of the price mechanism, which any alternative must perform, are ignored.

A final general point: this book is concerned with assessing policies which can be effected within the mixed economy and it does not attempt to question the overall political and economic organisational framework within which it functions. As a consequence, discussion of issues concerning the distribution of income or welfare will be tactical rather than strategic in nature. That is, we will accept for the purposes of analysis the current distribution of income and only attempt to assess the changes which it is within the scope of land-use planning to effect.

1.3 Outline of Contents

This book is divided into two main parts. Part 1 introduces the basic economic ideas which will underlie the analysis of planning policies later on in the book. Its aims are twofold. First, to identify the reasons why intervention by government in land markets may be justifiable and second, to develop a framework within which the effects of particular kinds of intervention can be analysed. Readers already acquainted with basic micro-economics will find most of Part 1 familiar, since it covers much of the ground included in introductory courses in economics. Where it differs is (a) in the emphasis on the imperfect workings of market processes, since it is these which form the basis for intervention by government in the physical development process; and (b) in the emphasis on spatial analysis. The latter is developed with the aid of a simple model of an urban economy, within which, initially, all economic decisions are made by individuals and firms. The role of the public sector is then developed by considering, first, the objectives of intervention and, second, the policy instruments which might be used to influence the outcome of market processes. The final two chapters of this part consider the problems of resource allocation within the public sector.

Part 2 shows how the ideas developed in Part 1 can be applied to the analysis of planning policies. Using the concepts developed in Part 1, Chapter 10 considers how different kinds of intervention used by planning authorities influence the workings of various parts of the urban economy. Chapter 11 considers a number of interactions between land-use policies and housing markets, Chapter 12 is concerned with the relationship between transport and land-use planning policies, and Chapter 13 with policies designed to influence the arrangement of land uses. The general aim of Part 2 is to lay the foundations for the evaluation of policies by identifying the kinds of cost and benefit which planning policies may produce.

2 INDIVIDUALS, FIRMS, MARKETS

Most land-use planners work within a mixed economy, consisting of publicly and privately owned firms and commercial and non-commercial organisations. In this kind of economy, the role of government is limited by the powers of control it possesses at any given time. Some parts of the economy may be under its immediate direction – e.g. such services as public health or fire protection. Others, such as rail transport or electricity, are controlled less directly through public ownership or regulatory bodies. Those sectors in which land-use planners are most interested – land and housing markets, the construction industry and other agents of private physical development – are influenced indirectly by a wide variety of detailed and general regulatory policies, most of which are not directly concerned with land markets at all, e.g. fiscal policies towards the total level of spending in the economy. By and large, these sectors of the economy consist of a large number of individuals and private firms each making their own decisions on when to buy or sell property, when to invest in new buildings, where to live and work, where to shop and where to provide shopping facilities, where to spend their leisure and where to provide entertainment facilities. In this kind of economy the case for intervention usually has to be made rather than taken for granted. Accordingly, this part begins by analysing the behaviour of free or private markets, goes on in later chapters to consider the arguments for regulating them and then later considers the implications of the analysis for the public sector.

In this chapter we take the individual consumer and consider initially how his wants may be satisfied by private firms. At this stage, we assume that the interests of the consumer are confined only to goods and services which have a price and which, therefore, private markets will supply. The 'economic man' which emerges is not a realistic description of the way any individual or group of individuals behave in fact, nor is it intended to be. But it will enable a number of the basic ideas which underlie much of the subsequent analysis in the book to be developed.

By making our starting point a situation in which government intervention is not necessary and in which markets work perfectly, our aim is not to propose such a situation as an ideal to which policy should aim. It would be just as illuminating, as far as the exposition of the underlying concepts is concerned, to consider a situation in which all decisions on production or consumption are made by one central authority, and then ask the question: which decisions, under what conditions, might such an authority feel free to leave to individuals or firms to make? Whichever way it is done, we can lay the foundations for considering the functions of markets and of the price mechanism in allocating resources, including land, functions which have to be carried out by political and administrative processes in their absence. In the following chapter the concepts developed are applied directly to the analysis of land markets.

The method of exposition we shall use is a traditional one in economics. That is to start from a very simple, and hence unrealistic situation, and then increase the complexity and with it the realism of the analysis. The simple situation may seem very far from the traditional concerns of planners, even when we have brought in additional assumptions. The aim, however, is not to build up a model of reality which will explain or enable prediction of the complexities of the real world, but to illustrate some basic ideas which can themselves be employed in analysing real-life situations. In later chapters we shall show how they can be applied to the type of problems which planners have to tackle. The exposition will be informal and non-rigorous; specialist economists may take it for granted. Those completely new to the concepts concerned may find the literature in the bibliography helpful if the exposition is too compressed.

Finally, one important simplification of terminology should be noted. In what follows we shall use the terms consumers or individuals on the one hand and firms on the other. In the first two cases, we will implicitly be referring to households most of the time and in the latter to any organisation, publicly or privately owned, which produces goods or services in response to the prices it may obtain in doing so.

2.1 The Individual Consumer: A Simple Model

The starting point of most economic analysis is the wants and desires of the individual. Some, but not all, of these express themselves in purchases of goods and services which have a money price attached to them and in the remainder of the chapter we shall concentrate solely on goods and services of this kind. This involves two important initial simplifications. First, we shall not be concerned with goods or services which are supplied by other means, e.g. through social, administrative or political processes. Second, we will assume that the individual is only concerned with the goods which he, and the household to which he belongs, consume. Later chapters will relax these assumptions and take into account some of the ways in which the individual affects, and is affected by, the consumption of others.

The ability of the individual consumer to satisfy his desires for those goods and services which are priced are limited by his income. Yet, we will assume, his desires for such goods and services are unlimited. In other words, he would always prefer more goods and services to less provided they were freely available. But he cannot buy as much as he would want, of everything he would like to have; that is, he is subject to a *budget constraint*. He must choose. How does he do this?

One way of answering this question is simply to say that he chooses that bundle of goods, out of all the possible bundles he may buy, which is most useful to him, gives him the most pleasure or seems the best value for money. These expressions can be rephrased into more formal language by saying that he tries to *maximise his utility* subject to the constraint set by his money income. Now to say this is to rephrase rather than answer the question. Can we derive a more useful answer? We may do so by using a simple diagram.

Diagram 1

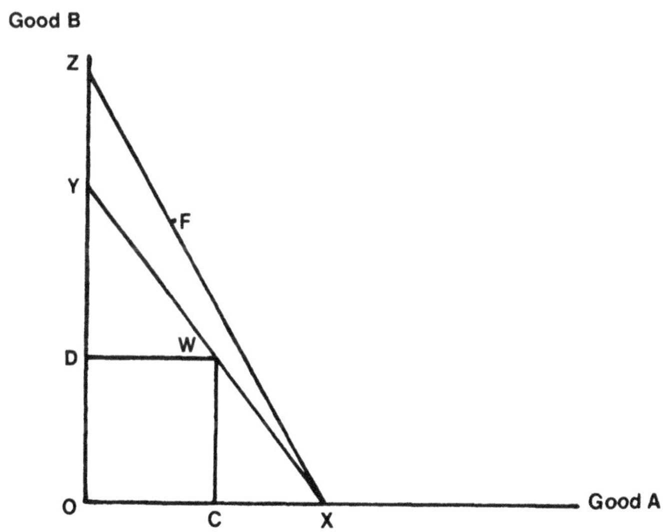

In Diagram 1, the choice facing a consumer with a limited income is shown, assuming that only two goods are available to him. If he spends all his income on good A, he may purchase amount X, while if he spends it all on good B, he may purchase amount Y. The line drawn between the two points X and Y is his *budget line* since it shows that combinations of A and B he may buy with the income at his disposal; for example, at point W, he can buy quantities C and D respectively. Which combination will he choose?

Intuitively we would expect him to strike some balance between the two, and not plump entirely for one. This intuition may be rationalised by invoking the assumption of *diminishing marginal utility.* This assumption implies that as the consumer spends more on good A, he gets less utility from each *additional* unit he buys. For example, if good A is footwear he would find it highly useful to have a fair selection for various weather and social conditions, but after he has purchased perhaps half a dozen pairs, he may well feel that additional pairs are of little extra use. Suppose then that in thinking about how to allocate his income between goods A and B, he initially goes for A, because his initial purchases of good A give him a great deal of utility. By assumption, as he spends more on A, the attractiveness of further units of A tends to decline and the case for spending on B tends to grow stronger.

As the consumer spends more on units of A, the utility he gets from each additional unit will steadily approach the utility which could be obtained from spending money on units of B and at some stage they will be equal. If he continues to spend on A, he would clearly be foolish – because he can get more utility by switching to B. The right course for him is to move along the line XY until he reaches the point where the additional unit of expenditure on A gives him equivalent utility to an additional unit of expenditure on B.

The rule he must follow is to so distribute his budget that an additional unit of expenditure yields the same amount of utility whatever it is spent on. If that condition does not hold, then he could rearrange his expenditures so as to increase his utility. The same rule holds if he can spend on more than two goods: however wide the choice open to him, he should still attempt to achieve that pattern of consumption at which an additional unit of expenditure would yield the same amount of utility no matter on what good or service it was spent. We will call this the 'equi-marginal rule'.

Let us assume he maximises his utility at point W. At this point he has so allocated his budget between A and B that no rearrangement can increase the benefits he enjoys from spending it. In other words a very small, or marginal, increment of expenditure on A or B would yield the same amount of utility to him. Now suppose that the price of the two goods changes, B becomes cheaper relative to A and hence he can buy more of it, provided his budget remains unchanged. This is shown in Diagram 1 by a shift in the line YX to the line ZX. The distance ZY shows the additional amount of B he can buy while still remaining within his budget constraint. We would expect that he would shift his consumption in favour of good B, e.g. move to point F, because at the new set of prices, good B is a relatively better buy. Nevertheless he still does not go overboard for B, since consumption of that too is subject to diminishing marginal utility, so he will move to the left of the diagram but still consume some of good A. He adjusts his pattern of consumption in the face of the prices he is faced with, not because his preferences have changed, but because, *given his preferences* and given the new set of prices, he can gain more utility from the new bundle of goods.

Diagram 2

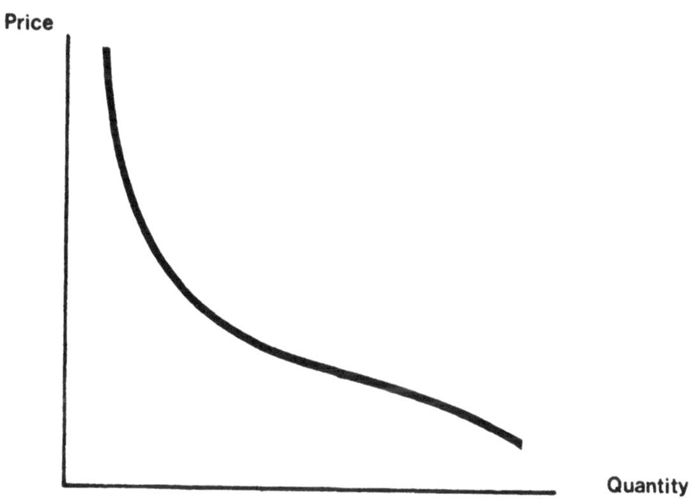

We can demonstrate this another way. Diagram 2 shows on the horizontal axis the amount the consumer is prepared to buy of good B, at various prices. These are shown on the vertical axis. The curve, known as the individual's *demand curve*, slopes downward to the right, on the assumption that as the price of good B falls, provided that the prices of all other goods and the money income of the consumer remain the same, he will buy more of it. The converse also applies: i.e. if the price rises, it is assumed he will reduce his consumption. The shape of the demand curve expresses the responsiveness of the individual to the price of the good concerned. It is shown to be very steep to the left of the diagram, on the assumption that the initial quantities are very important to the individual, and hence his demand is unresponsive, or *inelastic* to the prices he must pay. Normally demand is described as inelastic if a given percentage change in price produces a less than equal percentage change in amount demanded, e.g. if a 10 per cent price cut increases demand by only 5 per cent, then demand for the good concerned would be said to be inelastic.

As price falls further, the consumer is assumed to enlarge his expenditures on the good concerned fairly rapidly, i.e. his demand is *elastic* in this part of the demand curve and then as his consumption approaches the point of *satiation,* where additional consumption of this particular good offers no extra utility at all, a demand becomes inelastic again and responds very little to further price reduction. For example, the consumer may be fond of apples and may buy a modest quantity even when the price is high: when it falls to lower levels he rapidly increases his purchases. As it falls yet further he may still buy more, but his eagerness to do so declines until a point of satiation is reached and however low the price falls he declines to consume any more or even to pulp them for deep-freezing.

The actual shape and position of the demand curve will depend on the particular good concerned, the price of other goods and the income of the consumer. In the case of some goods, the demand curve may be very steep over its full length. This is probably true of the demand for salt, which is a necessity but which does not offer many opportunities for high levels of consumption. So however low its price falls, little more is consumed. In other cases, the demand curve may be very flat over its full range. This would be so for a good which is easily substituted for another. If A and B are very similar commodities, then any increase in the price of A will lead to a rapid increase in demand for B. For example, the demand curve of a commuter for bus travel might be very flat if, in a large metropolitan area, he enjoyed the alternative of tube travel. As long as he did not have a strong preference for travel by bus as such, and the journey times were similar, his demand for both forms of travel taken separately would be highly elastic. In this situation, we could say that the elasticity of substitution of A for B and B for A was very high.

As the individual's income rises, he can buy more of the available goods and services. In terms of Diagram 1, his budget line moves away from the origin in a north-easterly direction. Each of the points on his budget line at which he chooses to consume represents a higher level of welfare as he moves from left to right on the diagram. At any level of income one particular combination of goods produces more utility than any other. However, other bundles of goods would yield equivalent utility. The curve $I_1 I_1$ in Diagram 3 shows those combinations of goods

Diagram 3

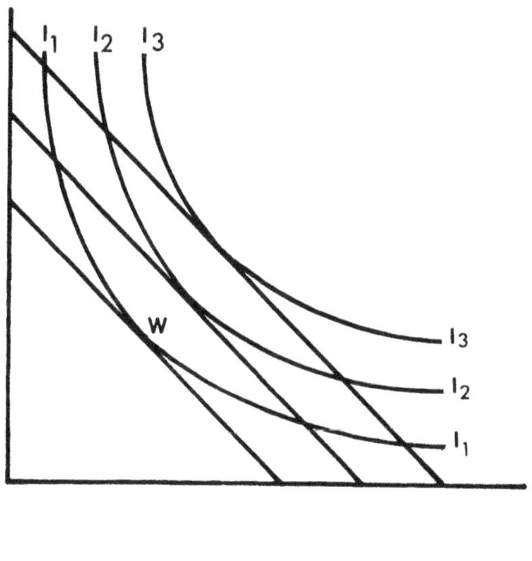

which yield the same total utility as the combination W. It is called an *indifference curve* because by assumption the individual is equally satisfied by, hence indifferent to, all the combinations of A and B which the line joins. The other indifference curves represent higher levels of individual utility.

In principle, the position and shape of the individual's indifference curves could be 'mapped' by suitable empirical work, but in the present context they are best regarded as ways of expressing different assumptions about the structure of an individual's preferences. The shape of the indifference curves in Diagram 3 implies that as the consumer moves away from his chosen point at any level of income, he requires increasing amounts of the good forgone if he is to remain at the same level of satisfaction. They are drawn such that as they approach each axis they become parallel to it. What this implies is that after a certain point, the individual cannot be compensated by increasing amounts of the other good and if he is forced to have less of the first good then his welfare declines. This would correspond to the consumer with a basic need for a given level of certain commodities who will only consider other items of expenditure when these are attained. In the case of two luxury goods, the indifference curves might touch the axes, indicating that he could be perfectly compensated by more of one good for the complete loss of the other.

As the income of the consumer changes, he is able to buy more goods (and services) but he is unlikely to increase his purchases on all goods at the same rate. Paralleling the notion of a price elasticity is the concept of *income elasticity*, or the responsiveness of demand to changes in the consumer's income. Not surprisingly, a good is described as *income elastic* if demand for it rises more than in proportion to a given change in income, and vice versa. It is usually found, for example, that demand for travel is income elastic, that is, as people's incomes rise, they spend a larger proportion of their incomes on it. In contrast, people tend to increase expenditure on other basic items, including food, less than proportionately; they are income *inelastic*.

This concludes our analysis of the individual consumer. Before going on to consider the firm, we will first draw out some of the conclusions of this simple model of consumer choice.

2.2 Implications of the Simple Model

Although the model of consumer behaviour is very simple, it illustrates a number of basic ideas which will feature strongly in the later sections of this book. The first of these is the notion of cost. In Diagram 1, no explicit money prices appear for the goods concerned. Nevertheless the diagram allows the costs of A and B to be determined in this way. We know, because the consumer's budget is limited, that he cannot buy all of A and B that he would conceivably want, since what he can buy is constrained by his budget to X and Y. Within those bounds set by his income, any purchase of A implies a reduction in the amount of B he may buy and vice versa. Thus the cost of A may be defined as the amount of B that has to be given up in order to obtain a unit of it. The converse also holds: the cost of B is the amount of A which must be given up.

This suggests a definition of cost in terms of *benefits forgone*. If the individual spends all his budget on A he cannot buy any B. To give some everyday examples: if he plants all his garden with roses, he cannot grow chrysanthemums in it: if he makes his career as a civil servant he cannot also be a member of the government, at least not in the UK. Choice between alternatives necessarily involves rejection of all but one. The most desirable alternative of those rejected is the cost of the chosen one, no matter whether we are talking of individuals, governments, of money incomes or careers. Choices of this kind are 'all or nothing', but the point still holds when we are considering other kinds of decision. The cost of another hour in bed is the benefits forgone from not spending the time in another way. The cost of extending the lawn is the reduction in the area of flower beds it entails. This definition of cost will be called subsequently *opportunity cost*, since to choose A deprives one of the opportunity of using the resources involved in producing A to produce B.

In everyday contexts, the question 'how much does X cost?' is usually answered in money terms. It would be odd to say that the price of a pound of new potatoes was a half pound of tomatoes. It would normally be easier to say it was 10 pence. But the answer 10p only makes sense because people are used to money as a general way of expressing what they must give up to buy a commodity.

The second basic idea illustrated in the simple model of the individual consumer is that of *economising* behaviour. The consumer in our simple model does not determine the pattern of his consumption with reference to preconceived notions of how much of this and how much of that he wishes to buy. He is assumed to behave in an *economising* way, that is, when the price of something goes up, he cuts down his demand for it; if it falls, he increases his demand. This economising behaviour can be seen as a continuous process of substitution and adjustment. His pattern of consumption is modified in response to changing relative prices because only by so adjusting can he make the best of his limited budget. His preferences are assumed fixed, but the expression of these in terms of purchases of goods and services alters in the light of the relative prices he is faced with.

The expression 'fixed preferences' can cause some difficulty and it may be helpful to elucidate it. By saying his preferences are fixed, we mean that the individual would respond in consistent ways to a change in any of the prices of the goods he buys, i.e. if the price of a good goes up and then returns to its original price, his pattern of consumption would alter and then revert to what it had been. Further, it implies that his pattern of consumption remains unchanged *unless* either his money income or the prices facing him change. A change in preferences would mean that his pattern of consumption altered irrespective of any change in his income or in the prices facing him.

Precisely how much of each available goods he buys is determined on the one hand by his estimate of how much benefit or utility he will enjoy from consuming each available commodity and on the other the opportunity costs which any act of assumption invokes, that is, by the rate at which he must *trade off* one commodity against the other. Before he decides to buy more A he needs to know how much B it will cost him. In Diagram 1, the rate of trade-off is assumed constant, i.e. the line XY is straight. This implies that for a given increase in the amount of A consumed, the amount of B to be given up is always the same. But the budget line might take other shapes such as that in Diagram 4 which reflects the fact that the rate of trade-off may vary. Suppose, for example, that the individual was choosing a house and that each axis in the diagram represented characteristics of the houses he was interested in, e.g. accessibility and peace and quiet. It is quite likely that he would have to sacrifice an increasing amount of accessibility in order to get a home which enjoyed perfect peace and quiet and vice versa, i.e. to find a house which had near perfect accessibility he might have to put up with increasingly noisy and unattractive environments.

Diagram 4

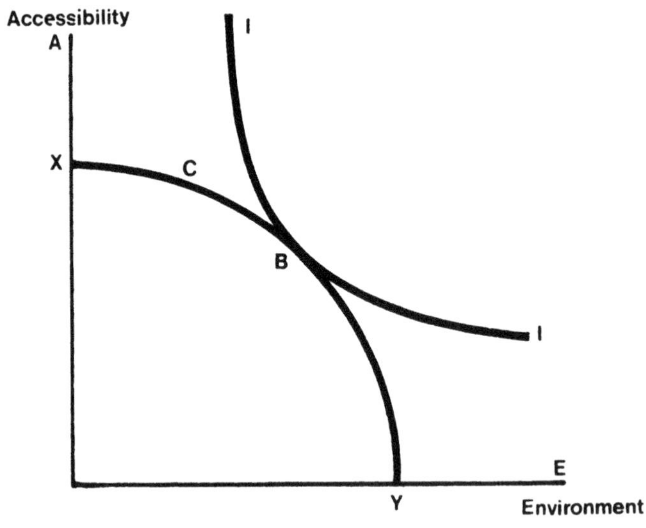

In this diagram the *rate* at which Environment (E) is traded off against Accessibility (A) changes as we move from Y to X. Starting at Y, he can gain large amounts of A by small sacrifice of E, but as he moves along the line, he must give up more and more of E to get an additional unit of A. Consider, for example, point C. A house represented by this point is *nearly* as good on accessibility as any house he can afford (i.e. the house at point X). But to buy a house at C he must sacrifice a large amount of environment to gain only a small improvement in accessibility. At point B, however, he gains a lot on the environment axis, at relatively low cost in terms of A. Where he finishes up will depend on his preferences: if he hates travel he may well finish up buying house D. The balance he strikes will tend to be influenced by his income. If his income rises and his budget line shifts to the right, he might strike a different balance. For example, if his income elasticity of demand for environment is greater than that for accessibility, he will tend to shift along the environment axis.

In the diagram, the shape and position of the individual's indifference curves reflect assumptions about his relative valuation, at different levels of income, of accessibility and environment. The curves by themselves do not determine the optimal balance between these two characteristics. This can only be done by relating the indifference curves to the budgetary possibilities open to the individual. Thus the optimal point is found by an interaction between the wants or preferences of the individual, the resources he can command and the relative costs of the goods he wishes to buy. Although, by assumption, his wants are boundless, the degree to which they can be satisfied is not. This is the basic economic problem.

As we shall show in later chapters, the concepts developed here have a wider application than the individual. The reason is this: that the simple theory developed in this section sets out rules of rational behaviour in the face of a general fact of human existence, the fact of scarcity. Resources are limited. The individual, and society like him, cannot have all he wants of everything he would like to have. The individual, and society, must choose. The theory sets out the rules which must be followed to make the most of the available resources. In the following section we see how this basic analysis applies to the producers of goods and services. Later, in Chapter 5, we will draw out the implications for a planning authority.

2.3 Producers

This section will sketch out a simple theory of producer behaviour, which in most ways closely parallels the theory of consumer behaviour developed in section 2.1. Like the earlier theory, this one is not intended to explain all features of economic activity in a realistic way, but to introduce some further basic concepts which will be used in later chapters. Paralleling the assumption that consumers try to maximise their utility, we assume that individual producers attempt to maximise their profits. They make profits by selling to consumers the goods and services which consumers want and are willing to pay for. We further assume that the producers of any such commodity consist of a number of firms which are small in relation to the output of each commodity and that there are no barriers to firms entering or leaving any particular line of production. In other words, there is active competition between firms to make profits. Problems of monopoly and restraints to competition are assumed away.

The firm, like the individual, is subject to constraints. If producers are in close competition with each other, then the price which they can get for the commodity they produce will be set, i.e. if some producers can supply at a lower price, those who cannot will go out of business. Given that price, they have two tasks, first, that of deciding *how* to produce and second, *how much* to produce. We take these questions in turn.

The firm is an organisation which brings together factors of production – land, labour and capital – to produce goods and services which individuals, like our consumer in the previous section, wish to buy. These factors of production themselves command a price, by virtue of their use in the process of production: land in an out-of-the-way location which has no potential for agriculture may command no price at all, while millions may be paid for land which is conveniently sited. Different categories of labour command incomes which relate to their skills, experience and other factors valued in the production process. We assume in the rest of this section that these inputs, or factors of production, command a price which relates precisely to their value in contributing to the production of goods and services.

In considering how to produce a commodity or service, the firm is bound by the available technologies. 'Technology' means not only scientific and engineering techniques, but also the availability of ancillary services such as transport, marketing and finance and management skills. These may allow production to take place in many different ways. For example, it may be able to produce using small amounts of capital and land and large amounts of labour. In this case, the production process would be said to be *labour intensive* and wages would form a high proportion of total costs. Alternatively, the firm might economise on labour costs by using expensive machines. In this case, the costs of capital equipment would form a large proportion of total costs and the process would be described as *capital intensive*.

To determine the best combination to use, the firm must go through a process identical to that of the consumer making up his mind about which combination of goods to consume. That is that the firm must weigh up the relative advantages to it of the various factors it can hire and employ the most efficient combination, i.e. that combination which minimises production costs for whatever level of production it decides upon.

Office construction is a good example of how factor mix can vary. If labour is very expensive, the building contractors will tend to employ lifting machinery, prefabricated materials and management techniques which allow careful control over the deployment of the work force. Where land is expensive, there will be a tendency to economise on it by building higher – at the price of incurring higher building costs; where land is cheap, the office layout may be more spacious and spread out over a larger surface area. If, over time, the relative price of the factors involved in office construction changes, then the way in which offices are built will also tend to change. If land prices continue to rise (and no alternative sites are available), then offices will tend to be built higher and higher. If labour costs increase, then greater efforts will be made to use mechanical aids which cut down labour inputs. These are all examples of *substitution* processes and in these, the firm mirrors the economising behaviour of the individual consumer in the face of changes in the prices of the goods he buys.

We noted above that the price or trade-off facing the consumer may vary. In Diagram 1 the trade-off was assumed to be constant and in Diagram 4 it varied according to the 'mix' of accessibility and environment. The individual may find it cheaper to buy in bulk rather than in small units. If he is buying a house, he will tend to get more space per pound the more expensive the house. How do these differences come about? Although firms can vary their methods of production, they are nevertheless bound by the available technology. It is this which determines the relationship between input of factors and output of product. This relationship, known as the production function, may vary as the following examples show.

In Diagram 5(a), the cost of producing a good X is shown as a straight horizontal line. This is a condition of *constant costs*, that is, the average cost of production stays the same, each additional unit costing

Diagram 5

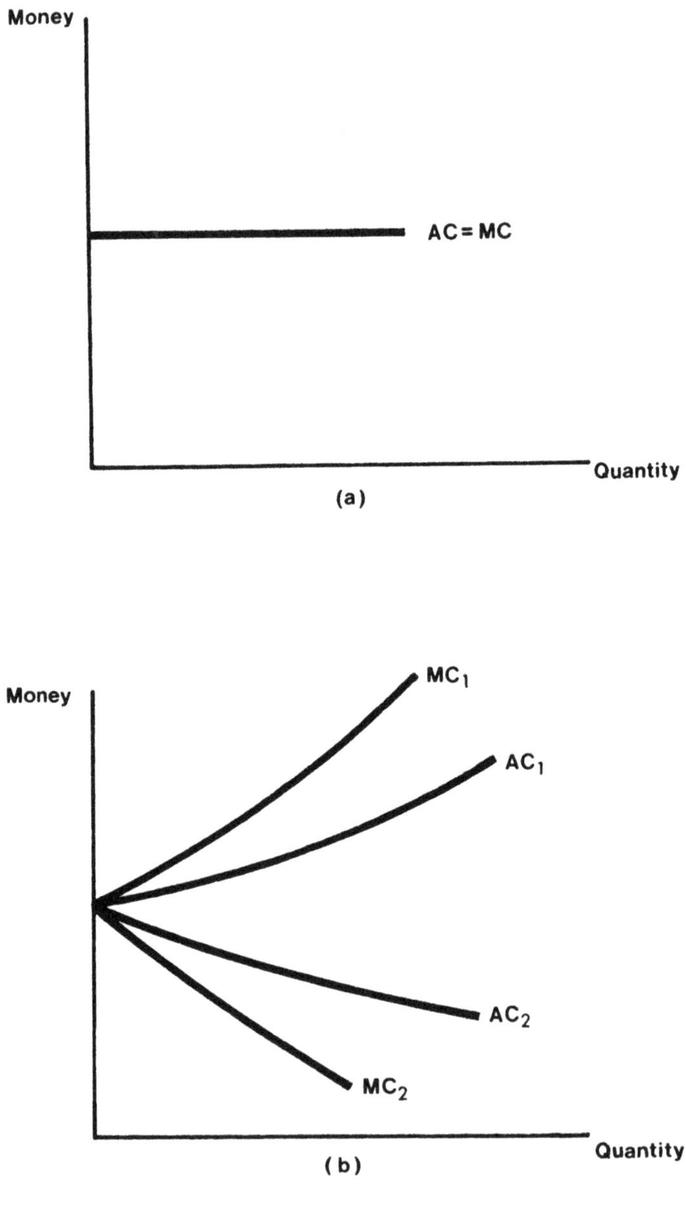

the same as the one before. Cost conditions of this kind underlie the (straight) budget line in Diagram 1.

Diagram 5(b) shows two average cost lines, one sloping upward and one downward. These show, respectively, *increasing and decreasing* costs. In the first case, we can say that there are economies of scale, i.e. as output increases average cost of production falls, and in the second case *diseconomies of scale*, i.e. as output increases average cost of production rises. Production processes such as steel processing or car assembly typically enjoy economies of scale, i.e. the cost per ton or per car produced are much lower at higher volumes of production than at low and usually, therefore, such goods are produced in bulk. In the case of most goods, the cost curve has a U shape, that is, they are cheaper per unit to produce up to a certain point and then become more expensive.

In drawing these curves, the assumption has been made that all the factors concerned are allowed to vary, i.e. at successively higher levels of production, increasing amounts of all factors will be employed. In many contexts the analyst needs to know how output varies when one factor is held constant while others vary. In most building operations, for example, variable quantities of labour and capital are applied to a fixed amount of land, i.e. the site concerned. Average costs tend to fall up to a certain intensity of development and then begin to rise. In the case of an office building, the structure has to be strengthened to support the greater height and extra lifts provided, which is expensive in itself and consumes valuable space. In these cases, we can say that at first use of capital and labour on a given site enjoys *increasing returns* and then is subject to *diminishing returns*.

Economies, or diseconomies, of scale are not only found within a single production unit. For example, if firms find it advantageous to be close together, they may be said to *enjoy external economies*. A single large plant like a steel works may enjoy very considerable economies of scale within its own confines. But in a large city, large numbers of relatively small institutions or firms of a very specialised nature are frequently found close together. They survive only because the size of the market in the city allows it. One example is the cluster of closely linked firms forming the financial and commodity markets in the City of London; another is the concentration of specialist suppliers and subcontractors in major industrial centres.

Where costs are not constant then it becomes very important to distinguish between *marginal* and *average* costs. Average costs are defined as the total cost involved divided by the total output. Marginal costs, however, refer to the costs of an additional unit of output and may diverge from the average. For example, where average costs are rising, as in Diagram 5 (b), marginal costs rise even faster, so that to the right of the diagram marginal and average costs diverge considerably.

The significance of this distinction will emerge in several parts of the later analysis. At this stage we will consider its relevance to the production decision of the firm. Given its price, how much of any commodity should a firm produce? Clearly it can only produce at all if its costs of production lie below the price obtaining for its product. But, given that its costs are sufficiently low, then in order to maximise profits it will devote additional resources to production up to the point where the cost to it of the additional resources needed for production equals the additional revenue which is brought in, i.e. to the point where *marginal* cost equals *marginal* revenue. For example, in considering how a particular site should be developed, a firm may have to decide whether to add an additional storey. If the rental per square foot is constant, no matter at what scale the development takes place, then it must balance the extra cost of the additional space with the extra revenue it will bring in, and go on adding storeys until equality is reached. In Diagram 6, this

Diagram 6

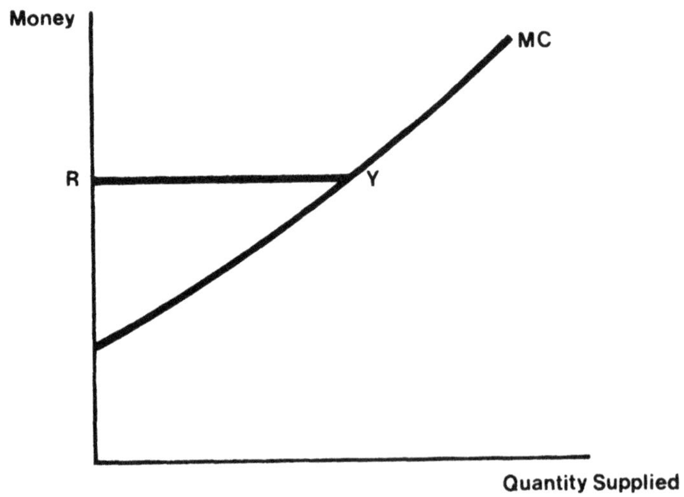

is given by the point Y. Such a rule closely parallels that we devised for the individual consumer. In both cases the correct point to choose – either of consumption or production – is set by *marginal* and not average conditions.

2.4 Interaction between Producers and Consumers

We can now consider the interaction between the two groups analysed, producers and consumers. Diagram 7 shows an aggregate consumer

Diagram 7

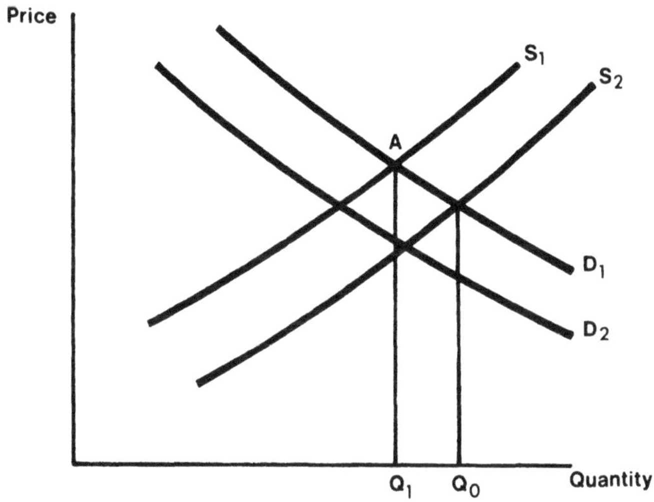

demand curve D_1 and a producer supply curve with rising marginal costs, S_1. The first of these requires a little explanation. Section 2.1 considered only one consumer. The curve in Diagram 7 sums up over all consumers or potential consumers for the good concerned. It therefore reflects the fact that some individuals are prepared to pay greater amounts for the good than others, e.g. those to the left would be prepared to pay very high amounts and those to the right very little, as well as reflecting the varying response of each individual consumer. The supply curve shows willingness to supply at a given price. It is drawn upward sloping to the right on the assumption that a higher price is required to elicit a large supply. For example, the supply curve of office accommodation would have this slope if building on any given site was subject to increasing marginal cost. In a given city, many sites would be involved, all of which would be subject to the same technical conditions of production.

The point A, where the supply and demand curve intersect, is the only point where producers are happy to continue to supply a quantity which consumers are willing to buy. At prices to the left of A, producers would find that they would make larger profits on the lower volume of output, but the price would be high enough to attract additional output. That is, at these high prices it would be very profitable to produce more – so new firms would come in to take advantage of the opportunities presented. To the right of point A the opposite would be true, i.e. producers could not produce these amounts and sell their products at a price which would recoup their costs. If, by chance, they got their production estimates wrong then they would have to cut prices to get rid of stocks and try again. These adjustments would feed back into the markets for factors of production in the following ways.

Suppose, for example, that due to a change in consumer spending, demand shifted to the left, to the curve D_2D_2; what is the consequence? At the new position of demand the old levels of production cannot be sold at the prices which producers will accept, supply has to be cut back, price falls a little as we have assumed a supply curve which slopes upward to the right. Behind these changes lie further adjustments. The volume of capital and labour employed in producing the good concerned will be reduced and redeployed elsewhere – eventually if not directly to supply the goods to which demand has diverted. In a simple economy producing only housing and food, such effects could easily be seen, i.e. an increase in demand for housing would lead to some land – and other factors – being transferred to housing from agriculture. In more complex economies the adjustments would be more difficult to spot, but the underlying processes would remain essentially the same.

Consider the opposite kind of effect, where the cost of supplying the good in question falls and the supply curve shifts to the right (e.g. through the introduction of more efficient production processes). Consumers will adjust to the new assumption possibilities opened up. As the price has gone down, they will tend to buy more, substituting it for some of these existing patterns of consumption. Producers will expand output and to do so increases their use of the factors of production required.

The precise extent and nature of these actions and responses will depend on the shape of the demand and supply curves. Diagram 8 shows two extreme cases. In 8(a) demand is perfectly *elastic*. If costs of

Diagram 8

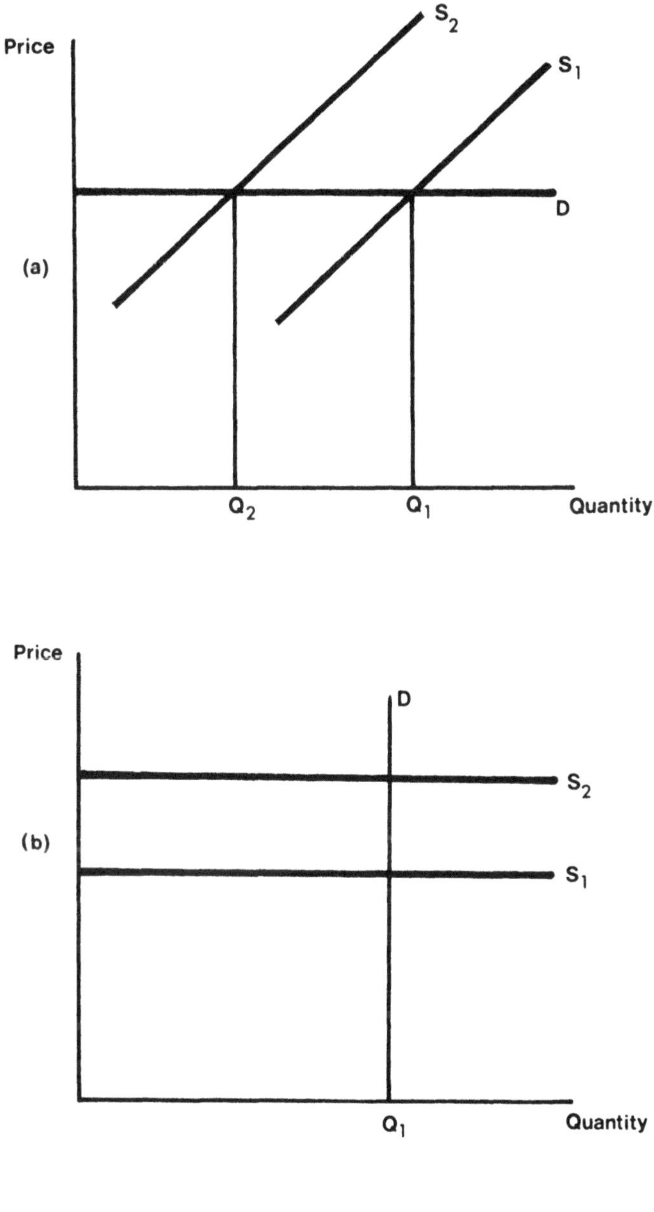

production rise, and all other costs and prices remain the same, then production would have to be radically curtailed from Q_1 to Q_2 as it would no longer be profitable to continue production near the previous output levels. In the case where demand is perfectly *inelastic* the converse is true, consumers pay more and producers produce the same as before. If the cost curves have a different shape, e.g. are constant or slope down to the right, then outcomes result which lie between these two extremes. That is, both producers and consumers must react to the change in demand and supply conditions.

This behaviour is reflected in turn in the markets for, and hence the prices of, factors of production. How are these prices set? Consider the demand and supply of a particular factor, labour, to a particular industry. The supply curve for labour starts some way up the vertical axis, since labour will be able to obtain rewards in other industries. As the industry seeks to expand its labour force it will have to bid progressively more, since it will have to attract workers who are less and less favourably disposed to work in it. If labour was indifferent between jobs, the supply curve would be flat, i.e. at the going rate, any amount could be hired. But if the industry offered unattractive jobs because of awkward hours or unpleasant working conditions, it would have to offer extra money to compensate for the extra *dis*utility of the jobs concerned.

Provided there are no restraints on its mobility, labour will go to those activities which offer the greatest net rewards, i.e. money income plus or minus any psychic benefits enjoyed. In this way, the bidding process of employers ensures that the labour is used in those activities in which it is most productive. By 'most productive' we mean that it can produce the most economic welfare or utility without regard to the specific good or service produced. The only reason why one employer can bid labour away from another is that the service or good which he produces is sufficiently attractive to allow him to do so. We can express this by saying that the demand for factors of production is a *derived* demand in that the factors are not wanted for their own sake but as inputs to things which are. The same is true of capital equipment or raw materials. Thus it is convenient to distinguish between final goods, bought directly by consumers, and intermediate goods which are produced only for further use in the production process.

If one good consumed by individuals becomes more popular, i.e. if its demand curve shifts to the right, then this means that the derived demand for the factors used in its production will also shift. The industry will, for example, have to bid up the price of labour, thus tending to put up the price to itself and also to other industries. This will have second-order effects of the kind discussed above, i.e. inducing expenditure on capital or other factors to substitute for the more expensive labour. This applies to the resource which is of most interest to land-use planning, land itself. The demand for non-agricultural land reflects the demand for housing, and for all goods and services which require land in their production, i.e. the demands of consumers for goods and services in general. At the local level it will reflect the different advantages which individual sites have in the production process. Land, like labour, is not a homogeneous factor, in that each parcel is slightly different from all the rest, but the demands for all parcels in a particular area are very closely related. Within a given area the price of plots will vary a great deal, but each potential user may compete for any of them. Thus everyone may wish to have a central site, but the effect of this is to so bid up the price that some have to reconsider and locate elsewhere. The higher price means that only those who find it most profitable to locate there will do so – perhaps because they can only survive if they have a very good catchment area for customers or for labour. At the same time, those who wish to stay there and who cannot afford the very high prices may economise on land by squeezing up on space, decentralising some activities, etc. In general, for example, one would expect space-intensive activities to locate away from high land-price areas and vice versa. These points are developed further in the following chapter.

2.5 The Nature of a Market

The previous section described the workings of a series of related markets for priced goods and factors of production. It wasn't necessary to fix them in a particular physical location. They were assumed to consist of all those who are purchasing or who may purchase, who supply or who may supply, depending on the price of obtaining the goods or services concerned.

A market can be defined as an institution which arranges for the production and exchange of commodities and services, including both final and intermediate goods. In doing this a market carries out a number of functions simultaneously. It determines how much shall be produced, who produces it and who buys it. This is achieved not by central fiat but through the interactions of separate decision-takers. No one of these alone determines what the price shall be and who shall buy and who shall sell. Nevertheless, the process of market interaction as a whole determines all these things. How does this come about?

The first point to consider is the role which prices have in influencing the decisions of the various actors in the processes described above.

Within a market, prices can be seen as indicators, signals or conveyors of information. If the price of a commodity needed in a production process goes up because its costs of production have risen, then the producer is 'told' that it is necessary to cut down use of that item if possible, i.e. to economise on it through substitution of others. If the price has risen in response to a shift in demand and if it is a commodity he himself produces or is able to produce, then the price signals to him that an increase in output may be worthwhile. Equally, the final consumer – or supplier of labour – is 'told' that it might be worthwhile modifying his behaviour when shifts occur in the relative prices he is faced with. Such signals may be obtained in different, though related, ways. For example, if demand for a commodity rises, stocks will tend to be run down, producers' order books will lengthen and queues will tend to form. These queues may be made up of housewives waiting for sugar or some other commodity suffering temporary scarcity, or of industrial buyers having to accept a long delivery delay for the machine they wish to install.

The second point derives from the existence of a large number of decision-makers. Each actor in the market can make his own interpretation of the significance of the prices or queues and decide what to do; how much to produce, where to produce it, where to trade it to, how to produce it, how much to buy, where to buy, etc. Where commodities are scarce, or in temporary short supply, and where this is reflected in the prices charged, then those who gain least from using it will cut down their use and in this way the shortage is eased. For example, since the recent rise in the price of oil, a large number of reactions have been triggered off. Some have been aimed at developing other sources of oil, some at building up supplies of other fuels, some at developing means of economising in the use of energy. Although encouraged by governments, most of these responses have been the result of spontaneous reaction from individuals and firms reacting to the new set of relative prices. These responses have been large and complex, but the basic motives underlying them are contained in the simple model of producer and consumer behaviour developed in this chapter. It is all substitution behaviour.

Another example is the market in second-hand houses for owner-occupation. This is a very complex market. There are a large number of participants, most of whom have a considerable range of choices open to them and the detailed workings of the market are influenced by a large number of outside factors including government intervention. This market produces an allocation of people to houses. Where I live is in part determined by my personal circumstances, income, job, my preferences for housing as opposed to other goods and my preferences for particular attributes of housing. The same is true of all other participants in the market. These various forces interact and produce a set of prices for houses which reflect the general strength of preferences for houses of different qualities: higher prices for houses in attractive locations, different prices for houses of different sizes and qualities. Relative prices will change in response to changes in job location, transport facilities and consumer preferences, so that if one kind of house becomes more popular, its price will rise until the numbers prepared to pay it are equal to the numbers available.

This familiar example brings out a central feature of competitive markets, that they are a *decentralised* way of reaching allocation decisions. The method by which nearly all public sector housing is allocated, which we will consider in Chapter 9, is basically different. All allocation decisions are made by the relevant housing department, i.e. it is centralised. In a competitive market, such as private housing, there are a much larger number of decision-makers, none of whom dominate the workings of the market and each of which has a very small influence on the final outcome. But the end result in both cases is an allocation of people to houses.

The market in second-hand houses is of a special kind since it is concerned only with the allocation of a given stock of houses and does not involve new production. It is, however, linked closely to the market for new housing. Here rather different considerations apply since producers as well as consumers are involved. If this market is working well, producers will build houses of the type and location which consumers demand. These demands for new housing will be determined by the preferences of individual purchasers and the nature of the existing stock of houses. For example, if the price of a given kind of house rises to a level at which it can be profitably supplied, then more will be put on the market. In those cases when prices have fallen below costs of production, then the reverse will apply. No new units will be built of the relevant types. In these conditions consumers as a whole may be said to be 'sovereign', i.e. they determine what kind of product market processes will produce. This is what is meant by saying that the market gives people 'what they want'. If producers failed to do this, then in the kind of markets we have been examining, their houses would not sell and they would go out of business. Even here, however, consumer wants are met only if conditions of supply allow it. If it is not possible to supply new houses of a given type for topographical reasons, then there is no way round the fact. As always, the satisfaction of wants is limited by the supply possibilities available.

We do not wish at this stage to come to any judgement about whether or not the price mechanism and market processes are better or worse than alternative means of allocating resources, nor about the realism of the assumption that consumers are sovereign. But before moving on to consider a number of reasons why market processes may not be satisfactory, we must consider briefly the conditions which must be satisfied if markets are to carry out well the functions described in this chapter.

Before a market can be said to exist at all, some basic conditions must be satisfied. Prime among these is the existence of information. By saying that there is a market in something, we mean that it is easy to find a buyer or a seller. For this to be the case there must not only be willingness to buy or sell, but potential parties to a transaction must be aware of the opportunities available. Markets in high-quality industrial shares in the Stock Exchange normally work well because it is easy to find what the going price is and to find someone who will buy or sell near that price. Thus, as far as information is concerned, a market may be more or less perfect. In the case of standard commodities like raw materials or steel, the market is very nearly perfect in *this* sense and unified throughout the world economy. For some commodities, e.g. second-hand carpets, the market may be highly imperfect, buyers and sellers finding it difficult to meet each other. In these cases there may be no market at all, even though there may be people and firms who would like to buy or sell, because no means exists of bringing them together.

The information on which markets work must be accurate. Because of their central role, this is particularly true of prices. As we have seen, the information they convey concerns the costs or alternative uses of the resources used in providing a good or service. If prices for any reason do not reflect opportunity costs, then the information they contain will be misleading, with the result that resources are not allocated correctly. For example, a price which is too high in relation to opportunity cost will lead to economising reactions for which no underlying justification exists.

Even where information is available, accurate and inexpensive markets may not work well if transaction costs are high. If the cost of exchanging a good is significant in relation to the value of the exchange for legal, administrative or other reasons, the market is likely to be rather sluggish – i.e. there are likely to be many fewer transactions than there are potentially useful exchanges. One example of this is the recent situation in the private housing market in the UK: the number of transactions has varied markedly with the availability of finance. In times of restraint only the lucky few with mortgage finance are able to make purchases. Even where no restraints of this kind exist, costs of transport will limit the extent to which profitable exchange may be made.

The various kinds of adjustment to changes in relative prices described above will only occur if there are no restraints which prevent them taking place. Such restraints may arise for various reasons: for example, to inertia on the part of individuals or firms. In other cases, they are due to statutory controls imposed for broad policy reasons. In yet others, they arise because individual firms have a much greater influence in the way in which markets function than the analysis in this chapter has suggested. Many of the markets with which land-use planning is concerned are competitive or if they are not perfectly so, the assumption that competition is free is not seriously misleading. Where it is not, it will tend to mean that the kind of market processes considered are rather slower to work through than they otherwise might be.

But in some cases, the restraints will be more severe. Individual firms may, through their size, be able to influence the outcome of market processes and so have a much greater freedom of action than the analysis in this chapter suggests. For example, if the supply of new housing were in the hands of a single supplier in a particular area, then the nature of the housing supplied and the prices at which it was supplied are unlikely to mirror the wishes of the potential purchasers in the way described above. A supplier in such a position may, as a benevolent monopolist, still try to supply what people want at reasonable prices, but it may equally well not be so responsive. Such non-competitive situations are the focus of much economic analysis, references to which can be found in the Bibliography. In many of the contexts in which a land-use planner is involved, however, it is the actions of the planning authority itself which modifies the nature of the competitive process between producers and it is these with which we shall deal in later chapters.

3 MARKETS IN A SPATIAL CONTEXT: A SIMPLE URBAN ECONOMY

The aim of this chapter is to use the concepts introduced in the previous chapter in a context of direct relevance to the interests of land-use planners. We shall develop, using a number of simple assumptions, a model of an urban economy and analyse within it how the various markets for goods and factors of production, particularly land, interact within it. This model, like the models used in the previous chapter, does not aim to reflect accurately the workings of a particular urban area, so that the results obtained from it cannot be transferred directly to a real-life situation. However, the nature of the forces analysed and the kinds of effects they produce are to be observed in any city where private land markets operate and in this sense the model, though highly simplified, is a realistic one.

Within this model, there is no planning system and no planning authority – in fact, no government activity at all. This simplification is made for two reasons: first, we are at this stage concerned with exploring the nature of the economic processes involved in urban land markets in the absence of intervention, and second, we have not yet provided the analytic base for justifying intervention. Following the basic value judgement expressed in the opening chapter, we want to see how private markets will work out before we consider the possible role of a planning authority. This latter task is taken up in later chapters.

The private markets discussed in this chapter are themselves much simplified. There is not space here to explore the basic economic justification of urban areas – the reasons why economic activities cluster together – nor to analyse very thoroughly the economic activity within it. We take as a starting point the fact that an urban area does exist, centred on an employment core, and by adding a number of assumptions develop some insights into the kind of city which may result and the nature of the forces determining it. The number of categories of participants in this economy are limited to five, employers, workers, builders, landowners and farmers, all of which work within the maximising framework developed in the previous chapter. In order to make the discussion manageable, the economy is assumed to be an isolated one which does not trade with any other similar economy. Similarly, we have abstracted from financial markets which, in real life, play a large part in the creation of physical development by virtue of the role of property and land as investment assets comparable to company shares and government stock. Although these are important limitations if we were analysing a current policy problem, the additions of these factors to the analysis would add little to the points we wish to bring out at this stage. With these and other omissions in mind, the next section is called 'A Simple Urban Model'.

3.1 A Simple Urban Model

We begin with some very simple assumptions:

(i) All employment is located in one central place and numbers of jobs and hours of work are fixed.
(ii) There are only two urban uses of land, employment and housing.
(iii) Housing is located around the central employment area in a way to be analysed.
(iv) Transport costs are related only to distance from the centre and are set at a constant rate per mile. There is only one mode of travel.
(v) There are four categories of participant in the urban economy; employers, workers, land and property-owners, and builder/developers. A fifth category is farmers who use land outside the urban economy.
(vi) No member of any of these categories dominates the rest, i.e. all markets are competitive. Equally, the remaining conditions for efficient markets hold.
(vii) Problems such as pollution or noise nuisance do not exist.
(viii) All workers live within the urban area and there is no migration in or out. They are able to move freely between jobs. Similarly all goods consumed are produced within it.
(ix) Workers live in the houses provided by builder/developers, but they do not own them. They pay rent to the developers who in turn lease the land for their development from land-owners.
(x) Workers prefer low-density housing to high-density housing.
(xi) There are no barriers to the conversion of land from agricultural to developed uses, or between any other pair of uses.
(xii) The utility of individuals is determined only by transport costs, housing services and goods purchasable with residual income. All workers earn the same income, but they have different tastes or utility functions.
(xiii) The land surface is flat and featureless. There are no amenity areas.

(xiv) Building costs are constant per unit output, i.e. as densities increase on a given site, the unit cost of housing remains constant. These costs include infrastructure.

(xv) There is no public sector.

Many of these assumptions will be relaxed very quickly and they are made primarily to simplify the exposition. Nevertheless, even with the framework provided by the above rather rarified economy, we can derive, by a process of informal rather than rigorous reasoning, conclusions which are needed in later analysis.

The first question to consider is how the price and allocation of land are determined within an urban area to which our assumptions apply. Let us assume for the moment that the demand by employers for land is perfectly *inelastic*, so that no matter what the price, they still buy the same amount. Workers, offered one point of employment, compete between themselves for land for residential use. Their housing demands are met by builder/developers, who decide in the light of their estimates of what people will be prepared to pay, how much housing to supply and in what location. To build these houses, the builders must compete with each other for use of sites, all of which are owned by the land-owning group.

Under the assumptions set out above, the most attractive sites for housing development will be those nearest to the employment centre, as we have assumed away in assumption (vii) any undesirable effects, such as pollution, which the employment centre might impose on housing uses. Since no parts of the land surface (assumption (xii)) are more attractive than others, then land is differentiated only with respect to travel costs or accessibility to the employment centre. The sites nearest to the jobs are the most accessible and will tend to be built on first.

However, not everyone can be housed on sites bordering the employment centre. Although assumption (xiii) implies that extra dwellings could be added on at constant marginal cost, a limit is set by assumption (xi) to the extent to which densities rise near the centre. This states that as densities increase, enjoyment of housing services declines. Accordingly, on sites immediately next to the employment centre, developers can provide housing at the same unit cost, but with reduced environmental attraction. Workers will only be tempted to live further out, however, if the price they have to pay for their housing is reduced, i.e. if rents are lower than in the centre, or if the quality of the housing they can get further out is higher, or by some combination of these two. Thus, in the sort of city described we expect to find two things: first, that the price of housing is lower at the edge of the city than at the centre, and second, that the density of housing is higher near the centre than at the edge.

The rents which result can be shown in Figure 1. Near the centre rents are very high, but they fall away rapidly, until at the edge of the city they are at the level set by the value of land in agricultural use. How precisely is the slope of the line in the diagram determined? To answer this question, we must consider the decision process of the individuals making up the demand for housing. Assumption (xii) does not describe their preferences very precisely. If people were very averse to high-density living, then they would be very reluctant to accept high-density dwellings near the centre but would prefer to sacrifice time and money to enjoy lower density. Alternatively, if they were happy with high-density living, then the city would tend to be more compact and the land value curve rather steeper. In practice people, even with the same incomes, will tend to have different preferences, so that those who liked high density would live near the centre and those who liked it less would tend to move further out, pay the price for it in terms of higher travel costs, but be recompensed by lower rents.

The shape of the rent surface curve will depend closely on the nature of the transport system. If transport costs are high, then the price of living further out, i.e. the price of space, will also be high, so densities will also tend to be high. If transport costs are low then the city will tend to be spread out as the total price of housing, i.e. rents plus travel, is low also. The shape of the curve is also dependent on the building technology assumed. If the cost of building high rose per unit added, i.e. if marginal costs were greater than average cost, instead of remaining constant then this would tend to reduce the density near the centre. Alternatively, if the unit costs of building fell with scale (marginal costs below average costs) then it would be possible to build densely and cheaply near the centre so that the inner site could remain competitive for longer with the outer ones.

The urban form arrived at reflects technological factors such as building and transport cost functions on the one hand and individual preferences on the other. For any given set of assumptions of the kind set out above, provided that the interrelations between the various markets for land were known with sufficient precision, it would be possible to predict how the urban area so described would be shaped, how large it would be and at what densities it would be built. Any one such set of assumptions would, however, be equivalent to looking at the area at one point in time. The rent surface described in Figure 1 reflects a situation in which the problems involved in adjusting supply to demand are assumed away, i.e. the figure ignores the point that developers may make mistakes and that costs would be involved in correcting such mistakes. For example, as the city grew, it might turn out that the inner parts had been wrongly developed for the new conditions which emerged. This possibility has been ignored. Thus the diagram is timeless, in the sense that it does not take into account the process of change and adjustment which would in fact be needed in any real city and does not allow for the fact that what is on the ground will influence the final outcome of the forces being studied.

Figure 1

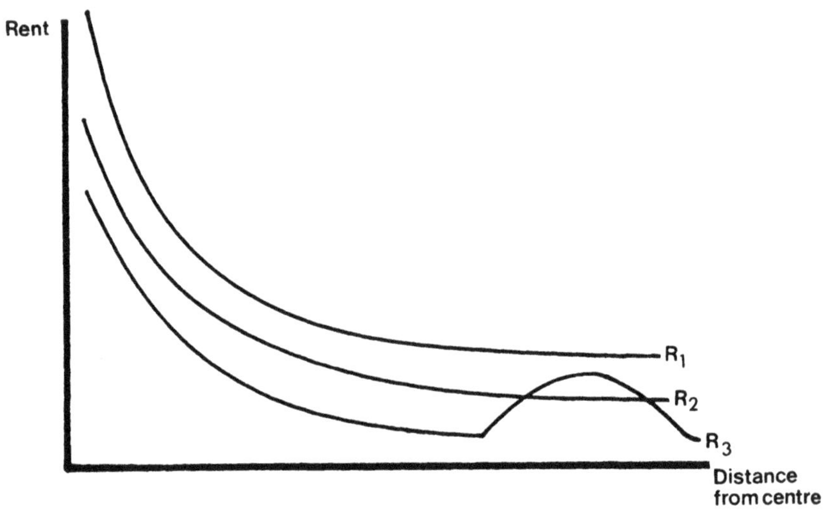

A real urban area cannot entirely escape its history and so a diagram of this kind represents a major simplification of reality. Nevertheless, we can explore in general terms how such a simple urban economy would react to changes in the basic economic factors determining it. The next few paragraphs consider the processes of adaptation involved, first by taking some of the basic assumptions of the model and examining the implications of changing them, and second, by looking at the various participants in the urban economy, to bring out the nature of the choices they are faced with.

We begin by looking at the implications of a change in the level of income per head. Let us assume that the demand for housing space is income elastic, i.e. expenditure on housing rises as a proportion of income as income rises. Using this assumption, we can predict that the city would tend to spread out, *provided that*, at higher income levels, individuals did not attach so much extra disutility to travel that they would attempt to cut down commuting. The outcome, in other words, would depend on the strength of these two elements in individuals' utility functions. In what follows, we shall assume, along with most empirical results, that overall the preference for extra space outweighs the disutility of travel so that the net result of income growth is a larger city in spatial terms. As we have assumed that preferences do differ between individuals, not all will follow this pattern. Some, for example, might give greater weight to accessibility as their incomes rose and prefer to live nearer the centre.

It follows from this that changes in the cost of transport by themselves will have implications for the city's size. If the price of travel falls, then the effect is to reduce the price of locations distant from the centre. This enables developers to offer cheaper dwellings at peripheral sites with the result that the city spreads out and the density of development declines. A new rent surface shown in the figure by the line R_2 would emerge. In a real city it would not of course take place immediately but would involve a long process of adjustment. This process would entail a modification in the stock of existing buildings and in the intensity of their use. There would be a tendency, once developers had reacted to changed transport costs by building more at the periphery, for inner-area rents to fall and for old buildings to be replaced with less intensive uses of the sites. This process would take time and resources, so if a sudden change in transport costs did take place it would take decades, even in the absence of other changes, for the capital stock to adjust. What the model suggests therefore is that if such a change did occur it would alter the relative profitability of different kinds of investment and hence the kind and spatial balance of developers' activities. In itself, it says nothing about speed of changes.

The same kind of effects would be produced by a change in building technology. For example, if the housing production function changed in such a way as to reduce the cost of high density relative to low, then building in the inner areas would be more attractive than previously. Similarly, any change in personal preferences would have consequences for the spatial pattern of development. If over time the attractions of accessibility grew, this would alter the relative profitability of inner- and outer-area investment – assuming still that all employment remained at the centre – and hence the shape of the city.

An alternative way of considering the implications of the simple model is to examine the behaviour of the various groups distinguished in assumption (v) and consider how they respond to the various situations with which they are faced. Consider first the employer. He is in direct competition with housing users and he must pay enough for his land to bid it away from them. The prices he is faced with depend on the outcome of the various forces we have considered. How much he is prepared to buy will depend on his own production function. If he finds it difficult to substitute other factors for land, then his demand will be inelastic and he will be forced to buy whatever quantity his production processes require. If he can adjust his pattern of production then he will respond to higher land prices by modifying his production processes. For example, he may be able to hold very low stocks and receive very frequent deliveries and so reduce his demand for storage space.

Once we relax our assumption that all jobs are at the centre of the city, however, the employer has the additional option open to him of locating his production facility elsewhere. Take the case of a small user of labour considering where to locate. He is faced with higher land costs in the centre and so gains directly if he moves to an area where land costs are low. But he may also be able to attract labour at lower wages. For example, if he locates in the periphery, then he may find it easy to attract sufficient labour from people prepared to walk to work. For these employees the costs of getting to work are reduced so they may be prepared to accept lower wages. If sufficient employers decentralise, then workers as a whole are faced with a choice of where to work. The result of this is likely to be differences in the wages available in different parts of the urban economy. Thus if the transport system is such that the centre has a relative accessibility advantage, then for any given level of labour demand it will be able to attract more people at a given price. If transport costs to the centre are high enough, then small centres may develop which offer lower wages – because the workers have lower housing costs at the periphery and lower travel costs. The extent of the wage differentials which emerge will be highly sensitive to the level of transport costs.

We consider next firms which continue to operate in the central area. They may find as the peripheral centres build up that their labour is being bid away from them. They may decide to move out, or they may decide to cut down on the use of labour, because this is now becoming an expensive factor to them, or they may decide to do something of both. They may decentralise certain activities, such as routine clerical jobs, and retain the higher levels of decision-making. They will tend to do this, for example, if the former requires categories of labour which are available throughout the urban economy and if the latter are scarce and hence require a larger catchment area to find.

If we introduce a range of industries, then it is unlikely that all would wish to locate in the centre, because as they will tend to use, by virtue of their different production processes, different amounts of the factors concerned, some will find it cheapest to operate in some locations and some in others. For example, a firm which uses a lot of land is unlikely to locate in the city centre where it is at its most expensive, but will seek more peripheral sites. In doing so it will have to trade off the lower costs of land inputs to its production process against any losses on other inputs, i.e. depending precisely on what transport system is available, the cost of other inputs such as raw material and labour may be higher. Thus, mirroring the individual trying to find the best housing location for himself, the firm will locate in that part of the area where its activities will be most profitable. Services dependent on demand from all parts of the urban area – e.g. specialist retailing – will tend to remain near the centre; other retailing activities dependent only on custom from a small catchment area will tend to locate near their markets.

Second, the worker. The decision he must make is 'where to locate': he is faced with various possibilities even within our initial set of assumptions with all employment located at the centre, running from high accessibility, high density and high housing cost to low degrees of accessibility and low densities and low housing costs. Following the analysis of section 2.1, the best combination for him will depend on his preferences and on the relative prices facing him. If he is averse to travelling, he may nevertheless choose a peripheral site if by doing this he can enjoy much better housing. If he is indifferent about different qualities of housing, he will prefer to live in the centre but will be dissuaded from doing so if rents are very high. He must trade off these various factors until he finds the best location in the city for him. If his income changes, then he will adjust his location according to the way his demand for housing and his aversion to travel is income-related.

These various possibilities can be illustrated using the indifference curve analysis developed in the previous chapter. If we take a small number of individuals we can assume that they are too small a part of the market to influence the rent surface, i.e. the rate at which accessibility is traded off against better environment is given as far as they are concerned. The houses they are able to buy are shown in Diagram 9 by the line XY. An accessibility preferer will be found at point A and an environment preferer at point E – their different preferences being illustrated by the different shapes and position of their indifference curves.

Diagram 9

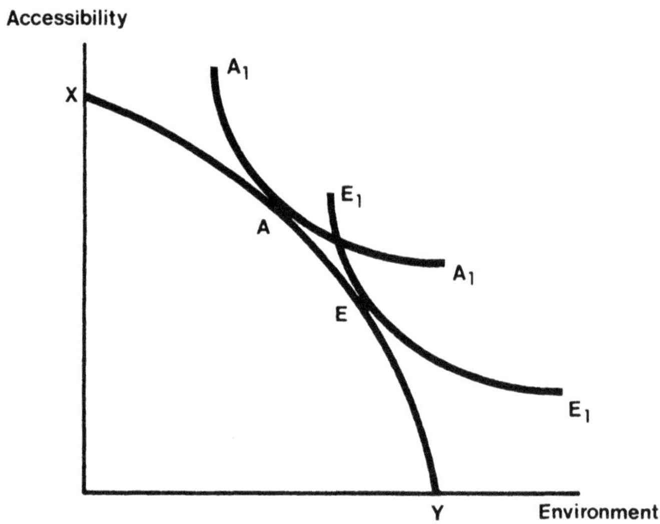

If assumption (xii) is relaxed and income differentials introduced, then differences in choice of location between income groups might be predicted. In large urban areas we would expect to find that the higher-income groups lived at the edge of the urban area, at low density, and that the lower-income groups lived at high density, near jobs, where housing was most expensive. The latter result follows from two considerations; first, the lower-income groups cannot afford long and expensive journeys to work. By assumption (iv), travel costs rise in proportion to distance, so to economise on travel, they must live near to their work. Second, land near jobs is the most expensive, so, given their income constraint, their only possible reaction is to economise on space. Upper income groups are free to locate where they wish by virtue of their purchasing power. Thus, if some are accessibility preferers and some not, then they would tend to be found at both inner and outer locations. Similarly, if employment decentralises, the balance of advantage changes for low-income groups and they too would be found at various locations, principally near the job centres.

Once there is more than one employment centre, then the rent surface will be more complex than in the monocentric city. Near the peripheral centres rents will be higher than otherwise because such locations will have local accessibility advantages. The rent surface would look like the third line in Figure 1, with a bump towards the edge of the urban area. Similarly, as noted already, the creation of peripheral employment centres will lead to differences in wage payments between different locations. Employers in the centre will have to pay employees sufficient to cover the extra travelling costs involved in working there. Their willingness to do so will in turn depend on the advantages which they enjoy from being in a central location.

This point is further developed in Chapter 12, but there is an important relationship between housing and job markets which we must note here. In the initial form of the simple urban model there was only one employment centre *and* the demand for labour was assumed fixed. As employment shifts to a number of locations, workers have the choice of where to work. This adds two complications to the discussion; first, choice of residential location is made more complex since it involves a trade-off between travel costs, housing costs, housing quality and different levels of money income. Second, a choice of whether or not to participate in the labour force at all emerges. The amount of labour supplied may depend on the accessibility of people to the jobs available. For example, at peripheral locations, some people, typically married women, may be so close to job opportunities that they will enter the labour force when they would not do so if they had to travel to the centre. Such people are trading off higher money income against time not spent working. Thus, the level of goods production in the city may depend on the distribution of land uses within it.

A final point about the nature of the decision facing the individual. As we noted in Chapter 2, we are using 'the individual' as a shorthand for a household. When a household consists of more than one person, then the choices to be made are more complex: nevertheless, some general points can be made which experience confirms. For example, larger households will, subject to their budget constraint, tend to prefer housing to other goods since their demand for space will be high and will therefore tend not to live at the centre of the city. Smaller, younger households, on the contrary, will tend to prefer central locations because their space requirements are less and their valuation of accessibility higher.

Third, the developer. His aim is to maximise his profits from building operations. On the one hand he is faced with the production functions for housing, i.e. within our assumptions constant returns to the construction activity itself but different land prices, and by the demands of workers for accommodation. By assumption, he seeks to put up buildings which promise to yield the highest rental value. If he does not do this, the landowner will offer the site elsewhere. The amount the developer can afford to pay for land depends on the difference between what people are prepared to pay for dwellings and his building costs. If this is small, then the payment to the landowner will be low, and vice versa. For example, at the edge of the city, builders may only be able to tempt buyers away from sites closer in by offering low prices with no margin left over for payment to landowners except what is necessary to bid away land from agricultural uses. Within the inner area, he will not be able to build unless he can meet the high rents which prevail there. This will only be possible if the difference between his building costs and expected revenue is larger. Thus as far as the individual builder is concerned, his bid for land is a residual, determined by his other costs. Whether the landowner will accept this amount depends on what others are offering.

If we relax the assumption that all houses are identical, then the builders' task becomes more complicated but it remains essentially the same as in the simpler case. That is, he must consider which of the various kinds of dwellings he may produce offers the greatest possibility for profit in the light of their relative building costs and the price of land in the area concerned. In some locations it may not be possible to build profitably certain kinds of house at all, e.g. at high land prices low-density dwellings would only be profitable if there existed a small section of the market willing to pay very high prices for them. Typically, he would have to use expensive land more intensively so as to keep unit costs down. Similarly at the edge of the city there would be little advantage in building high, since greater profits could be earned by different kinds of dwelling on the relatively large amount of land available.

All these decisions have to be made against a set of expectations about how the urban area will develop. As the urban area grows, either in income or population, the relative value of sites in different parts of it will change in response to the changing demands of the two 'demanding' groups considered above. When jobs are decentralising, there will be opportunities for profitable investment in commercial buildings outside the central area. If pressure on central area commercial and housing space grows, it will become profitable to demolish existing structures and put up new ones which make better use of the land under the new demand pattern. If pressure on housing space grows, then densities will increase and vice versa. If demand for one use rises relative to another, developers will seek to transfer land and buildings between them.

The demand curve for the use of a given site will shift over time. To put up the building which over time makes the best use of a site, the developer must take some view as to how demand will move. For example, he must estimate whether any pressure on central area space is best met in the central area or on the periphery, and at either location he must take a view on the appropriate density. He is, by assumption, seeking to maximise his profits, but the profit accrues over time. If he builds at high density in response to current pressures, he may find that what the building will yield – i.e. the rents people will pay – falls rapidly over time. Alternatively, if he builds at too low a density, he will find that his development yields less than it could have done.

Fourth, the landowner. His task in this model is straightforward. He makes his land available to the use and to the developer which is prepared to pay most for it. At the margin of the city, therefore, he will make his land over for urban development as soon as it earns him more in a developed use than in agriculture. Within the city he makes his land over to the builder who can use it most efficiently, i.e. can earn the highest profit, and hence pay the highest rent. If a building can be redeveloped to yield a higher rent, then he encourages the conversion. This role is simple enough, but it has important implications which are brought out in the next section.

Finally, the farmer. He, like the builder, must bid for land to be allowed to use it; he will be prepared to pay higher rent for land near to the urban area because it is accessible to the markets for his produce. But the amount he can pay is limited by the amount he can get for his produce and his costs of producing them. He must give way to other uses when they are able to pay for land a price at which agricultural production is not profitable.

3.2 The Supply and Allocation of Land within the Simple Urban Model

In a discussion like that earlier in the chapter, we can only describe the kind of forces at work in a free or mixed urban economy. We cannot attempt to predict particular outcomes or to describe precisely the workings of any particular urban economy, but we can say something about its general nature. The essential feature of the economy we have been describing is a continual balancing process. Producers and workers in their capacity as house users and employers continually adjust to the changes in relative costs or prices which face them. This description is of course a simplification of reality. Nevertheless, it reflects a number of important real-world processes which we shall discuss in more detail in later chapters. Because of the central importance of land to this book, we shall pull together now some of the points brought out in the previous section which relate to the demand and supply of land within the urban economy.

Within the simple model, the allocation of land between the two uses we have considered – employment and housing – in total and in respect of its spatial pattern – is the outcome of the interaction of a large number of factors, including both the technology of production and the preferences of individuals for different kinds of housing, for accessibility and for goods. The nature of the goods demanded determines the nature of the jobs involved. The precise production processes used depend on the price of the factors involved which in part reflect individual preferences directly and in part the spatial structure of the urban economy.

In the urban economy expressed in the assumptions listed above, resources, land, labour and capital are free to either physically move into any available location or in the case of land free to move into any use, according to which is the most profitable. In the case of land this means that all sites of comparable accessibility would have the same value, no matter what use they were put to. Any differences would reflect only the differential values accruing from accessibility or any other factor, such as visual amenity, where this is relevant. If amenity were highly valued by workers and if land similar in accessibility terms were available, then the amenity land would tend to command a higher price than the areas of equivalent accessibility. If the 'amenity' areas were scattered throughout the urban areas, then the rent surface which resulted would be much less smooth than that in Figure 1. Equally, if land was unattractive and expensive to develop, areas of low value would occur and further complicate the rent surface.

If there were some sudden changes in conditions within the urban economy, then differentials in land values between otherwise comparable sites would occur, but they would be temporary. We have not discussed transport very thoroughly yet and will not do so until Chapter

12, but a transport example is useful here. If, for instance, a new transport facility were added at one edge of the urban area, and if this had not been anticipated, then values in that area would be out of line with the new situation, until developers and landowners realised the nature of the new opportunities.

The important qualification here is 'and if this had not been anticipated'. In our urban economy, we have assumed that markets are working well in the sense that information is freely available. Thus, if the urban area is growing, changes in the relative advantage of different sites will be anticipated and will in any case tend to be slow. For example, if the urban area grows in terms of income and population, the absolute value of central sites is likely to grow, but may decline in relation to more peripheral sites. This process will be a slow one in all but exceptional cases. Any shift in values will tend to be gradual. But if there is some sudden change in demand, for example through a change in accessibility which has not been expected, the current values will be out of line with future earning potential and a sudden adjustment in values should take place.

At the centre of our urban area, employment and housing uses compete for the same land, and as employment moves to peripheral locations, competition occurs there also. Land is assumed to move from one use to another once a higher price emerges in the second use, as we have assumed that landowners are interested solely in maximising their money returns, i.e. they are assumed not to have a personal interest in the use to which land is put. Thus, for any particular use of land, in a given location, the supply curve is highly elastic, that is, landowners will withdraw their land from any use which cannot pay the going rate and supply it freely to uses which can. However, if we take the supply of central area land *as a whole*, then supply is completely inelastic, that is, however much is paid, no more can be supplied, since land by its nature is spatially specific. If demand increases because of income growth, the price of land must rise. Some users will drop out at the new price, move elsewhere and economise on space, and others will take over the space they have vacated.

Quite generally, within the model's assumptions, the price of land influences all decisions concerning its use. It influences the locational decisions of both individuals and firms and the use to which developers decide to put different sites. Where demand pressures are high, prices rise to induce the economising reactions discussed above. Where demand is low because the site concerned is unattractive or inaccessible, price falls to a level where some user will take on the sites concerned. Land will fail to be brought into use only when the costs of doing so, e.g. site preparation, rule it out. In these ways the price of land performs an economic function like any other market price, guiding decisions of all the participants in the market for it. It will only do this, however, if the participants in the land markets are themselves well informed. The prices they are prepared to bid and supply reflect estimates of rents obtainable now and in future years. When these are correct the price of land is an accurate guide to the way in which different sites should be used.

There is an important difference between the price of land and that of other prices, however, that the price paid for land is a *pure rent or surplus*. It represents a payment over and above what needs to be paid to keep the land in productive use. The reserve price of land to the urban economy is set by the price paid by agriculture. At the extensive margin of the city, i.e. its physical periphery, rent paid to bring land into urbanisation must be fractionally greater than this. From the previous section, however, it is clear that payments to the factor land in most of the urban areas are normally much greater than the minimum amount needed to bring the land into the urban economy. They comprise a surplus, or economic rent.

The essence of a surplus accruing to a factor of production is that its extent is determined by demand for that factor and not its costs of production. Thus the size of the income earned by landowners in this model is determined purely by demand and not by conditions of supply. In the calculation of developers bidding for land, the price of land is a residual element, after all other costs of construction have been allowed for. The demand for and value of land is derived from the markets for goods and services which require land for their production. Thus for the urban economy as a whole, land rents do not determine prices in that economy, but are determined by them. This is not true for any particular urban use. An individual use must meet the rent which other users are prepared to pay for a given site and in this sense rents do determine the final price of goods. For example, the price at which a manufacturer can produce in a central area location will be set by his production costs on the one hand and the rent he must pay on the other. But the latter will only be high as long as others are prepared to pay it. It is sometimes said that high rents are driving users out of a particular area. In the model's assumptions, this would only be true for a small part of the potential users of the area in question who are being squeezed out by incoming users prepared to pay more. It is the pressure of these demands which affects the price of the goods produced by the original user.

In this analysis the supply curve of land in a particular location within the urban economy is vertical, but it is horizontal to the urban economy as a whole since more land can always be brought into developed uses by outbidding agricultural uses. There are two circumstances in real life where such a supply curve to the urban area may not have this shape, but will be like those portrayed in the previous chapter, i.e. upward sloping to the right. The first instance is if landowners enjoy utility from owning land, i.e. if they are simultaneously demanders and suppliers. If landowners gained enjoyment from holding land or particular portions of land, then the supply curve would have the conventional shape, i.e. among the landowners at the edge of the urban area some would have a low supply price and others not. In these circumstances, they will have to be induced by extra payments to give up their land, even when agricultural prices have been exceeded. Second, if landowners have a different set of expectations about future values from other parts of the urban economy, they may not be prepared to supply at the prices at which developers are prepared to bid. In the model we have assumed that judgements on the future are shared and we have further ignored the function of land as a store of value. These are both important considerations when considering the direct application of the model to a real-life situation. A further important simplification should be noted, the assumption that land markets are competitive. This assumption has been made for expositional convenience in this chapter and it is not a bad approximation to the conditions which obtain in real urban areas. But again, it is a qualification to be borne in mind when interpreting real-life phenomena.

3.3 Concluding Comment

The urban economy described in this chapter can be seen as a set of interrelated markets. The outcome of this interaction is the production of final goods and services – which we have not analysed – and an allocation of land, and buildings on that land, to which we have given some attention. The various parts of this economy are related to each other through the demands for goods and factors on the one hand and their supply on the other. The essence of this urban economy is that, once change is introduced into it, it is in a state of continual adaptation. The various individual decision-makers within it, be it households, firms, landowners, make their own decisions, but they are nevertheless interrelated. Taken together, they produce a pattern of demand for land.

In the model, the key decisions, as far as allocation of land and the erection of buildings are concerned, are taken by the builder/developer. He makes these decisions in the light of the demands he perceives. These arise from the requirements of individuals, industry and commerce and they are expressed in prices obtaining in the markets for various categories of building. The risks he bears himself by committing resources to buildings which may, or may not, represent the best use of land and the other resources required. When changes occur altering the relative advantages of different sites and structures, the developer is led by the change in relative prices which results in altering the scale and disposition of the urban capital stock. His job is the more difficult the more rapid the changes and the more uncertain are the demands facing him.

In the model, we have assumed that the developer is a private agent, but as far as the definition of his basic role in the allocation of resources is concerned, this fact is immaterial. The urban area we have been analysing offers different 'bundles' of accessibility, space and money income. This is true of any real urban area, although of course the choices would be more complex. Nevertheless, the nature of the choices and hence the kind of decisions which have to be made remain the same if we were to assume that our simple urban model was organised centrally and all decisions on the use and allocation of land taken centrally. Any decision-maker, or set of decision-makers, is faced with the same technical possibilities. The production functions for construction and the costs of transport in relation to other goods would be the same and hence the basic trade-offs would be identical. The urban area would continue to offer different 'bundles' of accessibility, environment and cost.

What might differ between the market and the centrally organised economy are the judgements which are brought to bear on the relative value of different courses of action. Within the market economy described, the allocation of resources, including land, responds to the demands appearing in the markets concerned. The centrally organised urban economy could respond to different indicators of preference. This basic distinction between preferences on the one hand and technical possibilities on the other is one which is central to the analysis of later chapters.

The model and its variants described in this chapter have been developed using a number of simplifying assumptions. Nevertheless, although this necessarily limits the usefulness of the model as a description of reality, there is a fair amount of empirical work available which suggests that it does have considerable relevance to real-world conditions. For example, the rent and land value surfaces in many cities do have the shape suggested in this chapter and similarly wage differentials can be observed within the large metropolitan areas. But the main purpose to which the model will be used will be to provide a framework within which we can develop further the ideas introduced so far. The empirical material can be explored with the help of the Bibliography.

A final point. As we noted in Chapter 2, the purpose of this chapter has not been to suggest that because certain functions are carried out within a set of economic markets they are necessarily done well or best in this way. In the following chapter the reasons why markets may not work well will be systematically examined. Instead, the discussion has aimed to bring out four points: first, if in any given economy, private markets in land and production exist, they will tend to work in the ways analysed above, although to analyse a real-life situation it would be necessary to take into account a large number of the factors which we have assumed away, such as restraints to competition. Second, by setting out the ways in which markets do work, and the kinds of outcomes they produce, we can more clearly specify the reasons which might underlie intervention in those processes. This is the subject of the following chapter. Third, if intervention does take place to modify market behaviour, this chapter has given some indication of how markets might react. Chapters 6, 7, 10, 11 and 13 consider these reactions in more detail. Fourth, if intervention is to replace rather than modify those processes, then we have gone some way towards indicating the functions which any alternative set of policies or institutions must carry out. Chapters 8, 9 and 12 consider how these functions may be carried out within the public sector.

4 MARKET FAILURE

The previous two chapters analysed the nature of market processes, without coming to any general judgement on whether they are, from an individual or social point, desirable or not. This chapter goes on to consider some important and generally applicable reasons why the outcome of market processes may not be desirable. It will not consider all the possible reasons why markets may produce unsatisfactory results. Many reasons fall outside the scope of land-use planning. For example, the control of monopoly and restrictive practices is with few exceptions outside the scope of land-use planning authorities.

The main aim of this chapter, therefore, is to distinguish a number of general ways in which markets may fail which are particularly relevant to land-use planning and, second, to introduce the economic concepts which have been devised to describe and analyse them, when the conditions for effective markets set out above do not hold. In doing this, the scope of the analysis developed in the previous chapters will be enlarged. So far consumption and production have been seen as being self-contained or 'private' activities interrelated only through the workings of the price mechanism. This chapter extends the analysis to include interactions between producers and between producers and consumers which are not reflected in the price mechanism.

The cases to be examined can easily be recognised in the history of unregulated urbanisation and are familiar to all land-use planners. The main purpose of the chapter, therefore, is not to reveal examples of market failure, the effects of which have not been appreciated. It is to distinguish the various quite different reasons why such failures arise and hence why the outcome of private markets may not be acceptable. The importance of this is simple: that to be able to assess the merits of any particular policy, we must be clear what kinds of argument might be used to support it. As we shall see below, policies may be proposed with reference to different criteria, with the result that their justification is not always very clear and the case for the policy concerned either taken for granted or justified 'on social grounds'. What is meant by the latter phrase is frequently not specified. In this chapter, therefore, we shall consider systematically what 'social' grounds there may be for rejecting the outcome of unregulated market processes.

4.1 Externalities

We have seen how markets are interrelated through the workings of the price mechanism. If extra demands arise in one sector this is reflected in other sectors using similar resources. Firms wishing to expand may have to bid up the price of these resources in order to obtain them. The higher prices which result are reflected in the costs of all firms using the resources concerned. In a large number of cases, however, industries may impose costs on other industries, or directly on individuals, for which they do not have to pay. Such costs are defined as *external* costs, i.e. costs which are not felt within the firm which gives rise to them.

The classic example of this is the smoky factory chimney which forces householders to spend more on cleaning, damages the crops of nearby farmers and forces other industrialists to install air purification plant. If external costs are present then the supply curves used earlier must be redrawn. In Diagram 10 the total or social cost curve SC of the industry lies above the private cost curve PC by the amount of

Diagram 10

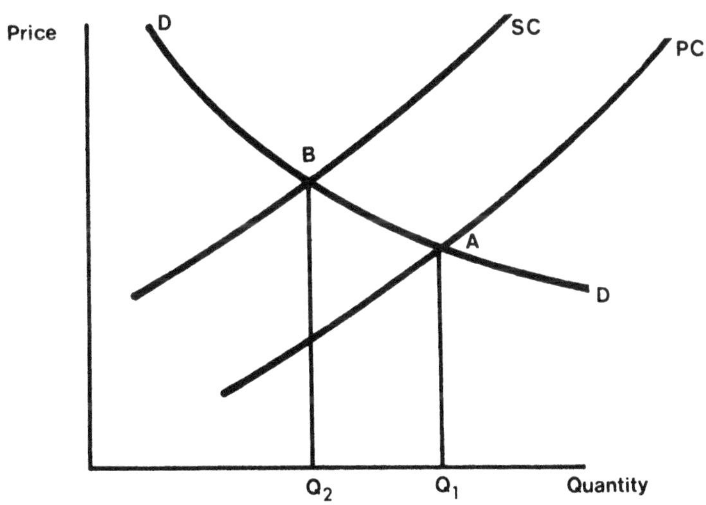

the external costs involved. Nevertheless, in an unregulated market amount A would be purchased since both producers and consumers would not take the social cost curve into account. Two issues arise here: first, is the scale of production right? Second, is production being carried out in the proper way?

One implication of the diagram is that the output of this particular commodity is too large by the amount Q_1-Q_2, for at Q_1 the total costs, including both the costs of the firm and the costs occasioned by the external effects, are greater than the amount which consumers would be prepared to pay. To the left of point B, however, the demand curve indicates that consumers would be prepared to meet the total social costs concerned were they required to. To the right of point B they would not. For example, in an amenity area a certain amount of mining might be tolerated because of the value of its output but not the full amount which those carrying out the mining might wish for. After a certain point – B – the social costs may be judged to outweigh the benefit.

In many cases the main issue, however, will not be the scale of output, but the method of production used. The process which is cheapest to the firm, reflected in the private cost curve, may not be the cheapest from the viewpoint of society as a whole. The smoke emerges from the factory chimney because of the particular means of heating used. This may be best, i.e. lowest cost, from the firm's viewpoint. The equipment required to eliminate the smoke nuisance will not be fitted because the benefits of doing so do not accrue, or accrue only in part to the firm itself.

Examples of external costs are very common and many of them are central to the interest of land-use planners. Smoke is just one example of the costs which producers may impose on people living near them. There may also be losses of visual amenity, traffic delays and noise, all of which are costs which in most circumstances do not fall on the activity giving rise to them. Similarly, individuals impose external costs on their neighbours; the individual extending his house may block out his neighbour's view, or the individual siting his house in a beauty spot may spoil it for others. The examples can easily be multiplied.

Not all external effects are unfavourable. Industry may bring with it benefits to other industry in excess of the services or goods it actually supplies. In these circumstances total social costs are below private costs and the industry concerned will, from a social point of view, tend to produce too little, because the revenue it receives understates the total advantages which extra output brings to society as a whole. One example of a favourable external effect is the general improvement of freight transport facilities in an area enjoyed by all firms as the result of the expansion of one of them. This may occur where freight transport enjoys economies of scale. The general increase in demand for transport allows transport firms to provide services to everyone at lower unit costs.

The existence of external effects does not in itself imply that market processes should be modified or controlled. The existence of some external costs may be regarded as inherent in any social context and possibly ignored on the grounds that people must take the rough with the smooth. But where activities give rise to external costs, or benefits, then there can no longer be any general presumption that private and social interests are identical. Production and consumption activities, where externalities are present, are necessarily *public*, not private, activities. Hence, although external effects may be trivial in some contexts, they provide one of the most powerful reasons for intervention by government in the workings of economic markets. This is particularly true of the market for land. The way in which a given piece of land is used is highly important to those users of land in the immediate vicinity. A large proportion of the problems which land-use planners face stems from external effects which are often acute in urban areas where activities are carried out in close proximity. The fact of proximity itself does not create external effects such as noise, nuisance or visual disamenity, but it does affect their impact. Thus what the individual decides to do with his land is of interest to all his neighbours whereas what he does within his house, what he buys for it and what activities he gets up to within it, are generally not. These may remain private activities. But as soon as he indulges in acts which have public consequences, such as building an extension or letting the exterior of his house run down, then his actions necessarily have a wider significance than his own, or his household's, utility function.

The introduction of external effects extends the scope of the individual utility function introduced in Chapter 1. Up to now the utility of the individual – or household – has been assumed to depend solely on the quantities of goods which they were able to buy, given their budget restraint. Once external effects are introduced, then this restriction must be dropped and the possibility recognised that the utility of the individual depends on his own private consumption, on the consumption pattern of his neighbours and of the means by which the goods he and others wish to buy are produced.

4.2 Failures of Supply: Public Goods

In the previous chapter it was assumed that producers could recover their costs by the prices they charged. But with some kinds of goods, they may find it difficult to do so with the result that the market fails to provide any incentives to their supply. Such goods have come to be known as *public goods*. This term can be misleading. First, a semantic point; many publicly produced goods are privately consumed, e.g. water or health care. So although they are made available by the public sector, they are not public goods in the sense defined here. Second, most goods have some public attributes and very few can be shown to have purely public attributes. The classic example of a public good is defence. Once the 'service' is provided to a given country, then no one can help but be defended. The defence for one is defence for all. But this is not true of all defence services. In some societies, and for some individuals, defence – or 'protection' – is a private good, sold and paid for like any personal service and enjoyed only by the person or persons paying for it.

In practice there is no sharp dividing line between private and public goods. Many quite ordinary goods have some public qualities. Certain kinds of information are of this kind. For example, the magazine *Which?* survives as the journal of a private association, but its availability in public libraries and through personal lending means that there is a constant risk that people will be disinclined to buy it, as the benefits it offers are available without doing so. People who do obtain benefits in this way are known as 'free-riders' and the supply problem it gives rise to often referred to as the 'free-rider' problem.

Where there are free-riders, the possibility of *exclusion* is important. In the case of national defence, exclusion is not practicable. But in other cases it may be, at a cost. For example, everyone with a TV receiver may pick up BBC transmissions if he is in the relevant area. BBC revenues are however guaranteed by a state-enforced payment system which no private firm could operate. Even this, however, does not extend to the 'free viewers' of neighbouring countries. Thus exclusion is rarely a purely technical problem. It would pay no one to put up a fountain in a public square unless he was able to charge for it. There is nothing by virtue of a fountain itself which precludes a charge which would allow only those who paid to view it, provided that a suitable screen could be erected. But this would be unattractive environmentally and perhaps dangerous to traffic. Thus, the obstacles to exclusion may be those of policy or practicality and little to do with the nature of the facility or service itself. In some cases, even with goods with some public qualities, private firms may be able to effect sufficient exclusion to make production viable, e.g. commercial publications are sometimes sent to a limited number of subscribers only and a very high price is charged.

The public good aspects of many goods are essentially trivial. The fact that if I buy a lawn-mower my neighbour will not because he will borrow mine, need worry no one. But there are many instances of public goods which are important to land-use planning. One example is an urban park. In principle it might be charged for and in this way the benefits derived from it would be expressed in a revenue flow sufficient to encourage private provision. But the firm (or public authority) could not charge for the benefits enjoyed by residents overlooking it, even though they might enjoy higher property values as a result of it being there. Accordingly, if the level of cash flow was relied on to determine the scale of urban park provision, under-provision would tend to occur since the revenue which firms might earn would systematically understate the benefits enjoyed by the existence of the park. This is the main reason why such facilities are rarely provided when development is left entirely to the private sector.

How effective the private sector can be in supplying public goods depends in part on the structure of the supplying industry. Suppose housing in an area was supplied entirely by a large number of private enterprise builders, each firm building on a fairly small scale. Each house would be provided with a modest amount of open space or garden. Suppose that large benefits would ensue if this space were 'pooled', i.e. if people got more pleasure out of a ten-acre space than a hundred one-tenth acre spaces. It would be unlikely for this solution to be reached without intervention by a planning authority because individual builders would have no incentive to bring it about, unless they could charge prices which reflected the extra benefit. In the circumstances considered it is unlikely they would, especially if the larger space had to be made available to everyone, not only the house-owners concerned.

A large common open space might be provided if developers were able to recoup in terms of higher house prices the profits they lose by devoting land to open space instead of houses. A single monopoly supplier might be able to do this. Such developments are frequently called exclusive. The word exclusive usually has certain social overtones. But in the present context it can have a precise technical meaning since the ability of the developer to obtain higher prices for the houses he puts up will depend on his ability through scheme design and other conditions to exclude all but the buyers of the houses concerned from the benefits of the open space. In this way he may ensure it is profitable to him to provide it.

The problem is more serious in regard to open countryside and other natural amenities. Firms may be able to – and often do – exploit unique and unusual natural amenities and so convert them into private goods. But the attractiveness of the countryside as a whole cannot be captured in this way. Nor can environmental features like clean air. There is no way in which demand may express itself in market behaviour for amenities like these. They may be destroyed or lost but they cannot be supplied in the way that other goods can be. As a consequence, the working of market forces, unless these are modified by measures of the kind considered in Chapter 6 below, cannot be trusted to ensure that the amount supplied is correct.

A final clarification. The public goods problem does not refer to the situation where specific individuals with low incomes or special needs are poorly served by the market mechanism. This reason for market failure is discussed below. It is distinct from the problem posed by goods with public attributes. These may be under-supplied no matter how high the income of those who would like to enjoy them.

4.3 Pricing and Adjustment Problems

In the previous chapter it was assumed that the prices charged by firms equalled the opportunity costs of the resources involved. For a large number of reasons, only some of which we can mention here, they may fail to do so. The result is that the prices which obtain do not do accurately the job identified in Chapters 2 and 3 of providing the appropriate incentive to suppliers to supply or consumers to economise. Where money prices and true opportunity costs do get out of line we may want to distinguish carefully between them, i.e. by talking about *money costs* on the one hand – what one actually has to pay out for something in cash – and *resource costs* on the other – what resources or factors of production are deployed (and hence benefits forgone in other uses).

Money prices and true opportunity costs may get out of line both for factors of production purchased by firms and goods purchased by individuals. For example, if a factor of production is in short supply, but if its price is controlled by agreement or by statute, then the true opportunity cost will be much greater than its apparent value. Similarly, if the factor is in excess supply, i.e. some of it not being used, but its price does not fall to reflect this, then the factor will be overpriced.

Instances where prices and true opportunity costs do get out of line are common. Some result from government intervention, e.g. price controls on key commodities or taxation – which tends to increase the money cost of resources or final goods above their opportunity costs – or subsidies, which do the reverse. In the private sector, prices of goods may diverge from true resource costs where, for example, a monopoly supplier fails to reflect marginal costs in the prices he sells at. This case is considered in Chapter 9.

The case of labour is important in a number of planning contexts. Here we can look at it briefly to bring out what markets may fail to work well in the presence of restrictions on the price of a factor of production. If the price is kept below that which would result from a free interplay between supply and demand, then the labour involved will be in *excess demand*, i.e. more of it will be demanded than is available at the going price. The opposite will also be true, that is, if it is kept above the price to which it would 'naturally' fall, then employers will have no incentive to mop up any supplies of labour which might become idle and have no incentive to move to, or expand production in, such areas. Without specific intervention this situation will tend to persist, with the result that the labour resources concerned continue to be unemployed.

The market, constrained in this way, fails to allocate them to productive activity and the workers themselves have a limited incentive to look for work elsewhere. Even if they are unemployed, the possibility of getting a satisfactory wage locally may deter them from moving to find work, unless the possibility is very remote indeed.

The result of this failure of price to reflect opportunity cost is that the adjustment processes by which factors of production move from one sector to another in response to changing demands for goods will be less rapid than we have tended to assume in the earlier discussion and may be very slow. This is true not only of labour but of other factors. For example, where rents are conventionally fixed for a long period of time, they may become very much out of line with current conditions, particularly during times of inflation. The result of this is that users hang on to properties from which they would be priced out, had prices adjusted, and are then hit very hard when their rents are raised. This has been observable in recent years in central London, for example, as leases of office space, sometimes fixed before the war, have fallen in and been renegotiated at many times their original level. The result is that urban structure changes less rapidly than if subject to 'perfect' market forces.

There are many other reasons why responses to changes in supply and demand conditions may be slow. Both firms and individuals suffer from inertia, so that they do not necessarily respond immediately to new opportunities for profit when they come along. Individuals may be reluctant to move because of social or other ties. Firms may be happy to continue where they are as long as they continue to make profits. In some cases, such obstacles to change may be so great that the kind of re-allocation and response to changing conditions normally assumed to occur may effectively never result. For example, there are long-established disparities in the level of employment between different parts of the UK (and even more marked differences occur in some other countries), and between different parts of metropolitan areas, which market forces have not eliminated.

Whether in situations like this we say that markets are inherently inefficient or ascribe their failure to restrictions on their working is not important in the present context. Most of the reasons mentioned in this section for markets not working well are the result of situations which may in themselves be desirable or have some desirable effects. The fact that national wage agreements may exacerbate local employment problems may be undesirable but be regarded as an acceptable cost to be set against the advantages of national bargaining. From the point of view of the land-use planner – or any other policy analyst – the important point is that as long as such policies are pursued within the economy as a whole, by government or other institutions, he may not be able to assume a ready adjustment through market behaviour to changing economic conditions – i.e. to shifts in relative costs, earnings or levels of demand. The fact that individuals may not move because they wish to remain in a community they value may be something to accept as a constraint on what is done. Alternatively the planner may wish to act so as to help along adjustment processes which might otherwise take too long. In either case, the fact must be taken into account.

In some cases the rate of change may be judged to be too rapid. For example, an influx of commercial development into an area might, in an uncontrolled situation, take over large amounts of inner-area housing peripheral to the commercial core which was occupied at fairly high densities. There might be no problem in terms of cost or land release in making good this loss of housing and there may even be advantages in older housing being taken over by a use which could finance its maintenance and repair. But in the short run, authorities, or the private market, may find it difficult to make good the loss of housing, so there could be considerable short-term disruption and hardship. Another example is given by changes in the distribution of jobs from existing locations to new ones. The pace and extent of change in the demand for labour may, for institutional or social reasons, be more rapid than the process of change in the housing sector. Consequently the kind of adjustment processes described in the previous chapter to changes in job location may not be feasible, e.g. workers may not find it possible to move into areas where demand for labour is increasing. A very uneven spatial pattern of demand for labour may result, with shortages in some areas and excesses in others, which persist in the face of institutional obstacles to their removal.

4.4 Imperfect Information and Failures of Co-ordination

In the previous chapter it was assumed that individuals and firms were aware, costlessly, of the opportunities available to them to make profits or to make their earnings higher. In the real world information is imperfect or incomplete. One result of this is similar to the restriction on market forces discussed in the previous sections, i.e. it hinders adjustment processes and hence the allocation of resources in response to changes in supply and demand conditions. To the extent that information is a public good, there will be no incentive for market forces themselves to work to overcome this deficiency. The cost of getting and distributing information and the time and effort involved in searching for and pursuing job opportunities all go to limit the amount of information available.

Lack of information has a particular relevance to land-use planning in cases where the choices made by individuals or the production plans of firms depend on others, in part or in whole, for their success. This problem is sometimes known as the *prisoner's dilemma*. This rather odd name refers to a problem of interdependence. The example is a dramatic one: the prisoner is faced with a choice, to be made in isolation; what he does depends on his expectations of what his fellow-prisoner, with whom he cannot communicate, will do. If the prisoner pursues his own self-interest, by confessing to earn commutation of sentence, his fellow prisoner will die. His fellow-prisoner is in the same position. If he confesses, his sentence is reduced to imprisonment and the first prisoner will die. But if both refuse to confess, then they are both set free since there is no evidence against them. But can the prisoners, unable to communicate, rely on the appropriate response from each other? The planning relevance is this: frequently movement towards some desirable end requires the simultaneous action of a number of individuals, who are not, for some reason, able to come to an agreement between themselves. A situation can then arise when it is in the best interests of each one not to pursue this course, while it remains in the interests of the whole that they should.

A good example is improvement. If an area is run-down, the individual doing up his house may run the risk of not getting his money back when he comes to sell because those who might wish to buy his improved house may not wish to buy in an area where everything else is dilapidated. But if everyone – or at least a majority – carries out improvements, then the benefits grow more than in proportion. The whole area 'goes up'.

Now this might happen – and has happened in London and in the older parts of some American cities – through the unco-ordinated spontaneous actions of separate individuals. Somehow areas have become fashionable and been upgraded. This came about because some individuals – enough of them – were ready to run the risk that their gamble would pay off and they would not be left, as some have been, as lonely and unsuccessful pioneers.

In some cases, however, the individual cannot take unilateral action to relocate even if he wishes. An example is a facility like Covent Garden Market, where a decision has to be reached jointly or not at all. Even in the case of groupings of firms, however, major changes in location, such as the relocation of the rag trade in London, have come about without formal co-ordination. But, as with the housing example above, this may reflect the fact that some individuals had very great incentives to move, e.g. were experiencing great difficulties in maintaining profitable operation and hence the risk of a move became worth taking. In the case of severely run-down areas, it is unlikely that anyone would be found taking a risk of this kind and nothing may happen to rehabilitate them in the absence of intervention designed to encourage it.

A further kind of difficulty can arise when firms are responding to a widely recognised shift in demand. Each may prepare their separate plans for expansion, while remaining ignorant of the plans of their competitors. The result may be, when all the extra capacity is available, that there is more than can be used at the prices obtaining when the plans were made. We illustrate this in Diagram 11.

If, in time period one, demand shifts from DD_1 to DD_2, price will rise to P_2 if supply cannot increase immediately to Q_2 because of the time required to finance, design and construct additional space. At price P_2, Q_3 could be profitably supplied and hence firms will tend to increase the volume of accommodation available in anticipation of the large profits which would be enjoyed at price P_2. However, if Q_3 is supplied then it will only be fully taken up at price P_3 which is much below the level which would justify the allocation of resources to the extra space concerned. The result in the short and medium term is a condition of 'excess supply', in which properties remain empty or prices are cut to P_3, much below the price at which any further space would be provided. The excess would only disappear if demand rose over time or some of the older stock, less attractive and more expensive to run, was withdrawn from the office market and converted to other uses. A good example is the recent office boom in New York which, helped by changed financial conditions, responded to pressure on space in Manhattan to the extent that a situation of over-supply was created and prices had to fall, in real and money terms, to clear the market.

Diagram 11

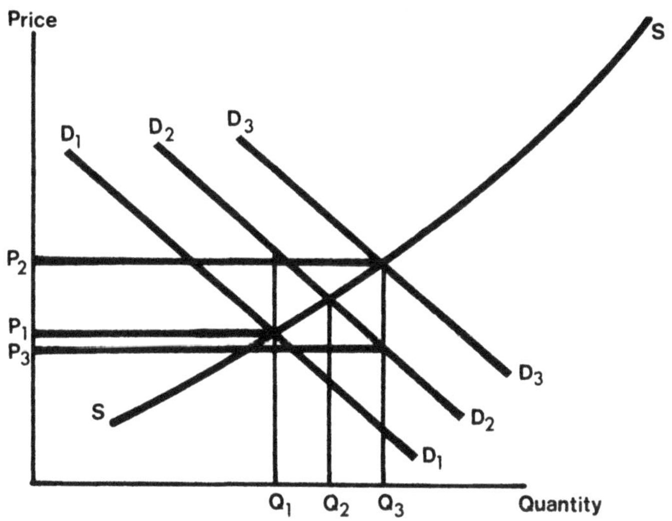

Imperfect information and inaccurate forecasts of future time periods may affect the efficiency of markets in other ways. We can take an example from the previous chapter. As urban areas expand, due to income or population growth, the best use of particular bits of land changes. At the periphery, builders, in deciding how to use the sites available, must estimate the growth of the area in the foreseeable future and attempt to estimate what is the best use of land within that set of expectations. For example, if they develop at low density, and if the city is expanding rapidly due to population growth, then they may well waste land in the sense that, had their expectation and those of their buyers been correct, they could have gained a higher return over time from higher density. Alternatively, if they build at a high density and the city spreads out due to transport improvements, with land values tending to be steady or even fall, they may find they have wasted resources in the other direction. Existing market behaviour may give little guide to how future prices will develop.

Where this holds, decisions made by private developers may not be the best possible, from the viewpoint of society as a whole; nevertheless, decisions are taken and developments proceed. In some instances, however, markets may fail to work entirely because of acute uncertainty about the future, i.e. a complete lack of the information relevant to decision-making. This may occur in the case of new development if suppliers of land are highly uncertain about the future demands and hence prices for land, or if developers are very uncertain about the price at which they may be able to dispose of their products when they are completed. Such a degree of uncertainty would arise in unregulated markets if consumer demand was highly unpredictable. In most cases, even in the absence of actual intervention, acute uncertainty of this kind will resolve itself, i.e. over time the trend in demand would become clear allowing supply decisions to be made.

Individual developers may be so influenced by uncertainty as to what other possible agents, public or private, may do that they take no action at all, and wait and see how the situation develops. In these circumstances, market uncertainty may persist, until the planning authority takes action to resolve it.

4.5 Paternalism and the Distribution of Welfare

In the description in Chapters 2 and 3 of how goods are allocated within a simple market economy, the economist's concept of demand has been used, that is demand is defined solely in respect of the price of the goods concerned and the ability and desire of people to pay for them. Such demand is called *effective demand* as it is backed up by purchasing power and actually realised. No specific level of consumption of a good is specified as being necessary or particularly desirable in such an economy. The pattern of consumption is left to the preferences of individuals interacting with the costs of supplying the goods and services concerned. Consumers have been assumed sovereign in the sense that the market responds to the pressure of their spending power. If people are prepared to pay for something it is supplied. The consumer is judged to be the best judge of his own interest and if he does things which appear foolish to others then that is no concern of theirs.

But for various reasons it may be argued that the consumer ought not to be sovereign. Some of these stem from arguments used earlier; for example, we may argue that people ought not to be supplied with certain drugs on the commercial market, in part because of the suffering and money costs they impose on others as well as on themselves. In the case of housing, it may be argued that people should not be allowed to choose poor housing, because of the health risks to society at large which result from insanitary accommodation. These two are examples of the externality argument considered in section 4.1. Historically, for example, the latter has been an important argument in favour of public regulation of housing markets.

Other arguments for restricting individual choice, however, are put solely in terms of the interests of the individuals themselves. Arguments in terms of lack of information were dealt with in the previous section, but there is only a narrow dividing line between such arguments and those which rest on assertion of the *inability* of people to see their own interest. To bring out the various strands of argument, consider the case of a developer applying for permission to a local planning authority to put houses near a motorway on a site where the environmental disadvantages would be considerable.

A case for refusing permission might be made on several different grounds. First, it might be argued that the developer would not be able to sell his houses at profitable prices, or if he did, subsequent occupants would not be able to do so. As a consequence the houses might remain empty, become derelict and have to be cleared by the public authorities, with the costs falling on them and not the developers. This would be an externality argument. Second, the individuals buying the houses might recognise the environmental damage, but be prepared to accept it, especially if the houses were cheap. Nevertheless, they should, it might be argued, be protected from it on the ground that they do not perceive their own interest best. Third, it may be argued that purchasers would not recognise the danger initially and should be protected from it, as they would come to recognise it in due course. The second and third of these arguments are paternalistic in nature but the implications of the two variants are very different. The first variant completely overrides individual preferences, the second recognises them but suggests that, in this particular case, the individual's choice is not well informed.

Thus paternalistic arguments may take two forms: either people do not recognise their own interest, but will do so if they are introduced to something – either by initial compulsion or by inducements, e.g. zero pricing for public open space. Alternatively, it may be argued that they may never recognise their own true interest and must therefore be compelled or otherwise to consume a 'socially approved' amount of the good in question, or, in some cases, where censorship or prohibition is involved, not consume any at all.

The second main ground for intervention to impose a specific pattern of consumption is distributional. The account in Chapters 2 and 3 of the workings of free market processes ignored people's different abilities to pay. But the fact that market processes do result in large differences in income is one of the most important reasons for intervening in them. Despite its importance, however, the distributional argument is not always easy in practice to distinguish from other reasons for intervention, as the example of housing standards illustrates.

It is frequently suggested that minimum housing standards should be guaranteed and supplied below cost if people are unable to pay for them. Such a view may rest on distributional considerations, but it may also rest on the externality or paternalistic arguments already considered. Historically, the externality argument has been important. In the nineteenth century the dangers to the rich from the bad housing of the poor were real enough. Clearly this point has less force today in developed countries where basic amenities are virtually universal. If so, then the case for laying down a minimum housing standard may be either paternalistic or distributional. One way of distinguishing between them is to ask the question: if money income could be redistributed up to whatever was the desired level, then would a case still remain for ensuring a minimum standard? If the answer is yes, then the case for intervention is paternalistic. If it is not, then it is distributional and it may be based on the judgement that for political or administrative reasons it is not possible to carry out the income distribution directly. In these cases, there is a case for intervention to ensure that everyone enjoys at least a minimum standard of provision.

The case for minimum standards is often expressed in terms of basic needs. But 'needs' arguments must be used with care. Attempts are often made to define the 'need' for office space or industrial sites. Now this may be a shorthand for saying: if so and so firms are going to come into the area, then about so much space will probably be built. But it can be a dangerous formulation in some cases. For example, a statement of needs may be taken to suggest that the amount concerned must be supplied no matter what the cost. This ignores the basic economising process which was described in Chapter 2. This showed that even for a given level of output, there is no unique set of factors which is absolutely required – except in those very rare circumstances where the technology of production is completely fixed. In the industrial context, the distributional arguments clearly do not apply as they do for individuals, i.e. no one would wish to argue, on distributional grounds, that firms should use a certain amount of a particular factor of production (this is from the viewpoint of the firm; it is a relevant form of argument in the case of individuals in reserved occupations).

'Needs' arguments are used where the market fails to supply, e.g. it is common to refer to 'needs for open space'. There is no effective demand, in the sense of a demand expressing itself in market processes, for open space in most urban areas, since there are few relevant markets. So there is no practical alternative to use of the term 'needs' to express the fact that benefits would accrue from providing it. But it does not follow that there are *distributional* reasons for providing it. Various possible interpretations of needs are discussed in Chapter 8.

There remain a large number of cases, however, common in land-use planning, where distributional concerns are of central importance. They do not all concern the broad income or social groupings which are the focus of debate at the national level about the distribution of income. For example, in a row of houses inhabited by people of equal income, distributional issues may arise where external effects are present. The proposal that one resident should develop his back garden and erect another dwelling on it necessarily raises a distributional issue: all the benefit will accrue to him but some of the costs will be borne by others. This might quite simply be considered unfair, in the absence of any compensation for the unwilling sufferers. A large number of planning issues are of this kind, i.e. they turn on whether it is fair on some people to impose costs for which no, or incomplete, compensation is given in order to benefit others. When something like an urban motorway is involved, these costs can be very large.

Many distribution issues in land-use planning centre round *ad hoc* groupings of people. In many situations, it is such classes as 'people living in a certain place' or people in certain sets of social or other circumstances – the young, the unemployed. In many circumstances groups are defined according to what they do, e.g. the 'commuter'. Another common kind of grouping occurs when people have different preferences, and where decisions have to be made as to how a particular facility should be used, between commuting uses which are incompatible, e.g. in the case of a stretch of water, power boat racing and fishing. The market would decide a problem of this kind by devoting the facility to that use which would yield the largest profits. But such an outcome may be considered unfair, on the ground that minority interests should be catered for, despite the fact that their level of demand is much below that required to justify provision in terms of the numbers concerned. Disparities of income add a further, if more fundamental, dimension to conflicts of this kind, but the latter would occur however successfully income had been redistributed.

One final distributional issue must be mentioned, that between generations. Decisions taken now on the level of investment, on the use of natural resources and on the layout of urban areas have consequences which spread over many years. The argument is often put that the interests of future generations should be taken into account since these are not reflected in current market decisions. For example, short-term interests may suggest the development of a beauty spot for mineral workings, providing extra jobs but damaging the area, perhaps irreparably.

To conclude: as we will be concerned with policies towards land use, we will not be considering the main instruments for the redistribution of income – i.e. national taxation and subsidy policies. Nevertheless, it will still be necessary to consider the implications of planning policies for different income groups, partly because income differences may be relevant even to small-scale decisions such as those mentioned above, and partly because some planning policies systematically impinge on certain income groups either by accident or design.

4.6 Private Response to Market Failure

So far this chapter has been concerned with classifying the various ways in which markets might fail. Before we go on to consider the ways in which a planning authority might wish to deal with them, we must first consider the various ways in which markets themselves respond to the kinds of failure analysed in the previous section.

(i) Information and Co-ordination

In a great many contexts market institutions develop to overcome information deficiencies. Some firms specialise in the provision of information to others on market trends, prices and contracts. The extent to which they do it may be limited by the public goods aspect of information, i.e. once it is published it is available to anyone with access to a photocopier. But experience would suggest that the market in information is sufficiently imperfect for firms to be able to make profits by supplying it. Some, for example, do so by selling information, suitably packaged, which is already available in official published documents.

The range of information available to the individual on many of the matters with which land-use planning is concerned is very wide and much of it is made available by commercial processes.

Market processes are sometimes able to overcome some of the problems analysed above through informally organised information flows or co-operative agreements, e.g. some small industries composed of small firms have managed to move location when *prima facie* it would appear difficult that they should manage to do so. Equally, groups or communities may be highly efficient in making available to all their members certain kinds of information. Thus an old-established community may find it easier to provide public goods through corporate voluntary activity than a rapidly changing or new community, such as that in a New Town. The notorious information system known as the old boy network may work equally well in an industrial community, in which news about jobs is passed by word of mouth. If such informal institutions are widespread, no intervention may be required, but they may have limited efficiency, missing out certain sections of the population. These may be defined by their personal characteristics, not necessarily by class or income. For example, the system may serve well enough long-established residents, but not visitors or newcomers.

The co-ordination by private firms of their investment plans where such firms are in competition raises some tricky issues which can only be touched on lightly. The competitive process assumed in Chapters 2 and 3 may not in fact exist. There may be collusion between firms, particularly when only a few are involved. Such collusion may be based on informal understanding alone, not necessarily formal agreements which in most countries would be illegal. The problem, which is more a matter of economic than land-use policy, is that the advantages which such arrangements may bring in terms of investment are bought at the price of reduced competitive pressures. But examples of private sector co-ordination can be found where these problems do not occur; for example, the need to concentrate a number of small firms may be met by a developer offering combined facilities. Shopping centres and industrial estates are two common examples. Typically in these cases the developer will try to limit the uncertainty he faces by making agreements with major individual retailers, sufficient to guarantee the success of the venture.

This is just one example of a large number of strategies which individuals and firms may adopt to deal with the uncertainty arising from incomplete information or poor forecasts. There are other very common ones. Individuals take out insurance policies against a wide range of risks. Firms may take out options, e.g. to purchase land when they are not sure they will be able to develop it. Both these examples involve costs as will most measures taken to eliminate or reduce uncertainty. But they do allow markets to function in circumstances where they otherwise might fail completely.

(ii) Externalities and Market Behaviour

Although we have defined external effects as effects which are not fully reflected in market prices, external effects are nevertheless one of the most important explanatory factors in determining how firms and households behave in urban areas and how land markets work. Typically in most urban areas firms cluster close together, e.g. the tight concentrations of garment workers found in New York, the London rag trade, retailing centres for particular products, or the cluster of banking firms found in London or New York and other major commercial centres. These groupings are largely explained by the existence of *external economies*. We noted in Chapter 2 that individual firms might enjoy economies of large-scale production; steel or car production are good examples. These benefits are termed *internal* economies because they accrue to the firm itself and do not spill over into the urban economy as a whole. However, the growth of a large production unit may lead to effects within the economy at large, e.g. the steel plant may place such demands on the local transport system that suppliers of transport are enabled to invest in large-scale facilities and provide frequencies of services which any shipper in the area concerned may enjoy. Similarly the benefits which accrue to individual small firms from being close together which they would not enjoy if they were separated. They save on transport costs by being close together, but also in more general ways, e.g. flexibility of meeting orders larger than the scale of one plant, or the development of specialists in particular kinds of service. For example, in large financial markets, it will be possible to get finance supplied or insurance offered on a wider variety of terms than in much smaller markets.

Although external economies are very important in explaining how urban areas function, we will not spend much time on them here, although at a later stage we will return to consider their significance in the context of policies which might, as a side-effect, tend to reduce their incidence. Generally, land-use planning policies are geared to dealing with unwelcome external effects which impose costs on those experiencing them. It is these that shall be our major concern.

Let us first consider how the existence of external effects would influence the behaviour of land markets and location of activities within the simple urban model. Assume that, in line with the historical experience of many cities, the initial location was determined by the major economic activity and that this activity imposed external costs through the noise and smell it gave rise to. The result of this would be that the land mainly affected by these externalities would have a lower value than land which, in other respects, was equivalent to it. This in turn would have an influence on the pattern of land use. For example, land uses, such as industry, which were not greatly affected by the external effects, but which were attracted by the relatively cheap land, would tend to utilise it, and those uses such as housing in which amenity is valued would tend to go on to the higher-value land.

In other contexts too there would be a tendency for market behaviour to result in a diminution of the impact of externalities of this kind. For example, the clustering of land uses referred to above and observable in all cities has been largely the result of market forces and not the intervention of planning authorities, since most developed before the advent of planning powers. The result of such clustering, if one land use imposes external costs on another, is to reduce the sum total of these costs below the level they would achieve in a dispersed location pattern, since they tend to reduce the scale of the interface between uses.

These are not the only ways in which market behaviour may reduce external effects. It is common for individuals using the general legal framework for contracts or other appropriate lègal machinery to deal with the kind of external effects which arise at very local levels. For example, residents of private blocks of flats or of housing estates frequently must agree, as a condition of their occupancy or purchase, to a set of conditions designed to reduce the level of external costs they might impose on each other. Some of these may concern matters outside the concern of the planning authority and refer to the standard of personal behaviour. Some such agreements, applicable to new developments, limit the extent to which individuals can alter the appearance of their property, or add extra accommodations and specify the standards of maintenance which is required. In some parts of the US, covenants are common which restrict the use of land to certain kinds of use, e.g. individual lot housing, and lay down standards for design, maintenance and exterior appearance. If these covenants are enforced, then the result is a reduction in the external costs imposed by individuals on each other in the developments concerned.

External effects cannot always be anticipated; consequently specific agreements to deal with them are not feasible. In some instances, the legal framework may allow individuals to take action to prevent external costs being imposed or to have them diminished. Under English law, for example, actions may be brought or, often informally, the help of the police invoked, to deal with very local externality problems, such as noise nuisance. But legal redress of this *ad hoc* kind will tend to be expensive and so not be of general use for most sections of the population. Both this and the cases covered in the previous paragraph bring out the point that the precise ways in which markets work are influenced by the legal framework within which they operate. As we shall see in Chapter 6, it is possible to envisage a more elaborate system of legal control of externalities which avoids the need for intervention by a planning authority in a wider range of issues.

Of those external effects which remain untouched by processes of the kind described many may be trivial. We must be careful to avoid the implication that because market processes are imperfect, due to the presence of external effects, that intervention is required on the part of the planning authority. It is simply not worthwhile trying to deal with every external effect. It is easy enough to point to a large number of examples of external effects, which there is no point in policy trying to deal with. My neighbour's plastic gnomes may cause me great aesthetic distress, just as any extension he proposed to build which cut down the view from my back window would do. But the former may be dismissed as *de minimis*. Some apparently minor matters may take on significance, however, depending on their context. For example, whether or not a resident in the Royal Crescent in Bath can paint their door a different colour to everyone else, or a house-builder in a national park use anything other than local materials, are both cases where UK planning authorities have felt they were justified in limiting the right of the individual to impose external costs on others, although, in the first case, the local planning authority's view was overruled on appeal. The dividing line between a trivial externality and a significant one is, in practice, very difficult to draw.

(iii) The Provision of Public Goods

Chapter 4 explained why market processes may persistently fail to supply certain kinds of good and we shall consider in this section how markets may be regulated in order to ensure their supply. Before considering the role of policy, however, we must see how market failure of this kind might be overcome without direct intervention by a planning authority.

In most communities, even in those where markets are dominant, a large number of activities are undertaken by formal or informal groups, seeking to provide services to themselves or to others, which are not available, or are only available at high prices, and hence only to some parts of the community. These activities take a great variety of forms – charities, sports clubs, political groups. Equally they arise for a variety of reasons; in part because the assumption that the individual is concerned only with his own interest does not hold, in part because very strong common interests – be it in human welfare or conservation – are sufficient to create a group, which overcomes, in part at least, the public good problem. Despite the fact that many of the benefits arising from the activity accrue to people in general – indeed largely for this reason – individuals are prepared to produce by voluntary effort the good in question. The point applies equally to private benefactors who in many cities have provided public open spaces and other municipal amenities and to those individuals who have donated funds, on a smaller scale, to charitable purposes.

Private grouping may be made more efficient through the use of the existing legal framework. The kind of procedure discussed above, e.g. covenants and other similar kinds of agreement, may be used to overcome the public goods problems, as well as the externality issue. For example, in private development land may be set aside for common open space, and not allotted to individual gardens. As noted already, this kind of development takes place where developers are able, through the nature of the design, to capture in the private of the dwellings they build the value to owners of their open space. They can only do this by making the public open space a private good through formal or informal restrictions on those who can use it. Such developments tend, therefore, to be small and often in a literal sense, inward-looking.

4.7 Concluding Comment

This chapter has identified a large number of reasons why markets may fail. The extent of these failures is determined not simply by the nature of the market processes outlined in Chapters 2 and 3, but also by the economic and legal framework within which they work. In some cases markets themselves develop institutions, e.g. insurance markets, specifically designed to overcome deficiencies in competitive markets. In some cases, restrictions on competition, possibly undesirable on other grounds, may overcome some of the problems such as those of co-ordination which arise in markets made up of large numbers of small firms. In other cases, government must step in and modify the framework within which markets work so as to bring the private and social interest better into line. How government may do this is the subject of Chapter 6. Before going on to means, however, we need to consider briefly the objects of intervention: if a planning authority takes policy measures designed to influence the outcome of market processes, what should its overall objective be and what are the measures of its success? These questions are the subject of the following chapter.

5 THE ROLE OF THE PLANNING AUTHORITY

In the previous chapter, a number of reasons were identified which might justify intervention in market processes. The aim of this chapter is to bring out some of the broad economic issues which underlie intervention in general and to develop a framework for the appraisal of particular planning policies. Here we are concerned with the general principles which should guide the analysis and formulation of advice on choices in land-use planning.

The model of the planning authority to be developed in this chapter parallels that of individual choice in two important ways. Just as the individual is presumed to maximise his utility, we shall assume that the authority aims to maximise social welfare and that it does so subject to various constraints. It is obvious that the process involved in maximising social welfare differs in a number of important ways from the individual trying to make the most of his limited means. In the first section of the chapter we will attempt to bring out some of the differences and also some of the parallels. The existence of constraints is straight-forward enough. The authority, no matter under what constitution, cannot do what it wants. It will be limited by its political powers and by the policy instruments available to it. It will be limited by the actions of higher levels of government. It will also be limited by the economic resources available to it and for this reason it too must go through the same economising process as the individual if it is to make the best possible use of those resources it does possess. The second and third sections of this chapter, therefore, will consider the rules which should guide an authority in making the choices entailed.

The simplifications of the real-life decision-making processes of firms and individuals made in previous chapters have been considerable and those made in this chapter will be greater still. Households and firms are political as well as social and economic institutions. Still more is a planning authority part of the political process and its policies cannot therefore be treated as merely technical matters. But planning authorities, whatever their formal role in the political institutions of the area they serve, do put forward plans or proposals for consultation which the community as a whole, or its representatives, must take a view or a decision on, and which affect most, if not all, of the members of the community. Such plans or proposals are frequently based on technical analysis by land-use planners and others and the guidelines under which such work is typically done is that it should reflect the public or community interest directly or as mediated through the established political process. Exactly how analysis should be related to the political process is one of the more contentious areas in contemporary planning discussion and it is one we will not try to tackle directly. Instead, the chapter will identify a small number of basic principles which should underlie the analysis of public policy if it is to serve any political process well.

5.1 The Objectives of Intervention

The model used in Chapter 2 to 'explain' or describe the behaviour of producers and consumers is frequently called the rational model. It presupposes that the individuals or organisations concerned attempt to maximise their utility or profits by looking at all available consumption and production possibilities and choosing the best set available. It is a model of choice. Individuals and firms are both assumed to have a single objective – to maximise utility or profit – and the problem facing them is to choose those courses of action which best further that objective. It is not difficult to see how this approach may be extended to a planning authority assumed to preside over the city examined within the simple urban model. Its task or objective can be defined as that of maximising the welfare of the people living in that city, subject, like the firm or individual, to the constraints acting on it.

An objective like this, however, may appear so general as to be meaningless. It certainly does not carry us very far. But at this stage, we will only make two points which help to clarify what is meant. First, it implies the value of any policy is to be judged solely in terms of the benefits or costs it brings to individuals. In this context, the term social is not meant to contrast with economic or political welfare. It refers solely to the aggregation of individuals' welfare. Second, it requires a careful distinction between final objectives which relate directly to the welfare of individuals – better housing and greater amenity – and intermediate objectives which relate indirectly to individual welfare, such as the containment of urban sprawl.

The aims of land-use planning are frequently expressed in terms which do not make it clear whether they are or are not final objectives. For example, one of the objectives of the Strategic Plan for the South East is to encourage the creation of city regions independent of London. The connection between an objective of this kind and changes in the welfare of individuals is not straightforward. The independence is not valued directly, although any reduction in commuting which its achievement would bring about would be. The authors of the plan had more in mind than commuting costs, but the formulation of the objective itself does not make it exactly clear in which ways the utility of individuals is expected to be affected by the promotion of this particular objective. In any particular case, these connections need to be made clear if we are to know what is, or is not supposed to form part of social welfare, and how the planning authority's actions are intended to promote it.

This still leaves open such basic questions as: how is welfare to be defined and measured? how is the welfare of citizen Y to be compared with the welfare of citizen X? exactly who is to count as a citizen? Here, we simply assume that there is some means available to the planning authority, be it political judgement or analytic technique, of combining the welfare of all those living in the city or affected by what goes on within it, just as it was assumed in Chapter 2 that we did not have to enter into an analysis of relationships *within* the household. The purpose of this simplification is to allow this and the following chapters to concentrate on the objective factors underlying social choice, i.e. the supply or production side of the urban economy.

Having defined the planning authority's objective, the next step is to relate this to the workings of the urban economy as a whole in order to derive a basic rule of policy evaluation. In previous chapters we have seen how market processes may create welfare by producing the goods and services which people want and also how they may fail, by not producing certain commodities at all, or by producing them in ways which are inefficient or undesirable from a social viewpoint. Despite these failures, we make the assumption that market processes of the simplified kind we have described do yield a positive amount of social welfare. We can illustrate this in Diagram 12.

The diagram is limited to two dimensions, so we can show social welfare to depend only on market goods on the vertical axis, and on non-marketed goods on the horizontal axis. The I_1 and I_2 curves show, like the individual indifference curves introduced in Chapter 2, those combinations of marketed and non-marketed goods which yield an equal amount of utility, i.e. which society as a whole would be indifferent between. The higher numbered indifference curves indicate a higher level of social welfare. In drawing such curves we are brushing over the questions raised above on the definition and measurement of welfare for ease of exposition.

The point M shows the amount of market goods which the market

Diagram 12

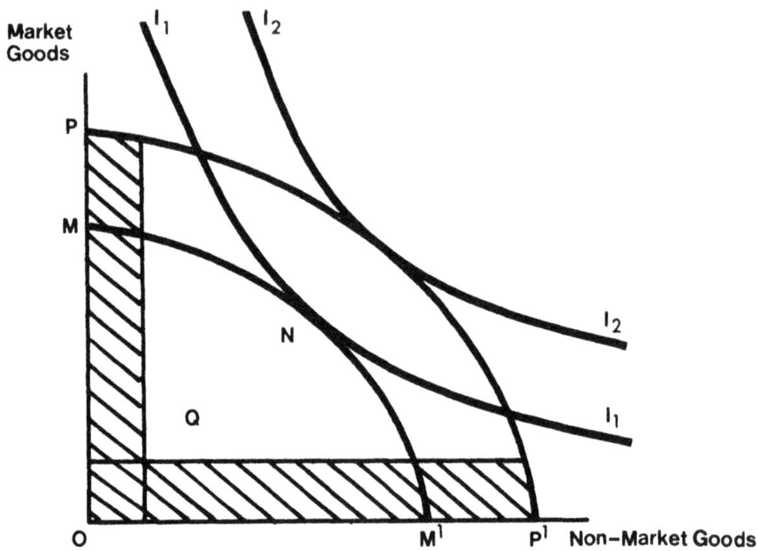

mechanism would produce by itself. It is the level of social welfare produced by the processes described in Chapter 3. That chapter took no account of any favourable external effects which the market process might produce nor of any production by non-market, but non-government, processes. But as section 4.6 showed, there are a large number of ways in which markets may react to such effects and reduce their incidence. If these are allowed for then the point M′ might be reached on the non-market axis. The line MM′, like the budget line facing the individual, shows what combination of market and non-market commodities might be produced, in the absence of any intervention by the planning authority. (For convenience, we are assuming away all other forms of government intervention, i.e. those not directly concerned with land use). This line touches its highest indifference curve $I_1 I_1$ at the point N, which is the point where the unregulated market processes achieve a social optimum. The general task of the planning authority follows directly: it is to find a combination of marketed and non-marketed goods which yields a higher level of social welfare than point N. Included in this is the possibility that it may wish to alter the distribution between individuals, as well as the scale of market or non-market production.

This formulation leads to a basic rule for policy evaluation: that the effects of a given policy instrument cannot be considered in isolation, purely by reference to desired effects. They can only be considered in relation to what would otherwise have occurred, in the absence of those policies. At the most general level the case for a land-use planning authority must rest on the assumption that it carries out functions which cannot be carried out, or would be carried out less efficiently, by other means. Markets are a means by which goods and services priced and unpriced may be produced, but the identification of market failure is not in itself sufficient to make the case for intervention in market processes for four reasons. First, we need to consider how markets themselves react to cases of market failure. As we have seen, even though external effects are effects which by definition are not reflected in prices, markets nevertheless react to them and frequently in ways which serve to reduce their importance. The same general point holds for other kinds of market failure such as imperfect information. Second, account must be taken of groups or individuals who do not respond to market forces or who act according to quite different criteria. The public goods problem, for example, may be overcome in this way, at least in some circumstances, examples of which have already been given. Third, as later chapters will show, some forms of intervention may create more costs than they do benefits. Finally, we must take into account the effects of other kinds of government policy, in particular the general legal framework within which individuals and firms operate.

This is a point which we shall develop further later on, but it is important to recognise that no land-use planning authority operates in a policy vacuum nor is it likely to be the sole government agency concerned with the problems of market failure discussed in the previous chapter. Other government policies such as taxation, property law and manpower programmes influence the scale and nature of the problems faced by land-use planning authorities. It follows from all this that if we observe the economy within our simple urban model at point N, which is at a higher level of social welfare than point Q, we cannot attribute the attainment of this point to the action of the planning authority. We would need to know first how far in the direction of N the urban economy could have reached (a) in the absence of any intervention and (b) given intervention outside the sphere of land-use planning.

5.2 Resources and Constraints

Let us assume that the planning authority is able, by whatever policy measures are available to it, to produce a higher level of social welfare in its city than unrestricted market processes or these processes modified by other policy instruments. We can show this with the line PP′, which shows the combinations of marketed and non-marketed goods which are feasible with intervention. The point P is shown above point M on the assumption that intervention might produce more efficient productive processes by means discussed in Chapter 6. The point P′ is shown to the right of the point M′ for the obvious reason that a greater part of the reasons for intervening with market processes is to ensure the output of non-marketed goods and services. The line PP′ connects all those points which under regulation might be produced; it is for the urban economy as a whole, the *production possibility frontier*. Beyond it production cannot take place, so all the area to the north-east of the line PP′ is *non-feasible*. How is the position of this line set? What are the limits under which the authority must work?

First, the position of the line PP′ depends directly on the volume of productive resources, or factors of production available within the urban economy and the efficiency with which they are used. If, over time, the population of the urban economy grows, or if, through changes in production techniques, existing resources are used to better effect, then the line PP′ may move to the right. In this way more feasible policy areas may be opened up and higher indifference curves attained. The possibility also exists, although it is one we shall ignore here, that the resources of the urban economy may be supplemented through grants from other levels of government. This in effect provides it with claims on the real resources of other such economies. Without grants from outside, the planning authority is subject to the fundamental constraint set by the productive potential of its economy.

It does not follow, however, that the planning authority will in practice be able to achieve any point within the line PP′. The authority is subject to constraints other than those imposed by available resources. It may, for example, be constrained by a higher level of government not to do certain things. The effects of such a constraint are illustrated by the shaded area in Diagram 12. This could be regarded as a policy constraint imposed on the authority by central government, that is to say that certain patterns of social production, e.g. very low housing standards or very high levels of environmental pollution, cannot be tolerated. In this case we might interpret the restricting lines as meaning that certain minimal or national standards had to be met. No production mix involving amounts *lower* than these standards is feasible.

Diagram 12, although very simple, nevertheless has a number of important implications for the role of the planning analyst. As noted already, we have assumed away in the shape and position of the social indifference curves a large number of essentially political issues. The main issues which remain for the analyst therefore lie in identifying the position and shape of the production possibility curve and the limits set on policies by contraints.

Rational choice entails, as we have seen already, knowledge of what is to be given up in order to attain a given objective. In the case of the consumer this problem is relatively straightforward to pose and solve, though not always. He may, for example, find it very difficult to determine whether or not a move of house will have acceptable or unacceptable consequences for other items in his utility function because the ramifications of the choice may be far-reaching. For a planning authority the task is much more complicated. We have already suggested that the urban area examined in Chapter 3 could be described as a system of interrelated markets. A system of this kind is relatively easy to describe in broad outline but it is tremendously difficult to predict its response in quantitative terms to measures affecting it. The implications therefore of any policy choices are typically difficult to unravel. It is the planning analyst's prime task to attempt to relate the effect of intervention, i.e. policy inputs to the urban economy, on the output, however measured, of that economy.

The next part of this book is concerned with developing the analysis of these interrelations. In Chapter 2, various *production functions* were described for privately produced goods and services. These described the relationship between inputs – resources and factors of production – and the output – steel, office space, houses. These relationships are determined by technological and organisational factors. Of central importance to the planning authority is the relationship between specific policy instruments and the response to them within the urban economy. It is with these responses that the next two chapters are concerned.

5.3 Efficiency and Distribution

The previous sections of the chapter have left to one side a basic distinction in policy analysis: that between efficiency and distributional effects. The production possibility curves drawn above reflected only the potential performance of the urban economy in producing total goods and services and was not concerned with their allocation between individuals.

In Diagram 12 any point within the area bounded by the line PP'O is an *inefficient* point, since, by assumption, it is possible to move by appropriate policy action on to a higher level of social production and hence on to a higher social indifference curve. Any policy which puts the urban economy on the production possibility curve is an efficient policy.

If an authority were to improve its management techniques and reduce the number of its employees, while maintaining the same level of service, it would, using common language, be said to be efficient. By maintaining its level of service, it has ensured that no users of the service are worse off, while, we may assume, the employees it no longer requires to produce that service can be redeployed to produce additional services elsewhere. Total production of goods and services can rise and the authority can dispose of the extra production as it wishes. In doing this it can pursue any distributional objectives it desires.

In these circumstances, the question of the efficiency of the urban economy can be considered separately from the question of the distribution of its output. In other circumstances the total of available goods and services is not in question; it can be assumed fixed. In these cases, the policy issues which arise are purely distributional. For example, if the price of second-hand houses in an area falls, sellers lose but buyers gain by the same amount. As long as the houses are retained in use, their services continue and no efficiency issues arise. That is, the performance of the urban economy in respect of housing services remains the same. The change in price of houses affects only the distribution of the costs of these services between two groups within the population.

Take a different case: I would like to build an extension to my house. This will inconvenience my neighbour, but as we are on good terms, I suggest that we slightly rearrange our land holdings so that he retains an area of private garden. He is happy with this and I go ahead and build my extension. He has not lost, indeed he may have gained, and I also have gained. Total welfare has increased therefore and as both parties are satisfied, then there is no need to worry about the distribution of that welfare.

Suppose, however, that I want to build my extension but there is no way through re-design by which the effect on my neighbour can be diminished. Suppose also that I value the prospect of the extension very highly as my family is expanding and if I do not have it, I may have to move elsewhere at some considerable cost in moving expenses alone. Suppose that my neighbour will only lose half an hour's early morning sunshine if the extension is built. Common sense suggests that the extension should be built because clearly my gains outweigh his losses. Nevertheless he does lose and has not been compensated for his loss by neighbourly agreement as in the earlier case. In principle, however, such compensation might be paid. Thus, because I would be put to great expense in moving if I did not get my extension, I could part with a considerable sum and still be better off with the extension than without it. If the situation was as described I would certainly be able to make the damage good to my neighbour. In this situation a position *could* be reached when everyone was better off, or no worse off than before, i.e. I would be willing to pay more to have the extension (after allowing for costs of construction etc.) than he would require to be compensated. But unless I actually did compensate my neighbour, then he would in fact be worse off.

This kind of problem is common in land-use planning. For example, in the case of an open space, there may be many competing groups wishing to use it. One group might be willing to pay more for it than another and hence potentially they could enjoy the use of the space and pay an amount to the losers sufficient to make them content with not having it. If this payment were made then both groups would be as well or better off than before. Total welfare could be increased. But if, as would often be the case, such payments could not be made, then the problem of deciding who should use the space would be primarily a distributional one.

In categorising policies, the extreme cases are easy; some policies can fairly readily be categorised as efficient or inefficient and others as being mainly distributional in impact. There remains a large awkward middle ground which consists of those policies which produce both gains and losses, and which do not in themselves allow any desired redistribution of benefits from gainers to losers to take place. Such policies can only be characterised in a conditional sense as socially efficient, since, whether they are or not depends on what weight is put on the direct distributional consequences of the policies themselves, and on any subsequent action which authorities might take to diminish or modify the direct and undesired distributional impact. For example, the distributional impact of a road otherwise agreed to be a very worthwhile use of resources may, in the first instance, be highly undesirable. But it may be possible through rehousing, moving grants, etc., to take care of these consequences indirectly. In cases like this there are *potential* increases in social welfare which may or may not be realised. Whether they are or not will depend on the nature of the policy instruments available.

5.4 Concluding Comments

The model we have used to 'explain' or describe the behaviour of producers and consumers is frequently called the rational model. It presupposes that the individuals or organisations concerned attempt to maximise their utility or profits wholeheartedly by looking at all available consumption and production possibilities and choosing the best set available. The same simple framework has now been applied to public policy-making. We have defined the task of the planning authority as being to maximise the welfare of its inhabitants, subject to the constraints with which it is faced. In order to do this, it must, like the consumer, attempt to make sure that its expenditures are correctly allocated between the various competing possibilities, i.e. no shift in budgetary allocation would produce more welfare, that it has the right balance, defined in the same way, between public and private expenditures, that its regulatory powers, to control or make up for the various market failures discussed are so used as to make any further adjustments of them unnecessary. The next four chapters consider how these balances should be struck.

Now it is evident that this statement of the tasks of the authority overlooks various important real-life features. Some reflect the limits of organisation and knowledge to which the authority like the household or firm is subject, which prohibit the careful examination of all relevant alternatives. Others reflect the facts of political life, that different groups will have different views of how social welfare is defined and that a great deal of activity will centre round the question 'who decides?' rather than 'how are the decisions arrived at?'

Various ideas have been developed aimed at redefining rational planning, which reflect the real-life limitations on the abilities of a real-life authority. The notion of 'satisficing' suggests that planners do not attempt to maximise or optimise total welfare but instead tend to look for solutions which are 'good enough' and take them in the right direction. Disjointed incrementalism similarly stresses the inability of authorities to make strategic decisions in a rational manner because much of the relevant information is simply not available. They involve effects too far removed from current experience and hence cannot rationally be calculated.

In the following chapters we will not explicitly back any one of these particular horses. We will rest on the assumption that in many practical situations analysts will be called upon to advise on the relative merits of different courses of action (although not necessarily all from an exhaustive list of alternatives) and that those receiving the advice will be interested in as systematic an account of the advantages and disadvantages of the alternatives presented as can be achieved. The customer for this advice may be a single powerful political figure, or it may be the public at large, via a consultation document.

We shall now consider the way in which these policies affect the economic system on which they are meant to act. As we have already noted, the measure of the effect of any particular intervention is the difference it makes to 'what otherwise would have occurred', and in Chapters 2 and 3 we have seen, in simplified form, the kind of forces with which a planner is faced in a mixed economy. These forces still exist when the authority is playing an active role in the urban economy, so we need to consider how these forces react to the changes made to the framework within which the authority operates. The rational authority cannot simply formulate its objectives in the right way. It must ensure that the measures which it uses to further those objectives do in fact produce the desired effects and do not at the same time produce such undesired effects as to make the policy ineffective or harmful. The essence of rational action is that the means selected are appropriate to whatever are the relevant objectives. In the terms we used in Chapter 2 to describe the technology linking the combination of factors to the resulting final product which the firm brings about, the authority must know the production functions it is faced with so that it can relate the inputs of public policy, be these general policies or specific expenditures, to the hoped-for outputs. This knowledge must rest on an understanding of how the urban economy, in the widest sense, works, and, in particular, how it will respond to the impact of public policy upon it.

We will not in this book go very far into the problem of how, in any particular policy situation, an authority should make the relevant forecasts; that is the subject matter of urban economics and related disciplines. What we will do in the chapters which follow is to consider the categories of effects and the general nature of the forces which an authority would have to take into account when rationally framing any land-use policy and hence the kind of information required for policy analysis. In the following chapter we shall consider various kinds of policy instrument designed to contend with the market failures discussed in the previous chapter and attempt to assess their general usefulness. We will then go on in subsequent chapters to discuss the specific impact of such policies on the way in which different parts of the urban economy function and attempt to identify the kinds of cost and benefit which should in principle be measured if such policies are to be properly appraised.

6 MANAGING MARKETS

Chapters 2 and 3 analysed the ways in which market processes work and Chapter 4 distinguished various reasons why the outcome of market processes might not be considered acceptable. This chapter will consider the kinds of policy instrument which government, not necessarily land-use authorities, might use to modify market behaviour, either to improve the workings of markets as markets, or to modify the impact of market behaviour on the community at large.

The aim in this chapter is to consider the general characteristics of the various means of intervention available to government. Although it will consider a number of practical planning problems as examples, we do not wish to argue for any particular policy, nor indeed, that intervention is required simply because market behaviour is not perfect. As noted earlier, some market imperfections are trivial or the costs to government of correcting them so considerable that intervention is not worthwhile. Furthermore, as Chapter 4 pointed out, some of the problems discussed in Chapter 3 may be dealt with without recourse to the machinery of government. Individuals, for example, may be able to sort out among each other some of the externality problems considered above by mutual bargaining and consideration of the rights of others. They may be aided in their ability to do so by the nature of the community in which they live, by its unwritten as well as by its written laws.

In general, however, this chapter is concerned with the ways in which governments can affect the outcome of market processes. The planning authority which appears in this and following chapters is not meant to reflect accurately the powers of any particular authority in the UK or elsewhere; it is a shorthand, expositional device. However, we shall limit ourselves to the kinds of policy instruments which most land-use planning authorities actually possess, or which, it has often been urged, that they ought to have at their disposal. For example, the second section of the chapter examines the effects of taxes and subsidies. The fiscal powers of local planning authorities are limited, although these kinds of policy instrument are frequently used, for example, in national policies towards the distribution of employment. But we shall not consider the powers which central governments typically have over the level of demand in the economy and over the taxation of private income, etc. In this way, the aim is to be realistic without being confined to particular institutional situations.

6.1 Providing Information

Chapter 4 identified a number of reasons why individuals and firms might make bad decisions because their knowledge of the consequences of those decisions was imperfect. The most obvious way to meet this kind of market failure is to make available the information which would allow the individual, or firm, to come to a correct decision. This might be seen as the minimum level of intervention in market processes, since it leaves the basic framework within which they work untouched. But precisely what sort of information should be provided?

Firms and individuals may make bad decisions for many reasons. Firms may choose the wrong production technique or individuals buy a house in the wrong location through underestimation of journey times to work. In the first case, the remedy does not lie with a land-use planning authority; in the latter it might. However, it does not follow that a land-use planning authority should make sure that individuals buying houses had full information. It would be expensive to anticipate and meet the needs of all the many individuals who might be thinking about moving house in a given area. Most would agree that it was up to the individual to obtain that sort of information for himself and if he failed to do so that was his fault. Only he knows that he needs the information and it would not be very difficult or expensive for him to obtain it. New house construction presents a different problem, the risk that through inadequate knowledge a house buyer may choose a house of faulty design. It would be possible, in principle, to provide buyers of all new houses with all the knowledge necessary to choose between various designs, but it would be very expensive and time-consuming to do so. It is cheaper to rule out, by making regulations about what houses should be built covering such matters as foundations, ventilation, damp courses, and insulation, about which the typical householder will not be well informed.

These examples indicate that simply because people may be ill-informed, that it does not follow that it is worthwhile having policies which make good their lack of knowledge. However, they do suggest two general criteria which should guide the decision on whether or not it is worthwhile providing information. First, the information should lie within the special field of competence of the land-use planning authority. The authority should be better informed than firms and individuals within its area about overall trends in population, incomes and employment, because these are the matters which it must itself consider in making its own decisions on intervention. The individual firm might find it useful to have information on these when assessing the demands it might be faced with. Within the simple urban model, information about the likely rate of growth of the urban area as a whole would clearly be central to decisions on what kind of development to put up and at what density. Nevertheless, there are limits to the value of information of this kind. While it is useful to the developer and any public agency responsible for infrastructure, it is not necessarily of much relevance to other participants in the urban economy. It does not tell the industrial or commercial investor what share of the market he might obtain or what his competitors may do. For a firm serving national markets, the local demographic and economic situation may have little significance. It will be more interested in national trends.

Second, the information must be relatively simple and easy to convey. Otherwise, the costs of making it available to those who need it may easily exceed the benefits they gain from having it. It follows from these two points that the range of information over which the authority has a comparative advantage as a supplier is restricted. The authority cannot have knowledge of the widely different circumstances of all the individual decision-makers within its area, nor can it have access to all the information which is available to them. The individual deciding where to buy his house, the developer deciding where to develop, the would-be shopkeeper deciding whether or not to take out a lease may be able to get together much better information relevant to the decision which they have to make than they can get from a single source, which must try to meet the needs of a large number of circumstances. Furthermore, discussion of the prisoner's dilemma and the problems of co-ordination indicated that much of the information which the individual decision-taker needed is about the intentions of others like him. The land-use planning authority will not have that information either, so although there are ways in which the prisoner's dilemma can be overcome, it is not normally through a provision of information alone. The information must be backed by other instruments of policy.

The ability of the planning authority to provide information to the rest of the urban economy of any of the kinds discussed is not simply set by matters of cost and relative advantage. Most developments require forecasts of future levels of demand and other factors which determine profitability. This, even within the simple urban model, requires forecasts of factors such as population and income growth and of the interrelations of the various markets within the urban economy.

It needs no stressing that despite the progress which has been made in understanding the urban economy, the forecasting problems remain severe. In cases where the factors involved do not lie within the special area of competence of a local planning authority, e.g. estimates of income growth, a planning authority will be dependent on other agencies for advance, none of which may be willing to take a long-term view.

If the authority's ability to predict the future in a way relevant to individual development decisions is limited, then so also is the value of any framework of assumptions which it may provide to guide the decisions of others and the higher are the chances of any given set of forecasts being changed. Obviously where development proposals involve a number of different agents who have to co-ordinate their activities in time and space, there are advantages in working to a set of common assumptions which a planning authority may provide. The problem this poses is that of getting the right balance between the advantages of a common framework of assumptions, and the losses from changes in it. Clearly, the more frequent the latter are, the less influence the former will have, as the 'information' they contain will be discounted if it is consistently found to be unreliable. There is something to be said for stability. Counter to this are the costs of change, once the change has to be made. If these costs tend to grow with time, and if it is correct to assume that the longer a set of assumptions has been in use, the less correct it is likely to be, the greater the adjustments to change have to be.

We have been implicitly assuming that information is only conveyed in the form of firm assumptions and statements of intent. However, though the fact that an authority cannot decide whether or not to build a given road may cause hardship to individuals and lead to wasteful investment by firms, in other circumstances, the individual decision-maker may be helped by a statement of possibility, since it makes it clear that he must fall back on his own judgement as to what must be done and he can make his own assessment of how the authority itself may react to changed circumstances. For example, if it is possible that a large new factory will come to a town, no one may know a year or so before it does that it is definitely coming, but the possibility may be acted on by, for example, suppliers of services to the production process concerned. They may take the chance that the factory will in fact arrive; that particular uncertainty would be one among many which they would have to deal with.

In other words, the existence of uncertainty about the context in which individuals operate does not in itself make a case for a central authority providing a specific forecast of what is expected to happen. The individual, even though faced with only a partial picture of the whole situation, may nevertheless have a comparative advantage in relation to those decisions he himself must make. It will often, therefore, be the best policy to let the market absorb uncertainty and not attempt to remove it by centrally based estimates and forecasts, which are themselves liable to error. In this case the role of the authority will tend to rest on the provision of up-to-date analysis of market and other trends, rather than forecasts as such. It may usefully aim at increasing the general understanding of events in its area while leaving their interpretation in terms of forecasts to those actually making development decisions.

In many situations the most important kind of information which the authority can provide concerns its own intentions. Where authorities are active in modifying market processes by means to be discussed below, then knowledge of their intentions is obviously important to other participants in the urban economy. As we shall see, land-use controls can affect the relative and absolute values of different parcels of land or property. The same is true about decisions concerning the provision of new infrastructure. Chapter 3 noted, for example, that additions to the transport system could alter the pattern of accessibility and consequently the desirable pattern of investment. Further, external costs arise as much from public decisions as from private, so individuals may be affected through disruption, severance or noise from the direct action of the planning authority. Equally, in all those situations where private and public action is complementary, failure by the planning authority to provide a framework of information will inhibit the workings of the private market. The most obvious example of this is the blight which can affect an area when the intentions of the public authorities towards it have not been declared or, if declared, not acted upon.

Where the authority is actively intervening in market processes in order to modify their outcome, then the forecasts it makes will reflect its views on how successful such intervention is likely to be. If, for reasons analysed below, its policies are not likely to be successful, then any 'information' of this kind may be counter-productive or simply irrelevant. It will be counter-productive if the authority fails to meet the targets it sets, yet other parts of the urban economy act under the expectation that it will. For example, public agencies may respond and provide infrastructure but the complementary private investment may not materialise. It will be irrelevant if the targets involve the response of the participants in the urban economy, yet no action is taken to induce it. This is likely if the looked-for response depends on agencies acting against what they perceive to be their own interest. In this case the provision of information alone is unlikely to alter their behaviour.

In summary, the provision of information, which at first sight seems an obvious and uncontroversial role for a planning authority, is only appropriate in a limited number of circumstances. There are relatively few kinds of information in the provision of which a planning authority is likely to have a comparative advantage and these are only of subsidiary importance to many of the decision-makers within the urban economy. Perhaps the most important limit to this role, however, is set by the authority's level of understanding of the urban economy and hence its ability to predict its development. Without such understanding its estimates of the factors are likely to be no better – and no worse – than other participants in that economy.

6.2 Dealing with External Effects

(a) Taxes, Subsidies and Compensation Payments

The previous chapter identified the existence of external effects as one of the main reasons why the outcomes of market processes may not be acceptable. This section considers a number of ways in which policy can take account of them and consequently improve, from the social viewpoint, the efficiency of markets.

The first kind of policy instruments we shall consider are taxes and subsidies. Chapter 4 showed how, if an industry gave rise to an undesirable externality, the social costs of that activity exceeded the private costs involved and vice versa, i.e. if it gave rise to external benefits, then social costs would lie below private costs. In the first case the price of the product produced by that industry would be too low and in the second too high. The result is a situation in which the price incentives facing producers are not correct. In the first case they tend to produce too much and in the second too little. Probably more important, they may use the techniques of production which are not best from the viewpoint of society as a whole.

Taxes and subsidies may be used to bring private and social costs into line, as Diagram 13 illustrates. The diagram shows the total private and social production costs of an industry. The curve SC_1 reflects the extent of the external costs it gives rise to. These have been assumed for convenience to be a constant amount per unit produced. At the point where the demand curve cuts the private cost curve, i.e. the point where the firm itself would be willing to sell, total social costs are in excess of private costs by the amount AB and they exceed what consumers would be willing to pay. That is, at the level of output at which the firm would be content to produce, the price to the consumer would be too low. It would fail to reflect the total, or social, costs of the output level concerned.

Diagram 13

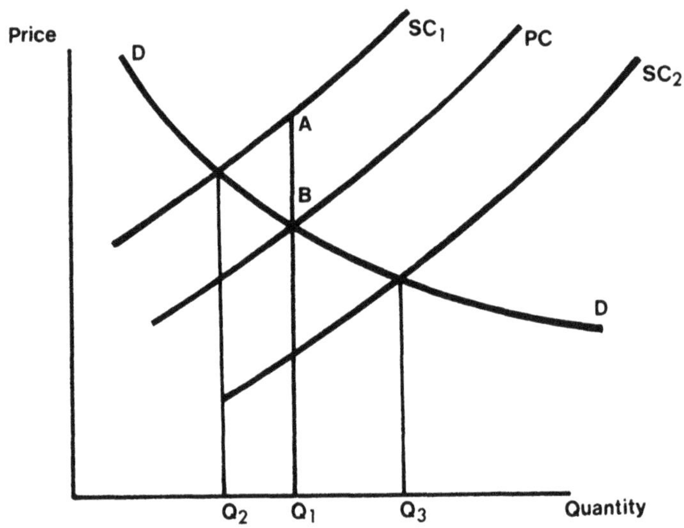

If the tax levied on the sale of the goods in question equals the amount of the externality its production gives rise to, then the price to the consumer would equal the social cost. Demand would fall to Q_2, and at this level of output willingness to pay, as expressed in the demand curve, would be equal to the total costs involved. At this point, marginal social cost and marginal social benefit would be equal. The diagram also illustrates the situation if the marginal social cost curve lies below the private cost curve. This is shown by the line SC_2. In this case, if production is to take place at the point where marginal private and marginal social cost were equal, a subsidy would have to be given to the producer of the good concerned so that his supply curve was reduced to SC and demand increased to Q_3.

The effect of the tax and the subsidy is to *internalise* the externality;

that is, it produces a situation where, as far as the firm is concerned, there is no distinction between the cost (or benefit) it imposes on others and those which it experiences directly itself. The initial effect, as we have seen, of internalising the external effects is to modify the total level of demand for the good in question. However, the nature of the adjustments which markets would make to the imposition of a tax, or the granting of a subsidy, depends closely on the precise way in which the tax or subsidy is administered and the extent to which it is related to the external effect concerned.

The significance of this can be seen by examining further the smoky chimney example introduced in Chapter 4. Let us suppose that it was possible to estimate that each unit of production from the factory concerned cost the households living near the factory £1 per year in extra cleaning bills and that the product concerned sold for £100. It is obvious that if a tax were imposed equal to the amount of the external cost, the effect on the level of demand would be very small, even if demand was very elastic. If, for example, we assumed an elasticity of 3 – a very high figure – demand would fall by only 3 per cent, which might be regarded as negligible. However, the reason why the tax appears so ineffective is that its imposition is unrelated to the externality concerned. Let us suppose that the factory was taxed according to the weight of the dirt which neighbouring households had had deposited on them. The effect of such a tax would probably be considerable, for even if it did not affect very much the total level of production in the plant, it would affect the way in which it carried out that production. It would have an incentive either to install smoke-cleaning equipment or to adopt a new production which did not give rise to such dirty side-effects. As a final alternative it might move to a site where no one was affected by the smoke it produced.

The same points are equally relevant to the use of subsidies. For example, if the external benefit resulting from a production process were not very closely related to its total level of production, then the use of an overall subsidy would be inefficient in a way analogous to the previous analysis. However, if the problem to be solved was a failure of supply or public goods problem, i.e. if the total level of production was too low, because the firms concerned could not charge all those benefiting properly, then a subsidy linked to production levels would be a possible solution.

In many contexts subsidies and taxes are alternatives. Consider, for example, the case of farming practices which threaten to damage the appearance of the countryside, e.g. the removal of hedgerows to allow the use of large-scale equipment. Farmers could be taxed if they used the offending techniques or taxed in relation to the length of hedgerow destroyed, or alternative farming techniques which preserved hedegrows could be subsidised to make them more attractive. The same balance between amenity and farm production could be reached by either of these routes, i.e. the same length of hedgerow could be preserved. Thus the efficiency effects could be the same, but the distributional consequences would be very different. If a subsidy were paid, taxpayers would have to bear the cost of preserving the amenity. If a tax were levied, farmers or those purchasing farm products would have to do so.

One further implication of this analysis can be considered by looking at another example, that of congestion. The users of roads, parks and countryside impose costs on each other simply by getting in each other's way, when the facilities concerned begin to fill up. We show this effect in Diagram 14 which illustrates the demand for a park. Up to the point A, there is no congestion and people are completely unconstrained by the presence of others. The cost curve, which is made up only of the

Diagram 14

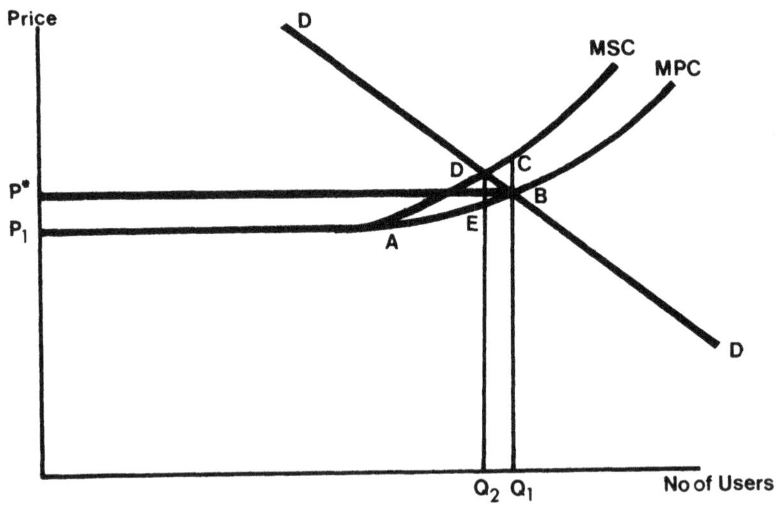

entry fee, is horizontal. But after a certain point congestion begins to make itself felt and each user experiences a cost, or loss of utility, from the presence of others. Hence the private cost curve begins to rise. But the social cost curve rises even faster, since the private cost curve does not take into account the costs additional users impose on others. For example, we assume that at point B, the user concerned must pay P_1 like all other users, experiences a disutility equal to the distance $P_1 - P^*$ and imposes costs on others equal to B – C. Marginal private and marginal social costs can be brought into line in the way we have explored above by the imposition of a tax DE. This fixes the use of the park at point D, where marginal social costs and marginal social benefit are equal. An important point which emerges from this analysis is that at usage level Q_2, congestion is not eliminated completely. In other words, at the socially correct level of use, some congestion will remain.

Why this is so can be seen by considering the position of those users to the left of Q_2 and to the right of A. Their position on the demand curve shows that they would be prepared to pay a greater amount than the total costs concerned – the costs of congestion they cause plus the entrance fee. Beyond point Q_2, this would not be so – costs would outweigh benefits. Thus it would not be desirable to eliminate congestion, as this would reduce the overall level of benefit gained from the facility concerned. The total level of benefit is maximised only at the point where the marginal conditions hold and marginal social cost equals marginal social benefit.

In some contexts external effects can be dealt with through payment of compensation. Detailed provisions vary, but in a number of countries, payment can be made when public sector projects such as road-building or redevelopment impose costs on individuals. For example, in the UK, businesses bought out by compulsory purchase orders receive compensation for loss of profits. Recent legislation has given people seriously affected by road noise the right to be compensated for the nuisance they suffer.

Compensation payments of these kinds are closely related to the use of taxes to internalise external costs. In the case of road-building, if the compensation payments are assessed correctly, they serve to bring home to the construction authority in monetary form the costs they are imposing in order to achieve the intended transport benefits. As far as the authority is concerned, these payments are on a par with payments for cement and labour. That is, they are provided with an equivalent incentive to economise. To give an example: if a choice of routes existed, the fact that one entailed greater compensation would tell against it just as would higher construction costs.

Arrangements like this may allow a correct balance to be struck between the interests of those proposing a development, the firm or the road-building agency, and the wider social interest. In some cases, however, compensation payments may be paid and not have that effect. This will be so if individuals are compensated by government but not by the party giving rise to the cost. The individual is in the same position but the offending party is not, as it is not liable for the payment. It therefore has no incentive to avoid giving rise to the cost concerned. Noise nuisance at airports is a useful example. This could be treated by taxing the creation of noise itself, e.g. by having a landing tax in relation to emitted noise levels or, as at London Heathrow, subsidies may be given to reduce the burden of the noise on those suffering it, in this case through double glazing grants. The important difference between this case and the previous one, however, is that production of the external effect is not affected by the policy instrument used as the airlines themselves do not bear any of the costs of the double glazing scheme. They have no incentive from this source to reduce the noise their aircraft make.

Schemes of this kind suffer from further limitations. By their nature they must be expressed in general terms with the consequence that not all individuals are likely to be adequately compensated for a given change, if, at the same time, others are not being overcompensated. We can take the example of a row of houses each affected by a road proposal by the same amount in physical terms. The importance which the individual attaches to this will vary. Equally, while all individuals have the option of motion of moving house, they will attach different values to their houses, depending largely on the length of time they have spent in it. Such variation cannot be reflected in a standard *tarif*, which must inevitably entail a degree of rough justice.

Despite these problems, there is potential scope for extending the compensation principle. Various rights concerned with nuisance are embodied in the legal system, for example, prosecutions may be brought against those imposing excessive noise costs on others. Implicit in this is a basic right to peace and quiet at least during certain times of day. These could be extended to have greater relevance to land-use planning. In the case of the two neighbours, one of which wishes to build an extension, the present situation in the UK is that the objector has a right to state his case against the proposal, but not a right to be compensated for the losses he suffers. If, however, all individuals were invested with rights to be free from certain nuisances, then an alternative arrangement would be possible under which anyone infringing, or threatening to infringe, such rights would have to bargain with the person or persons whose rights were threatened. In this situation, no one need accept an infringement of his rights, unless he felt himself adequately compensated. There are obvious problems of practicality with a system of this kind, e.g. the definition of the scope of the rights concerned. In particular it would be difficult to define the interested parties to be given rights when the ramifications of a development may be very wide. In the case of an extension, the loss of sunlight experienced by a neighbour might be obvious but not the aesthetic loss experienced by a passer-by. For this reason, probably only some cases could be settled in this way. But the nature and adequacy of compensation arrangements obviously affect cases where the planning authority itself is involved, specifically those which involve the imposition of large losses on a small number of individuals. A more thorough-going compensation system would reduce or eliminate the conflicts such cases entail.

(b) Regulations

The vast majority of policy measures used by land-use planning authorities to deal with externalities, particularly external costs, are in the form of regulations. These may specify where certain activities take place, how buildings should be designed, whether certain pollutants can be emitted. Although like taxes and subsidies, they set the framework within which market forces work, they do so by setting precise limits on what may or may not be done by prohibiting specific developments. Where should the limits be set?

The previous section has provided the necessary rule, that the output of the activity giving rise to the externality, or the level of the externality, should be set at the point where marginal social benefit and cost are equal. In principle, a regulation may be used to set output, or the level of the externality concerned, at that point. In the case of the smoky chimney, an estimate might be made of the point at which the cost of preventing omissions by the installation of the relevant equipment was equal to the benefit of getting cleaner air and the level of emissions regulated to that level. In the case of the congested park, a regulation might be set for its use which said that no one should be allowed in once Q_2 have been admitted. This would have the same effect as a tax as far as numbers enjoying the park was concerned, although it would have a different distributional impact, since if a tax were levied to bring private and social costs into line, users would have to pay more for the given level of benefit and different users would enjoy the facility.

Calculations of this kind are satisfactory in the individual case or where a large number of similar cases are involved. But they are less satisfactory if a large number of different kinds of users, in different circumstances, are affected. Regulating activity can be carried out on a case-by-case basis. Generally, however, it is a characteristic of the use of regulations or standards that decisions are taken centrally, at local or national level, which may then not fit the facts of individual cases very well. For example, in the case of the smoky chimney, a standard might be set which permitted emissions only up to a certain level. The benefits from having the standard at that level might vary a great deal from area to area, because of different population densities, and so might the costs. If different firms use different production techniques they have to pay widely varying amounts to meet the levels set. Consequently, a level which was too low in some areas, i.e. the costs of meeting the standards outweighed the benefits, might be too high in others – the benefits outweighed the costs. In these latter cases, too much pollution is permitted and in the former, too little.

This example brings out two characteristics of regulations: first, within the limit set by the standard, no incentive is created to diminish the externality to which it is directed. If the standard is complied with, that is sufficient. To take another example, regulations are in force in all countries limiting the maximum size and weight of vehicles to avoid the excessive damage or congestion which very large vehicles would give rise to. But such regulations do nothing to reduce the damage or delays which vehicles just below the statutory limits cause, although if these external costs are related to vehicle dimensions, then clearly it would be desirable that all users of the heavier vehicles should be given some incentive to reduce their use of them.

This leads directly on to the second point: that regulations, if approved in a blanket fashion, do not allow the individual decision-taker to make the best of his own particular situation. For example, the regulation which forbids the use of 100 ton vehicles does not allow a possibly very small body of users the opportunity to use such vehicles at all, no matter how great the advantages may be. They are not in a position to trade off their private benefits with the social costs involved, in the way they can do if the external costs were brought home to them via a tax related to size of vehicle. The same issue arises with individuals if preferences vary. For example, people indifferent to noise nuisance do not gain from a regulation which prevents houses being built near noise sources. Instead their choice, and hence their potential welfare, is reduced.

A discretionary case-by-case system of regulation can avoid this problem, but only if used in a way which reflects variations in individuals' circumstances. This would mean in the case of high buildings that exceptions would be allowed if a specially strong case could be made. If general standards are employed in coming to a decision, they will not be able to take such special circumstances into account. The significance of this point must be judged, however, in relation to the analysis in Chapter 4 of the reasons for intervention. If these are paternalistic, then a general regulation is likely to be the appropriate instrument of policy. But if intervention is based on any of the other grounds distinguished, this does not hold. Any general policy could then only be justified on grounds of administrative simplicity.

In extreme cases there may be no advantage of allowing such a trade-off. For example, if there was widespread agreement that very high buildings should not be allowed in a given area, there would be little point in setting up a tax schedule relating tax paid to building height, since the tax for buildings above the maximum permitted level would be so high that no one would pay it. It is far simpler to make a regulation. In other situations, however, when the balance of advantage is not so clear, the problems of setting the right level for a regulation may be severe, and a tax, or subsidy solution, might be attractive. For example, in the fuel example discussed in Chapter 2, there was obvious advantage in using fiscal means to discourage use of imported oil, because of the large numbers of decisions affected and the wide variety of circumstances in which these decisions would have to be taken. It would make little sense to forbid the use of oil in quantities over 1,000 gallons per user; since the requirements of users vary so widely. A tax, however, naturally bears harder on heavy users than light users and will tend to produce the effect desired without imposing what would possibly be very high costs on those who would find it difficult to change their fuel if a regulation forbade its use entirely.

As noted already, the problem facing an authority using general regulations is that of striking the right balance. The general rule is clear, that the balance should be struck at the point where marginal social cost and marginal social benefit are equal. Diagram 15 illustrates this. It shows two curves: the benefit curve rises to the right, reflecting the increased benefit to be gained from a more intense control over the emission of a given pollutant. The cost curve, however, also rises to the right, and at point A cuts the benefit curve. To the right of point A costs outweigh benefits.

Many of the practical problems involved in measuring both costs and benefits of measures of this kind will be examined later. Here, however,

Diagram 15

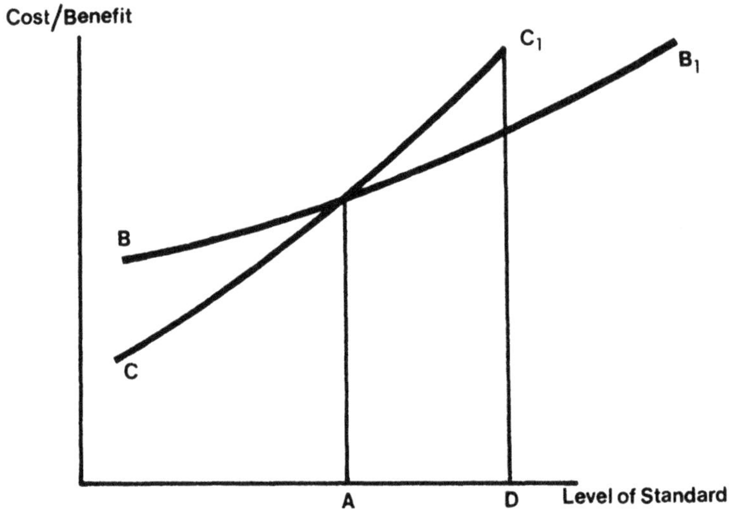

we want only to bring out a general point which applies to most regulations. This is that the benefits of a regulation are usually more apparent than the costs. For example, a planning authority may be very clear that it does not want high buildings in its area. It is quite convinced that they will damage visual amenity severely. It may, therefore, be tempted simply to make a regulation or enforce a general planning policy to that effect.

A policy of this kind may seem to be costless. The costs, however, of a regulation of this kind are hidden and may be difficult to disentangle since they tend to be felt throughout the urban economy. If high buildings are forbidden, more land will be required for commercial uses, or existing uses will have to take place at a higher density with resultant pressure on space and lower efficiency. If more land is used, there might be extra transport costs, increased servicing costs for statutory undertakers, loss of agricultural production and countryside amenity. If some development takes place at higher density, there may be extra construction costs, reduced enjoyment from housing and lower public urban open space standards.

None of this proves that the high building regulation is not worthwhile; what it does show, however, is that the task of setting the level right is a difficult one, much more complicated than the simple making of a regulation – which may have no direct cost to the planning authority itself – would suggest. This point applies to all regulatory activity. Later chapters, particularly 10 and 11, examine a number of common examples.

6.3 Provision of Public Goods

In most cases, the provision of public goods will fall to the public authorities. But in some circumstances, provision can be achieved by modifying the behaviour of private markets. We have already noted that when external effects are favourable rather than unfavourable, a subsidy may be useful in inducing output to the right level. Few public goods are perfectly public; consequently there is usually some scope for private firms to make available a limited supply which a subsidy may further encourage. The public good benefits of farm land cultivated in a certain way may, as we have seen already, be retained by subsidy. In this case, taxation of the offending farming practices was also a possibility.

Subsidy is not, however, the only way in which private markets may be induced to supply public goods. In some circumstances, depending precisely on their legal powers and bargaining skill, planning authorities are able to exact public goods from private developers as the 'price' of obtaining planning permission. If the authority operates a discretionary control system over changes in the use of land it may, either formally, or informally, require developers to provide open space when they put up private housing developments or make land available for public uses. More generally, authorities may impose conditions on developers concerning the detailed design and layout of their developments. These may concern details of the houses themselves which might give rise to external costs, but they may go further and set down the characteristics of housing developments of a public goods nature, e.g. road space. This is discussed in more detail in Chapter 11. Developers can be induced to supply public goods of other kinds. The precise procedures vary a great deal but the basic principle is the same, that the planning authority, to the extent that it controls whether or not the development takes place, bargains a share of the total profit from the development and takes its share in the form of goods supplied.

There are two basic limitations to such procedures. First, as long as planning authorities are not able to receive cash payments in return for the right to develop, then the public good benefits received may be of low value. If authorities could receive benefits in either form then the point would not hold. Consider the case of a commercial redevelopment.

The developer may offer £1m, 100 units of public housing or some open space. The authority would be rational to choose the open space if it has already intended to make some available and if it would have cost it more than £1m. If, however, it could get the space more cheaply, then it should choose one of the two remaining alternatives. If housing would normally cost more than £10,000 per unit then this would be the best choice. Thus where the cash or kind choice was available, the 'kind' alternative would be chosen where the developer was able due to economies of scale in his development or some other similar factor, to supply at low cost. The corollary is that it would be unwise for an authority to make a benefit in kind a condition for permission if the alternative of a cash payment was available.

Second, the ability of the authority to make deals of this kind is limited by the profitability of the development concerned. Where development or redevelopment offers only normal profits, i.e. a level of profit only just sufficient to encourage the development to take place, then there is no surplus profit for the authority to tap. This point must be considered in relation to the earlier analysis of the way in which land prices are determined. Within the simple model, these were seen to be a residual, with the landowner tapping any exceptional profits. This followed from the assumption that there was sufficient competition between developers to achieve this.

Thus, under this assumption, the scope for extracting planning gains in either cash or kind is determined ultimately not by the developer's profit but by the surplus accruing to land. In the case of much development, and redevelopment in particular, no such surplus may exist. Whether it does or not will depend, as the analysis in Chapter 4 shows, on whether the planning authority has adopted a restrictive policy towards development of the kind concerned.

In the case of general policies, the same analysis applies but in a slightly different form. A planning authority may for example require developers to provide certain amenities of a public good nature. If these are sufficiently costly, the surplus accruing to landowners may disappear, i.e. developers' bids are reduced to zero. The consequence in this situation may be more severe. If the conditions are such that developers are not able to pay a price for land at which landowners will supply to the use concerned, the development may not take place at all or its scale may be reduced.

This leads to a final point. To the planning authority the methods considered here may allow certain facilities to be provided free, or at low cost. The question, from the viewpoint of society as a whole, is whether such procedures are efficient, i.e. whether the gain to the planning authority's budget is at the expense of its constituents. To the urban economy at large, facilities gained by exploiting planning gain are not free goods as real resources will be used in their production. The brief analysis above suggests that only in certain circumstances will advantages in terms of real costs ensue, i.e. when costs of provision are lower than average due to particular circumstances in the developments concerned. In other cases, the real costs of such policies may be very high, e.g. if an authority requires the provision of certain facilities when the particular circumstances of the development make it expensive to do so, e.g. the provision of housing units in an otherwise purely commercial development. The cost of the housing may in itself be high; in addition it may be, due to its location and surroundings, of low value to potential occupants.

7 THE EFFECTS AND LIMITS OF INTERVENTION IN THE URBAN ECONOMY

For the various reasons distinguished in Chapter 4, a land-use planning authority may wish to modify the outcome of market processes. The previous chapter considered the general characteristics of the various policy instruments which the planning authority might use to effect such modifications. We will now consider how the use of such controls is likely to affect the behaviour of markets within the simple urban model and how the effectiveness of such controls is determined.

In the real world, the range of external effects with which land-use planners may wish to deal is extremely wide. So also is the range of policies which are employed. Some of the most important of these lie outside the range of what are traditionally thought of as land-use planning instruments. As we have already seen, property law, laws relating to nuisance and other procedures, statutory or non-statutory which allow individuals to treat other individuals in respect of damage done to them, all determine the scale of the problem falling on land-use planning authorities. In considering how any markets work, or how public authorities behave, we must assume the legal framework within which we are working. This is of central importance to the treatment of externalities. Our starting point is that the existing legal framework does not deal adequately with external effects.

Either by reference to the legal framework in general or legislation relating to land use in particular, planning authorities may, according to their particular jurisdictions, make a wide number of different interventions in market processes. The nature of control varies a great deal and with it the potential to modify market behaviour. This chapter aims to bring out some general issues using as examples kinds of control which most land-use planning authorities exercise. The purpose of this examination is to pursue the general point made in Chapter 5, that the prime aim of the analyst should be to provide an understanding of the relationships between the various objectives which planning might pursue and the resources available. To do this we need to develop an understanding of the way in which markets are affected by different kinds of intervention and hence the kinds of cost and benefit which can arise. We are not concerned with development of a critique of any particular policy, but rather with seeing how to identify what effects are relevant to the examination of policies in general.

7.1 Land Use Controls within the Simple Urban Model

We begin by considering how the various types of control affect the workings of the urban economy, taking first taxes, subsidies and compensation payments, and going on to consider the impact of regulations.

If it were administratively possible and costless to levy charges, taxes, grants and subsidies and require payment of compensation according to the principles set out in the previous chapter, then the urban economy could work essentially along the lines discussed in Chapter 3. All external effects would be internalised through the imposition of taxes on undesired externalities and through payment of subsidies where favourable external effects occurred. Problems of undersupply of public goods would be overcome through subsidy or through the grant of exclusion rights, where this was practical. This approach will be called the fiscal system of management.

Essentially then the system would remain one of decentralised decision-making, but with the fundamental modification that the price information which the individual decision-makers were faced with would have been modified to take into account external effects. On this model of management of the economy the main task of the authority would be to estimate the social costs and benefits arising from private acts of production and consumption, to set up the appropriate financial framework and then let market forces work through the consequences.

Administrative complexities apart, such a system would place considerable demands upon the authority. It would have to make explicit judgements about the value or disvalue to be attached to all the externalities physical development gives rise to. In areas where amenity value was attached to agricultural land in excess of its market value, a tax would have to be set to reflect the difference between private and social valuation. This tax would have to be paid when land was converted from agricultural to developed use. The price set would have to vary with conditions of demand and supply in the relevant markets. For example, if pressure of demand on scarce amenity land was increased, and some was made over to development, then the value of the remaining land would have to be adjusted upwards.

Subject to the analysis of 6.1, there would be a role for the authority in the provision of information about broad trends in the urban economy, changes in land use, income and employment etc., since this information, if accurate, would improve decision-making under any system of control or management. There might also be a need for policy intervention to deal with some of the other problems discussed in section 4.3, where market forces themselves are not working efficiently, e.g. those arising from adjustment lags, problems of co-ordination and deficiencies in information of the kind which cannot be overcome by its simple provision.

Under this system, those activities which gave rise to significant unfavourable externalities would react by taking measures to reduce them and individuals and firms would respond to the changed structure of the land market in the ways already discussed. To give some examples: developers would tend to choose sites where the burden of externality taxes was low, thus avoiding land with public good characteristics, such as amenity areas. They would only develop such land if the benefit in terms of higher prices and profit were sufficient to overcome the burden of the tax. Firms would tend to site activities which did not give rise to external effects wherever suited them most for other reasons, e.g. where accessibility was good or land cheap. Firms which did give rise to external costs might have to go to remote or expensive sites.

It is not easy to predict in detail what the effects would be in terms of land-use patterns, but it seems probable that the outcome would be different from both the tightly regulated UK land market and the (in most respects) much freer US market. In some cases juxtapositions of land uses would appear which do not do so now. Uses which are thought to be incompatible under the highly managed UK market might be found together because some industrial or commercial users took steps to cut down on the externalities they gave rise to and so made themselves acceptable to residential neighbours. In other cases, there might be more separation, where the taxes induced firms to move out of areas of mixed land use.

A fully worked through system of urban management of this kind is unlikely to be realised, but it is not a model which should be rejected entirely, for three reasons. First, it may be possible to realise it partially through tax or subsidy measures in particular cases: a recent proposal for the use of fiscal measures to correct for pricing failure is examined in Chapter 10. Second, it makes explicit the kinds of judgement which authorities must make under a regulatory system. Few authorities would, for example, care to produce a tax schedule to impose on developers, graded according to the amenity and conservation value of the land concerned. But, as we shall see, such values are implicit in regulatory policies. Third, it provides a backcloth to the appreciation of alternative kinds of policies aimed at achieving similar ends.

The main general point to bring out is that it represents one basic approach to land-use planning, that of setting up a framework of incentives and disincentives within which individuals and firms make their own decisions. This strategy contrasts with those regulatory approaches which require intervention in each decision which has social, as well as private, implications. Some further points of contrast will emerge below.

Within this approach to the management of urban land, the movement of land between uses remains free. The desired balance between uses is determined by market forces, as in Chapter 3, but the information, especially the cost information, within which such a managed market works alters the effective outcome. Where controls over change of use of a regulatory nature are exercised, markets work in a different way.

As noted already, the majority of controls exercised by land-use planning authorities is in the form of regulation. These are very diverse, however, ranging from the broad strategic controls typified by the zoning ordinances common in the US which specify in detail how large tracts of land should be used, to the case-by-case approach which UK local planning authorities employ against the background of broad land allocations and general policy contained in development plans. In the UK, nearly any change in the way in which land or property is used is subject to control, provided it is likely to give rise to a change significant from the viewpoint of other members of society. Nevertheless, the system is potentially very flexible, since it allows changes of use to be considered on a case-by-case basis.

Because of the wide range of institutional contexts in which planning takes place, it is not easy to generalise about the impact of specific policies. In the following paragraphs, therefore, we will bring out some general points which are common to a large number of regulatory policies. To do this two basic assumptions will be made: first, that the urban area 'described' in the simple urban model of Chapter 3 has a planning authority which controls changes of use; second, that it employs this power by zoning broad areas for particular kinds of use and by exercising a detailed case-by-case approach over any changes of use within these zones, i.e. there is no outright prohibition of change of use. This crudely approximates to the planning powers exercised by UK and many other planning authorities.

Let us assume that in the first instance an initial allocation of land to various use categories had been made, that this was arbitrary or based on very insufficient evidence, and that the discretionary control was used very sparingly so that in effect each land use operated in a different market. It would not be surprising if different land values emerged in each of these markets. For example, if demand for commercial land had been underestimated, it would be unsurprising to find that land in commercial uses had a much higher value than land in other uses. If, on the other hand, demand for industrial land had been overestimated, the converse result would hold – land values would be low in relation to others in comparable locations. Following Chapter 3, the implication would be that the efficiency of the urban economy would be increased by a transfer of land.

The authority might react by facilitating transfer of land to those markets where land values were high from those where values were low. But let us suppose that it decided not to do this, on the grounds that to do so would impose external costs on users, e.g. householders would lose out if neighbouring land were handed over to industry or commerce. The effect of this policy can be shown in Diagram 16.

Diagram 16

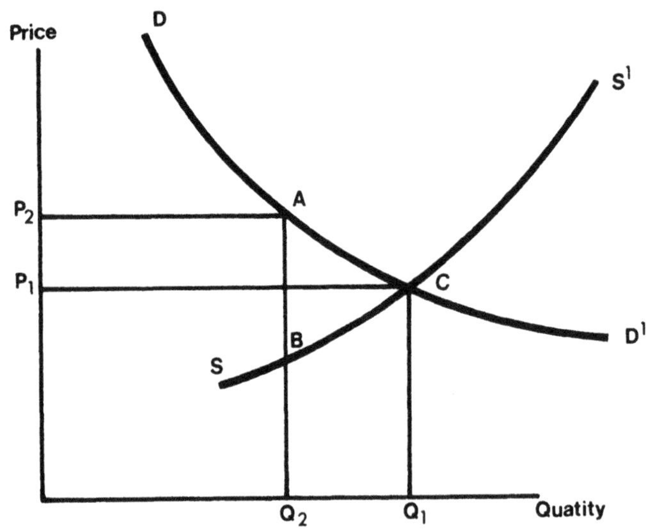

In the diagram, the familiar demand and supply curves are shown, but instead of the point of equilibrium being at C – where it would be had the markets been free – the effect of the control is to restrict supply to Q_2 and hence send the price to P_2. At this point, the price is higher than the equilibrium price by the amount P_2-P_1. This has various effects, some on the efficiency of the urban economy and others distributional. The former are discussed in the following paragraphs. The latter are discussed in the following section.

In response to the rise in price, economising reactions can be expected in respect of the 'scarce' land use of the various kinds described in Chapter 3. In the case of industrial sites, this means that firms would find it less profitable to have spacious layouts for their factories or storage and that in the case of commercial uses, there will be a tendency to build high and economise on space by lowering space standards per employee and moving routine tasks out to other areas. Some firms would not be able to compete at all. If housing were the restricted use, densities would tend to rise and the size of each housing unit fall. All these reactions have real consequences, either in the form of commitment of resources or in the form of a direct loss of utility to the persons affected. The central economic issue which any such control raises is: do the costs imposed on those using land made scarce by control outweigh the benefits which stem from the control? In the previous chapter we devised the formal rules for answering this question, i.e. that at the margin social costs and benefits should be equal. In the present context this rule implies that the price difference which emerges between the rationed and the non-rationed use should reflect the extent of the divergence between private and social cost.

If the social costs associated with the expansion of a particular use were high and hence the social benefit from preventing its expansion also high, then a large price differential would be appropriate. One good example is the price differential between agricultural and other uses which obtains in the UK. Within the simple urban model, this would emerge if the planning authority attached a value to the preservation of agricultural land and reflected this judgement in a restrictive land release policy. The price differential which emerged would, if this was the only consideration, reflect the relative value of land conservation on the one hand, and better (or at least lower-density) housing on the other, as well as lower prices for the goods produced within the urban economy. A regulatory control could in these circumstances continue to be exercised according to the marginal rules. The rational authority would release land until the marginal social cost and benefit were equal. If, because of increased effective demand for housing, the housing benefits of more land release grew, this would shift the equilibrium point and land would be released until balance was again reached. Alternatively, if the value of agricultural or amenity land grew over time, a more restrictive policy would be appropriate.

Now in this case the connection between the control and the desired effect, i.e. a general economising on land, is clear and direct, since the land price encourages the required reactions. As noted above, a similar effect could have been achieved by taxing the conversion of land and setting the price at a level which reflected the divergence between private and social benefit in any development decision. The tax would be set equal to AB in Diagram 16.

The distributional implications however would be different. Under the regulatory system Londoners receive the high prices resulting from the policy: with the tax, they do not. Let us suppose, however, that the externality in question is not associated with land use as such but with pollution of the atmosphere. In this case a general land rationing policy is of little relevance, since the economising reactions of the firm would have little to do with the externality with which policy was concerned. Little control is as blunt an instrument in this case as a general tax on production. To achieve a given level of pollution control by these means would therefore be highly inefficient.

This follows directly from the fact that such a land-use control does not alter the basic behaviour of the firm or its motivations with regard to the externality in question. What it does do is lead to a wide range of adaptive behaviour, which it is not easy to predict. The individual refused permission to alter his dwelling on the grounds that it imposes excessive costs on his neighbours may simply accept the loss, or he may move with only small expense to another area where he can make the desired change or to a house with the required characteristics. The firm may move elsewhere, or it may simply economise on space in the various ways available to it. The control may be ineffective in relation to the objective of reducing pollution but it may nevertheless impose costs. The analytic problem is to discover precisely what the costs are of reactions to the control.

The planning authority itself has a direct perception of the benefits but not of the costs to other elements of the urban economy. This holds true no matter if the regulatory policy is applied in a blanket manner or on a case-by-case discretionary system. In the latter case it is easier to get at the facts of a particular proposed change, but it is no less difficult to assess the consequences of refusal. In principle, an understanding of the workings of the urban system as a whole is required to predict the consequences of policies of this kind. Refusal of permission to transfer land in a particular location will have greater or lesser effects on the demand for land in all locations. In the case of the individual applicant, the effect will be minimal. The main problem here is estimation of the loss the individual suffers from not being able to do what he wants. But in the case of a large user of land, the main problem may be that of estimating the consequences in the urban area as a whole of refusing or allowing a change of use. For example, the indirect effects of releasing or not releasing additional land for industrial or commercial development may lead to changes in employment levels, incomes and travel patterns as well as land use itself. Some specific cases are considered in Chapter 10.

Whether or not restrictions on the switching of land from one use to another are justified and their effects calculable, one sharp point of contrast with the fiscal system of management should be noted. The effect of such a control is, as noted, to erect a price differential between the rational use and other uses. This differential will prevail as long as the demand conditions which give rise to it. The control, by itself, does nothing to modify the pattern of demand away from the rationed use (or rationed location) in other directions. The pressure to convert land in the non-desired direction remains. This would not be true under the fiscal system.

The pattern of land values which emerges from the two kinds of management also differs. Where regulatory controls are in force, the land values will vary: (a) for a given site according to the use allowed; (b) as between similar sites (i.e. sites identical in terms of accessibility and environment) according to the use allowed. Under the fiscal model of management, the values would be similar in basic structure to the simple urban model. Under regulation the result is a very uneven land surface with sharp difference between values under different uses. The differences do not, as in the simple urban model, stem from differences in value to the user, but depend on the control. Such differences can persist in a regulatory system when this works to limit the supply of land to particular kinds of use and in particular locations. The forces tending to even out such differences, described in Chapter 3, are not able to work through to remove them.

7.2 Distributional Effects

The analysis introduced in the previous section is of direct interest for its distributional implications. One important effect of a restrictive control on supply of land use is to give special value to all land already under that use and hence a special gain to all those enjoying an interest in that land. If markets are working perfectly, landlords would be able to charge a higher than average price for their land and earn a supernormal return on it. If they were not able to do this because of lease agreements, then the sitting tenants would enjoy the gain. Equally, a special gain attaches to anyone who obtains permission through a discretionary control system to transfer land from a non-scarce to a scarce use.

The nature of this effect has already been illustrated in Diagram 16. If land supply were unrestricted, the amount Q_1 would be supplied at price P_1'. If supply is reduced by control to Q_2, price P_2 results. The difference between P_1 and P_2 is the extent of the supernormal profit. How large this difference is clearly depends on the strength of demand for the use of rationed land. The mere fact of a regulatory control on change of use is in itself insufficient to produce supernormal profits for landowners. Land for commercial uses may be administratively rationed in a particular area but if there is no demand in that location, land prices will be unaffected.

As noted already, these distributional effects stem directly from the nature of regulatory control. A fiscal control on the lines of that described above would, in general, not produce them, except at times where the control was not properly adjusted. Nevertheless, there are circumstances where similar effects may occur. For example, a subsidy may be used to promote a certain kind of development on the ground that the social benefits from improvement exceed the private. One recent case is the improvement grant policy which has enabled local authorities to make payments to house-owners for the installation of amenities and other modernisation works. The initial effect of this was to reduce the cost to those purchasing older properties of bringing them up to acceptable standards. In certain market conditions, the result was to increase the price of such properties in such a way as to reduce the incentive effect. In other words, some or all of the subsidy leaked into land values as owners of properties likely to be bought for improvement realised the enhanced value of their property.

Whether or not such leakage will occur can be analysed using the familiar supply and demand diagram. In Diagram 17 the supply curves represent the conditions under which owners of older properties will put them on the market. Curve S_1 shows conditions of perfect elastic supply, i.e. at the going price an indefinite number will be supplied, S_2 perfectly inelastic supply, and S_3 an intermediary case. Which circumstances would be reflected in these various curves? Clearly in total the supply of older properties is fixed and cannot be increased whatever price is offered. S_2 is in this sense the appropriate representation of the situation. If it were, then all the subsidy would go into the property values, i.e. it shifts the demand curve from D_1D_1 to D_2D_2 and the price of older properties from P_1 to P_2.

Diagram 17

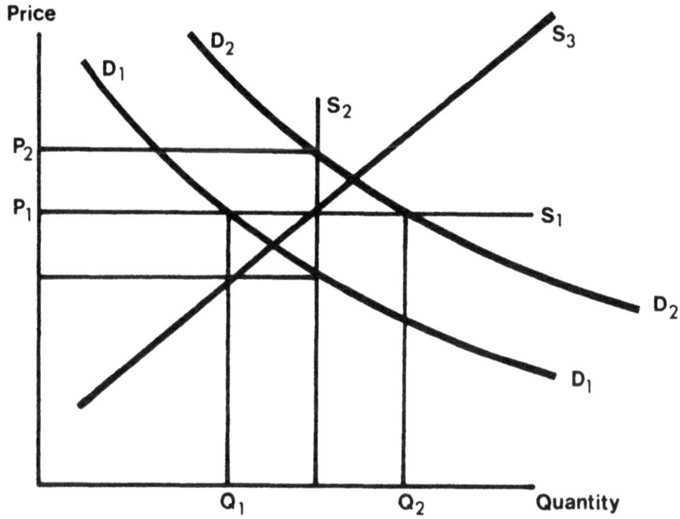

However, if the demand for improvement was low at any point in time in relation to the total stock of improvable houses, then the supply curve might be more realistically represented by SS_1. For example, if the effect of the subsidy was only enough to induce a small number of owners to make improvements, then the effect on the price of the properties as a whole would be insignificant. In this case, there is no leakage into property values and subsidy has a maximum effectiveness. If the curve were like SS_3, then the effect of the subsidy would be dissipated, but not lost entirely.

These consequences of control are straightforward enough at a general level, although in any particular situation the actual effects might be difficult to judge because of rigidities in land and property markets due to lease and rental agreements. For example, permission may be obtained for a change of use, but it may not be possible to effect the change of use immediately. However, as the improvement case showed, the distributional effects of controls on the urban economy are difficult to unravel. To help in their analysis we will introduce a basic distinction between the initial and the final incidence of a policy measure.

To illustrate this distinction, we will consider the example of a tax on the sale of a commodity. Take curve S_2 in Diagram 7, page 35, as the supply curve of the industry producing the commodity. The curve S_1 shows the imposition of the tax. This has the result of reducing demand for the commodity from Q_0 to Q_1 which has the consequence that resources going to produce the amount Q_0 minus Q_1 are redeployed into other uses. Thus, if we ask what has been the effect of the tax on the redistribution of welfare, we cannot simply say: the consumer of commodity X, because, although he pays more, manages to escape some of the burden of the tax by reducing his consumption. Some of the burden falls on producers and factors of production. Only if his demand curve for the good in question were perfectly inelastic would it be true that the consumer paid all of the tax. This is shown in Diagram 8 (b), p. 37. In the contrary case, where his demand is perfectly elastic, shown in 8(a), the full burden is born by the producers in the sense that they must cut back production from Q_1 to Q_2 but the price remains the same. If their supply is perfectly inelastic, i.e. is vertical, then they must accept a fall in earnings equivalent to the whole of the tax. For although they are worse off, they still get something for what they supply. Quantity supplied remains at Q_1.

We can apply this simple analysis to land markets by considering what the effects would be of imposing a tax on the use of land for a given purpose and one which forms only a small part of the total demand for land. We assume initially that all land could be used equally well for any purpose and that it is free to move from one use to another. If the activity concerned is to continue then it must pay the tax, which will be reflected in the final price to consumers. Owners of the land would continue to offer land to this activity at whatever was the going rate, according to its accessibility and any other special features it may possess. Let us suppose, however, that the tax was imposed on only some land in the area concerned and not throughout. Then the activity would tend to move from the one to the other, to escape the burden of the tax. In doing so, certain extra costs might have to be incurred, e.g. higher labour payments or extra transport, but nevertheless some of the burden of the tax could be shed. However, suppose that the land in the area concerned could be used for no other purpose than the activity in question. If this were literally true, i.e. it had no reserve value at all, then in effect its supply would be perfectly inelastic to the activity in question. The owners of the land would consequently have to reduce their price – otherwise the user would move elsewhere, where his overall costs would be lower. The amount which the owner of the land could continue to ask would depend on just how readily the activity could move away.

In this example, although simple, the question of the incidence of the policy is nevertheless very complex. If the effects of the tax were to be predicted, a very large amount of information about the workings of the relevant markets and the supply and demand curves would be necessary, not only at the time when the tax was imposed, but over time, as the necessary adjustments actually took place. Indeed, the fact that markets are imperfect and subject to delays and lags means that the actual process of determining the incidence of a tax is made even more complex.

This example enables one important general point to be made. In considering the effects of any policy it is rarely sensible to consider only the initial impacts. It will frequently be helpful to distinguish between the initial and ultimate incidence of a policy measure, and, possibly, between the initial and final stages, and various intermediary 'rounds', as the initial impact works through the system.

The significance of this point depends very much on the nature of the policy instrument concerned. In the case of the perfect fiscal system, we would not need to trace through incidence effects to ensure that the outcome was the desired one provided that the tax or subsidy reflected all the relevant externalities. If this condition does not hold or if regulations are in use which bear indirectly on the problem in hand, then it is necessary to consider the second and third round effects in order to see whether or not the objectives of the intervention are in fact being achieved or are being subverted by the various kinds of reaction analysed above. This condition is, however, a very strong one. Our discussion of the fiscal system above deliberately glossed over the practical problems of implementing it. In Chapter 10, a case is considered which brings out the point that fiscal solutions are likely to suffer from the same evaluation problem as regulation.

7.3 The Limits of Management

The earlier sections of this chapter and Chapter 6 as a whole have been primarily concerned with the ways in which authorities can modify market behaviour to achieve certain policy objectives. Although, as we shall see in detail in later chapters, these policy instruments can be powerful, the extent to which authorities are able to achieve the outcomes they wish to promote is inherently limited. These limits are set in part by the nature of market processes and in part by the characteristics of the instruments which authorities have available to reflect their policy intentions.

Markets, as we have seen, are made up of individuals and firms making their separate decisions on the allocation of resources. They are adaptive processes, shifting the incidence of a tax here, adapting to a regulation there. The first and prime requisite of successful intervention in market processes, therefore, is that it should be based on an understanding of how the market will react to whatever the measures which change the framework within which it works. Without such understanding, at least on a partial basis, there is a risk that intervention will produce fewer benefits than hoped for, be completely irrelevant or even be counter-productive, i.e. produce effects exactly the opposite of the desired ones or side-effects as undesirable as the problems which intervention was initially aimed at avoiding. As the discussion in section 6.1 showed, the ability of the authority to make the necessary forecasts is likely to be limited, in part because of the inherent complexity of the urban economy, in part because of the difficulty of forecasting relevant factors, such as income growth in the country as a whole, which lie outside that economy.

Perhaps the most notorious examples of failure to take market reactions into account have occurred in housing markets, particularly in those countries where public housing programmes have been small or non-existent. Prices controls have frequently been introduced in large cities, with the distributional objective in mind of keeping down the price of accommodation to the poorer groups in the population. Nearly uniformly, this has set in train reactions which have made the housing situation worse for the groups concerned: landlords, finding no profits in retaining housing in controlled tenancies, have attempted, legally or otherwise, to transfer their property into markets where they can use it more remuneratively. No new units of accommodation have been provided because it is not profitable to do so; maintenance has not been carried out for the same reason. The quality and quantity of the stock has declined and, where the public sector housing programme has been insufficient, no new housing opportunities have opened up. The result has been that bad housing conditions have remained, and have probably been exacerbated, for some or all of the population which the regulation was intended to protect.

The same kind of problem can arise with the regulation of the provision of commercial property: following the analysis of the previous section, if the supply of office space is limited by a planning policy, then its price will tend to rise (see Diagram 16). The rise may in itself have effects of the right kind, i.e. it may discourage people from locating in the area concerned. But it will bring with it a large capital gain, due entirely to the monopoly created by the control on supply. As the diagram shows, suppliers of office space will be able to earn more than the price they would be willing to supply at, i.e. make *supra normal* profits, and these higher rents will be capitalised into the market values of the properties themselves. The benefits of the policy in terms of the distribution of activities can only be attained at the cost of failing to meet distributional objectives. How serious a problem this is, from the distributional viewpoint, depends, of course, on the nature of the tax system in force. In the UK, for example, recent tax changes have been designed specifically to tax away gains of this kind. The presence of taxes of this kind reduces the conflict between distributional and other objectives, but a regulatory control cannot by itself resolve it.

Other conflicts may arise. For example, one reaction to the higher prices produced by control over quantity may be to control the price of accommodation. The question this poses is: how should the space concerned be allocated? As Diagram 16 shows, at price P_1, Q_1 units of accommodation would be demanded – however, due to the control, only Q_2 units are available. If the control is inefficient, black markets will tend to develop or key money will be paid. In those ways, the extra value created per unit of accommodation will be transferred into capital payments for entry into accommodation, not directly into the rentals themselves. However, if the control is so effective that these market reactions are not allowed, then the allocation problem becomes more severe. Sitting tenants enjoy a large benefit (as do sitting tenants under rent control of housing), but those outside the control, i.e. new firms, then find it very difficult to get space – as do firms who wish to expand. The result is a random subsidy to existing firms and a restriction on the competitive and innovative forces within the markets concerned. The advantages in terms of reduced price levels will be bought, if the control is rigid and maintained for a long period, at some costs in terms of lost productive efficiency.

In the cases just considered, the policies concerned, while producing desirable effects, also produce undesirable ones. These conflicts might be overcome by the use of superior policy instruments, e.g. in the case of housing, the effects of rent control of privately rented accommodation may be alleviated by public building programmes or they may be replaced by housing grants to the individuals concerned, which makes it possible for them to pay market rents. The limits set on market management by the policy instruments available are set by various factors – all are familiar. In part it is a question of administration. For example, in considering whether regulations, subsidies or taxes were the better forms of intervention, their relative administrative cost and convenience would clearly have to be weighed very carefully. Regulation may allow great flexibility and discretion to the authority using it, if it is able to act on a case-by-case basis.

In part, it is a question of budgetary constraints. In the case of subsidies the financial resources of the authority go to determine the limits to their use. If its ability to subsidise is restricted, or its ability to finance the relevant construction programmes insufficient, then the dangers of counter-productive intervention are all the greater because it may not be able to make good the problems which its own intervention has given rise to. In part, it is a question of the available policy instruments being imperfectly adapted to the problem diagnosed. In the case of a tax there may be no precise way of relating it to the externality concerned, such as damage to the environment or congestion. If a regulation is aimed at avoiding a specific externality, such as pollution, its effect may be very attenuated if its main impact is not on the emission of the pollutant itself, but on the process leading to it or on total production of the good concerned. Similarly, control of traffic congestion which does not work directly on the trips themselves, but less directly through the land uses giving rise to the trips, may be a very imperfect instrument. These cases are discussed in more detail in later chapters.

A final point: if the authority is unable to replace market processes either for financial reasons or because of lack of powers and rely on regulatory measures, then it has to accept the basic limitations of these powers that they do not basically change the pattern of motivation of the market they wish to regulate. As section 6.2 brought out, regulations may be successful at avoiding certain extreme and undesirable outcomes, e.g. the despoliation of beauty spots or the worst excesses of urban sprawl, which are both cases where social costs exceed private costs because of the externalities they give rise to. But they do not of themselves divert the market into directions which they themselves would like to promote. It is for this reason that regulatory planning is often called negative, in that it rules out certain options to individuals and developers, but it does not create any new ones or alter the balance of attractiveness between existing possibilities.

7.4 Land Use Controls and the Market Economy: Summary

In the next chapter we will go on to consider how public authorities may replace market activity and make the relevant decisions themselves. Before moving on it may be helpful to run through the main points which have emerged from this and the previous chapters on the functions of markets and the ways in which they may be regulated.

First, a planning authority may regard the market as a way of reaching a large range of decisions within the area of its responsibility. One example of this is the market in second-hand housing, within which individuals' mutual interaction produces an allocation of people to homes. This may not be the best possible allocation, but there may be no practical means of improving it. If this were so, then it could be regarded as an appropriate area for non-intervention.

Second, markets may fail for a large number of reasons, of which external effects is probably the single most important category. These may lead to conflict between the aims of the planning authority and the activities of unregulated markets. These conflicts largely arise from the inadequacies of the framework within which markets operate. Relevant action to improve this framework may lie outside the field of land-use policy itself.

Third, where authorities aim to manage markets, or where they carry out policies of their own, then they must take account of market reactions to their policy measures. This requires an understanding of the operation of market forces. If authorities do not have this, then their plans run the risk of irrelevance or, more seriously, of being counter-productive. Because of the complexity of the urban economy, this requirement is a stringent one and it imposes strict limits to the actual scope for useful intervention.

Fourth, intervention in market process itself entails costs. These are not only the costs of administration – the direct costs falling on the authority – but the costs which firms and individuals experience as a result of the intervention. These costs are frequently 'hidden' and are not easily identified; they arise in part because of the direct loss of utility imposed by control, in part from the reactions of markets to controls which limit their behaviour, and in part through the effect they have on the efficiency with which markets work.

Fifth, the distributional consequences of intervening in market processes are particularly difficult to estimate. The very nature of market processes, in particular their adaptive nature, tends to mean that the initial effects of intervention are passed on, so that the ultimate incidence of a policy measure is difficult to identify.

Sixth, the available policy instruments are frequently not perfectly appropriate to the ends they are intended to serve. They will therefore tend to have undesired and undesirable side-effects. In this chapter the fiscal system has been used as a model of how policy ends and means might be related. But in practice these and the other kinds of policy instrument are likely to be imperfectly related to the problems in hand.

Finally, if market processes are to be replaced, because markets are thought to be inefficient or because they are thought to lead to undesirable income distribution, the basic functions of markets still remain to be carried out. Alternative procedures have to be found to come to the decisions which markets of their nature carry out; what is produced, how much is produced, by what means and who enjoys the results of that production? How these decisions may be reached within the public sector, in the absence of markets, we consider in the following two chapters. Subsequent chapters, particularly 10 and 11, will explore with specific examples the points summarised in this section.

8 THE ALLOCATION OF RESOURCES IN THE PUBLIC SECTOR

For convenience, the existence of a public sector was assumed away within the simple urban model. But now, having analysed various ways in which private markets may be managed, we must consider the issues which arise when they are replaced. The only reason identified so far for the existence of a public sector supplying goods or services is supply failure due to the public goods problem discussed in section 4.2. This is important in a number of land-use planning contexts such as open space provision, but there are many other reasons why governments decide that certain goods or services shall not be provided by private firms. In some cases, such as health or welfare services, the reasons are primarily distributional. In others, the main reasons lie with conditions of production. Many of the services central to the process of physical development such as water, sewage, gas and electricity, enjoy economies of scale and competition between suppliers is difficult, if not impossible, to arrange. Typically, therefore, such services are provided by public bodies or by private firms subject to close and detailed regulation.

In some cases, particularly those where public ownership is motivated largely by supply conditions in the industry concerned, public enterprises may behave very much like private firms. That is, they too must buy factors of production and must sell their products at prices which produce sufficient revenue to cover the costs they incur. If they have monopoly power, then the problem of raising sufficient revenue may not be a difficult one and this may lead to some of the problems traditionally associated with monopoly such as neglect of consumers and technical inefficiency, which are not our concern here. However, such public enterprises remain subject to the financial discipline imposed on them by market conditions and so retain a rule to guide their allocation of resources: they may invest and expand their scale of production as long as they satisfy the constraint that they should cover costs or make reasonable profits. This is not, as we shall see in the following chapter, a very precise rule, as it still leaves open a number of options to them, but it does set some limits to the allocation of resources in the activity concerned. This and other pricing rules will be considered in the following chapter.

In other cases, however, governments wish to see goods and services supplied at zero price, or at a price much below cost of production; examples range from refuse collection to urban parks, to health and education. In these cases there is no financial rule to guide the allocation of resources, since there is no financial constraint specific to the service itself to set limits to the scale of output. However, wants are infinite and resources scarce in the public as well as in the private sector so even though the market processes are, by assumption, not working the functions of markets still have to be performed. Market processes, as we have seen, result in a pattern of outputs and allocation of productive resources which reflect the interplay of the large number of individuals and firms which make up the markets concerned. When governments take over responsibility for part – or all – of the economic life of a country, alternative ways must be found of allocating productive resources between the competing claims made upon them. We are therefore faced with two problems. How do we decide that the scale of output should be for publicly produced goods and services? How should that output be allocated between individuals?

The purpose of the present chapter is to consider a number of different ways in which the first of these questions may be answered. The following chapter will consider the second. The first section of this chapter introduces the concepts of consumer and social surplus criteria, which economists have developed in recent years to provide guidelines for the allocation of resources in the public sector. We will then go on to consider a number of alternatives. In most land-use planning contexts it is customary to talk of needs for goods and services not provided by the private sector. Section 8.2 analyses the concept of needs and brings out a number of possible meanings, some of which are very close if not identical to the economist's concept of surplus and others which are not. In some cases, needs are defined by professional or technical criteria, expressed in terms of standards of provision. In other cases needs are defined primarily in terms of distributional objectives, that is, they are concerned with those groups of the population which are not adequately supplied from market processes, not with the way in which the total supply of the good or service in question should be determined. The final section therefore considers distributional criteria for the allocation of resources within the public sector.

Before considering these different approaches, however, we will set out in formal terms the problem with which this chapter is concerned. If the public sector supplies services for which it sets prices which cover costs, then its financing problems are similar to those faced by a private firm. But where services are supplied below cost, it must divert spending power from individuals by taxation in order to finance their supply. Using the terminology developed in Chapter 2, the opportunity cost of deploying resources in the public sector is the private consumption which is lost in order to finance them. Thus, to ensure that the correct volume of resources is being devoted to public sector uses, the rule is that any extra expenditure in the public sector should produce at least as much benefit as would result from those resources being enjoyed by private individuals spending their own budgets.

This rule is, of course, a simple extension of the equi-marginal rule which was developed in Chapter 2 for the individual consumer. It has a further application within the public sector itself. If the budget of a planning authority is determined by some external body, e.g. the central government, then if it is to make the best use of the resources over which it is given command, it too must try to ensure that under each type of expenditure for which it is responsible, a given increment earns the same return. That is, it must try to reach a position where no re-arrangements of its expenditure pattern can result in an increase in the welfare generated by the available budget. This rule applies to all resources in general and land in particular. For example, if the planning authority wished to abstract land from other uses to provide open space, then it should do so to the point where it considered that the gains from more provision of open space were equal to losses from other uses.

The equi-marginal rule may seem at first sight to be of little help. It says nothing about how a position where benefits are equal shall be recognised. This is a valid criticism; to use the rule we need ways of applying it empirically, a problem which there is not space enough to tackle. However, although the rule may appear innocuous and non-controversial, some of the criteria we consider in the later parts of the chapter run counter to it, or can do so if they are misapplied. Our main task is to consider the *kind* of criteria we wish to apply to the allocation of resources within the public sector.

In principle, the institutional context is not relevant to the determination of the optimal rule for resource allocation. In practice the existence of a range of authorities, each responsible for spending in a particular area or on a particular function, makes it more difficult to apply. In what follows, we will abstract from the institutional complexity of the real world and assume that the planning authority employed in the analysis so far is responsible, unless otherwise stated, for all services provided at zero price and that these have to be paid for out of local taxation.

8.1 Consumer and Social Surplus

We have seen how the expenditure decisions of individuals in private markets, which reflect their willingness to pay for services and goods, can be seen as providing the information which guides private firms on what and how much to produce. If the public sector does not charge for what it supplies, this source of information dries up; how can it be replaced?

This problem can be approached during the concepts introduced in Chapter 2 for the analysis of private markets. In that chapter we used the concept of a demand curve to express the varying amounts which individuals would be prepared to pay for a given good or service. In private markets, they would actually have to pay, but although, by assumption, they may not have to do so in the public sector, they may, nevertheless, be willing to pay if they were required to. We could, therefore, draw a kind of demand curve for the good in question, which would illustrate potential willingness to pay. This is done in Diagram 18 which also shows the cost, C, of supplying the good in question.

The costs of supply reflect the value of the resources concerned in alternative uses, on the assumption that the public sector must compete with the private sector in the market for factors of production and that their value in turn reflects willingness to pay in the markets for final goods and services. These are points we established in Chapter 2. If we could establish the position of the demand curve then we would be able to establish the point, labelled A in the diagram, where individuals would be prepared to pay sums equivalent to the value, by the same test, of those resources in other uses. This test has already been used in defining the point at which regulations should be set, i.e. the point where marginal social benefit and marginal social cost are equal.

In private markets, consumers are not usually required to pay the whole of the amount they would be willing to pay for the goods they buy. This would require not only a different price for each consumer, but also a different price for each unit of the good in question. The latter result follows directly from the fact that the demand curve slopes downward to the right so that the amount people would be prepared to pay is much higher on initial units of consumption than on later ones. As individuals are not in fact charged in this way, they enjoy a *surplus*, the extent of which is measured by the difference between what they

Diagram 18

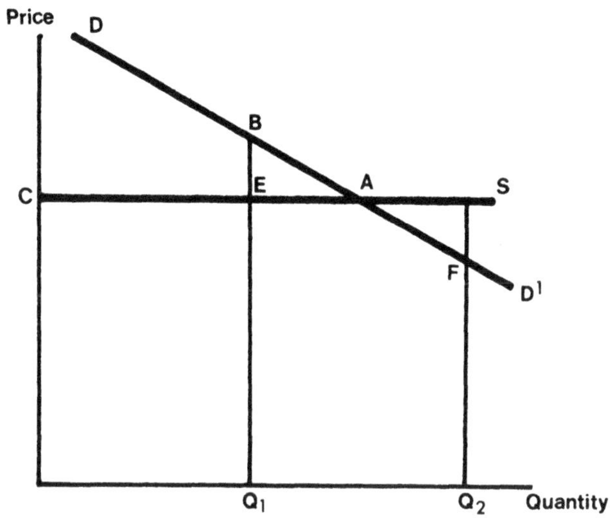

are asked to pay and what they would be prepared to pay.

If public sector services are provided at zero price, then the surplus consumers enjoy is given by the total amount individuals would be prepared to pay for the services in question, i.e. the whole of the area under the demand curve. In most practical situations we are concerned with a change in surplus and not the total. For example, suppose that output of good X is currently at Q_1 and we must decide whether or not output should be increased to Q_2. Then as a measure of benefit, to be compared with the costs of achieving the increase in output, we could take the change in consumer surplus which would result. In the diagram this would be given by the area $BAFQ_2Q_1$: the relevant cost would be ESQ_2Q_1.

It is obvious, however, that not all the effects of increasing output from Q_1 to Q_2 will necessarily be caught up in such a measure of benefit. The demand curve is defined only in terms of those who would be prepared to pay for the good in question. It would not include all those affected by any external effects arising from its production. For example, expansion of output may involve major construction works, which could have widespread effects, some favourable and some unfavourable. Accordingly we might wish to extend the scope of the surplus measure to include all those affected by the change in question, that is, we would try to estimate the *social* surplus and then compare it with the costs of achieving the change.

In either the restricted or the more extended form the surplus measure mirrors the criteria employed for the allocation of resources in the private sector in two important ways. First, it is based on the preferences of individuals, and second, it takes evidence of willingness to pay as the best indicator of those preferences. The first of these embodies a political judgement, i.e. it rejects the pure paternalism argument. The second is a mixture of technical and political judgement. It is technical to the extent that it asserts that other evidence on the desirability of allocating resources in the public sector to particular uses is less reliable. It is political to the extent that it embodies an important distributional judgement, since in the simple form we have introduced the surplus measure, where the strength of the individual preference is determined by a measure which reflects differences in income and not merely intensity of preference.

The importance of distinguishing the various assumptions underlying the surplus measure is this: that when we come in the following sections to discuss alternative criteria, we need to be clear in what respect they differ from the surplus measure. The latter may be rejected on the ground that the individual preference is irrelevant or that the individual preference is not adequately reflected in a willingness to pay test or that it does not adequately take into account differences in income. Such arguments reflect quite different viewpoints: the first may be a paternalistic judgement, the second a technical one and the third a view on distribution. With these considerations in mind we now turn to some alternative ways in which the allocation of resources between competing uses within the public sector may be determined.

8.2 Alternative Criteria

(a) Needs

We have already seen in Chapter 4 that 'needs' may be used in different ways. In the case of an urban area planning for industrial expansion it may be necessary to consider the 'needs of industry' in respect of land, water and power, but in none of these cases would there typically be a problem of the kind we are concerned with here. In these examples 'needs' is another way of talking about the likely level of effective demand for the services in question. The problem, for those concerned with their provision, is to make the right decisions about the level and kind of capacity to install. This interpretation of needs we will subsequently ignore, as it corresponds to the demand concept used in previous sections. Nevertheless, it is important to recall the point that needs arguments can be misapplied in this kind of context and used to justify expenditure regardless of its opportunity cost and the specific benefits expected to flow from it. This point is particularly relevant where, as in the cases just considered, there are no problems of practice or principle in the way of applying a willingness to pay test.

In other cases 'needs' is a way of referring to the public good problem. For example, it is common to talk about the need for urban open space. There is not, under present institutional arrangements, an effective demand for public open space in urban areas. It is possible to consider charging higher local taxes for houses near to parks. But since such charging policies are in practice rare, there is no way of measuring a revenue stream to guide the allocation of land within urban areas to open space.

If 'needs' reflect the public good problem, and not other considerations, then the criterion discussed in the previous section is relevant, i.e. the 'needs' reflect potential, but not realised, demand. But the case for provision based on 'needs' is sometimes founded on quite different considerations. The first of these is paternalism.

In talking about the 'need' for open space we may reject the willingness to pay basis of the surplus criterion, on the ground that individuals are insufficiently informed of their own interest to be willing to pay for it at the time when decisions must be made. Not all forms of this argument lead to a rejection of the consumer surplus criterion. Individuals may be insufficiently informed of their own interests for various reasons. At a given point in time, few are fully aware of the benefits to be gained from a new investment in transport or an extension of the amount of urban land given over to parks, but we may nevertheless be fully aware of the value to us of the *kind* of benefits these facilities create – easier travel, pleasant view, etc., because we experience these in other surroundings. If we are, then our preferences remain as relevant as before. In other words, if a decision had to be made on the scale and layout of open space provision in a new urban area, in which, by definition, there were no consumers to consult, evidence on the appropriate scale and form of provision could be built up on the basis of consumer reaction to provision in other circumstances.

As noted already in Chapter 4, individual preferences remain relevant in relation to another form of paternalism distinguished in that chapter. It is sometimes argued that people should be induced to experience something because after experiencing it they will come to accept that it was worthwhile even if at the time that was not their view. This form of paternalism can be tested against the response of individuals in the 'after' situation. For example, surveys have been carried out of people who have been moved, generally against their will, to make way for transport projects. Some of these are found to change their view on how the move would affect them after they have actually experienced it and such evidence is clearly relevant to a decision which involves forcible displacement. But the alternative form of paternalism which argues that in some cases people must be protected from their own preferences, made to have certain things for their own good and deprived of others, cannot, as a matter of logic, be justified in terms of evidence relating to what people say they would like or demonstrate a willingness to pay. Hence the justification for expenditure on projects on these grounds must be based on quite different evidence, e.g. the harmful consequences which follow from allowing people to do what they wish or the benefits which accrue from getting them to do things they otherwise would not.

Paternalism may further run into conflict with the assumptions underlying the surplus criterion to the extent that it takes the form of asserting that minimum levels of consumption should be adhered to. If minimum levels of expenditure are fixed, then the workings of the equi-marginal rule have to be modified. The minima act as constraints on the application of this rule in the same way as regulatory measures. That is, they must be satisfied before the equi-marginal rule can be applied. How this works is considered in the following section.

The second reason for rejecting the consumer surplus interpretation of 'needs' is distributional. Although it may be accepted that individual preferences are relevant to the allocation of public sector resources, their expression in terms of willingness to pay may be unacceptable, simply because it gives more weight to the rich. Consequently some other way of measuring the strength of preference or some modification of the willingness to pay criterion must be found. This and other problems associated with welfare distribution are taken up in the final section of this chapter.

(b) Standards

In many land use planning contexts, and quite generally in the public sector, the allocation of resources is determined by reference to standards. These relate to details of road design such as carriageway widths and curvatures, the amount of open space provided, the size of school playing fields and many other examples. They have enormous influence on the construction, appearance and layout of physical development. How do they relate to the consumer surplus criterion?

In principle there may be no conflict. Diagram 15 showed the cost of applying a standard at various levels and the benefits from doing so. At some point shown as A in the diagram these curves intersect and a standard set at that point produces the same result as the rules set out above. However, if the standard is set at a point higher than A such as D, then because the costs are shown as being higher than the benefits, the implication is that welfare could be increased by lowering the standard and putting the resources saved to other uses. The same evidence might be used to determine the position of benefit with the level of the standard as to determine the position of the demand curve considered in the previous section. That is, the benefit curve might be derived by considering what people would be prepared to pay to have the standard concerned set at various levels. In many circumstances, the costs of attaining a given standard vary from place to place or location to location. For example, the cost of providing main services varies enormously from urban to rural locations, so that the comparison of the cost and benefit curves in the two areas would have very different results. In these circumstances the scale of the disparity between costs and benefits might be reduced, setting up a range of standards which more or less accurately reflect these variations.

Design and layout of the physical environment require a very large number of decisions, ranging from minor technical details to major determinants of the performance and cost of the facilities concerned. It would not be practical to calculate, for each and every design, the correct level to which each aspect of the design should be set. Standards can therefore be regarded as rules of thumb, which save the burden of excessive computation entailed by a strict application of the equi-marginal rule. In this light there is no necessary conflict between use of standards and use of an economic criterion, provided that the standards concerned are checked from time to time.

Conflicts do arise, however. The discussion so far has paralleled that of regulations in Chapter 6 and the parallel can be taken further. For in practice there are two problems with output standards which are very close to the problems arising with regulations. First, they can inhibit the search for the best pattern of expenditure through ruling out alternatives, and second, the point at which they are set tends to be determined arbitrarily or by reference to criteria which we shall want to reject. Let us take these points in turn.

Standards, like regulations, rule out certain areas of possible choice; if everyone must have a certain amount of X or a certain quality of Y, then two consequences follow: first that some options cannot be considered, i.e. lower amounts of X and lower qualities of Y cannot be traded for more of Z. Second, the speed at which an authority is able to make progress in tackling the problems it faces is determined for it. Let us take the case of a public housing authority, which would like to provide an extra 1,000 units; at the standard of housing which is laid down, it can only produce 100 units per year and stay within its budget. It follows that it will take the authority ten years to meet its target. It is a simple matter of arithmetic to show that the higher the standard, and hence the higher the cost per unit, the longer it takes to meet the target.

Diagram 19

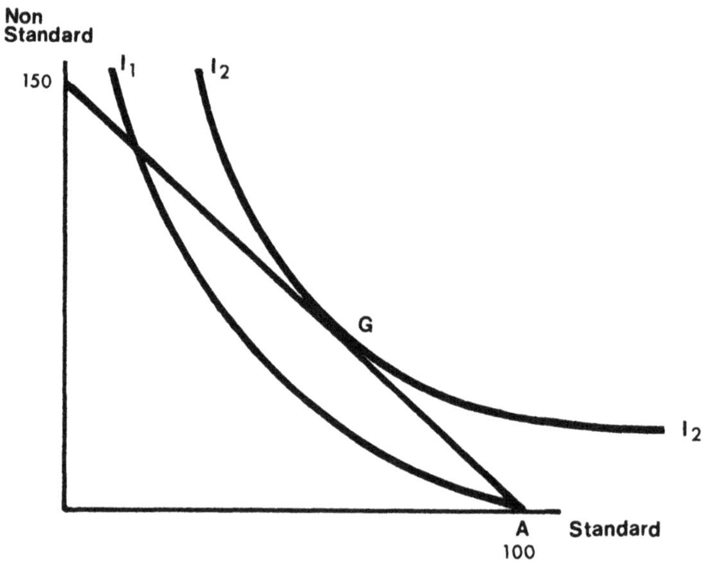

We can illustrate the issues using a form of the diagram first introduced in Chapter 5. Diagram 19 shows the production possibilities open to the housing authority. If standard houses are built, 100 units can be provided each year as against 150 lower standard units. The authority may prefer a balance between the two extremes, shown by point Q, which is on indifference curve I_2I_2. If it is compelled to produce standard houses, then it must produce at point A, which is on a lower indifference curve. In other words, from the authority's point of view, it is forced to accept an inferior solution. It might come to this view, for example, if it attached very great weight to getting people out of extremely bad conditions into something which was adequate.

This trade-off between standard of provision and the speed at which something can be done cannot be avoided, no matter where the standard is set. The authority's view of what was adequate might differ from the level which individuals or other authorities might consider to be so. The first general point to bring out is that if the standard is determined externally, then the solution or choice is effectively determined without reference to the local facts or to local preferences.

The second point is that resources are committed to the attainment of these standards. These have an opportunity cost like any other expenditure. If the standard is set in the way described above by a careful balancing of marginal benefits against marginal costs then this is recognised. Frequently, however, standards are proposed without reference to the implications for public or private sector outlays incurred in attaining them or without evidence being offered to justify their being set at one point rather than another, i.e. their costs are not identified.

Although in principle they can be determined by reference to individual preferences, in practice standards are usually set 'professionally'. For example, roads and other urban infrastructure are often designed according to engineering criteria; buildings and urban layouts according to architectural criteria. As a result, standards are frequently paternalistic in nature. That is, they assume the right 'mix' of public output and the right balance between public and private expenditure without reference to the preferences of the individuals who subsequently use the facilities concerned or who have to meet, directly or indirectly, the costs of meeting them.

Of course, to assert that complex structures should be designed in relation to the preferences of those who are to use them is in itself too glib. There is no easy connection to be made between the design of new public sector housing and the tenants in the existing stock; from the preferences of the present inhabitants of an urban area to the amount of parkland laid out in it. In the remaining parts of this section we will consider in more detail how technical criteria can diverge from the economic principles discussed in section 8.1.

(c) Capacity

The scale of most physical facilities – roads, parks, sports facilities –

are defined in terms of capacities. For a lane width of road, the capacity may be said to be so many vehicles per hour. The capacity of an airfield may be so many aircraft movements, or so many people through the terminal. Capacity has a strong intuitive appeal and in many cases has a very simple meaning, e.g. the capacity of a bottle. The bottle will hold one pint, no more and no less.

In the planning contexts in which capacity is used, capacity is frequently used as though it had a rigid quantitative meaning of this kind. For example, stated capacities of roads are often given as though they represented an absolute limit on the number of cars which might use the road concerned. In fact, before UK highway capacities were revised recently, it was common for roads to be used at two to three times their rated capacity. It is clear from this that highway capacity is not defined in the way in which the capacity of a bottle may be defined. Nevertheless, the capacity figure is often quoted in which it would suggest that, if capacity is reached, then no more traffic could be handled and more investment would be required. But this is clearly wrong, if it is possible for a road to handle two to three times its rated capacity.

An alternative definition of capacity can be derived using the analysis of congestion costs introduced in Chapter 6. There it was pointed out that the private and social costs of using a particular facility may differ, in the way shown in Diagram 14. This diagram suggests a definition of capacity as that level at which the additional user imposes more costs on others than he enjoys in benefits himself. These costs will include any direct maintenance costs, disutility, e.g. time delays imposed on other users and any other costs suffered by society at large, e.g. in the case of countryside, losses to farmers or damage to flora.

This definition says nothing about the physical ability of the facility concerned to handle more users. For example, if the diagram referred to a road, it might be possible to get more vehicles along it, if at lower speeds, or in the case of a tourist attraction, more people round the relevant exhibits. But it is a commonplace that as the numbers involved and the speed at which viewing has to take place rises, enjoyment rapidly diminishes. Physical capacity in this sense may well lie beyond the point defined by our definition. However, other kinds of definition lie well to the left of capacity in the sense defined above, e.g. many highway definitions implicitly assume a definition of capacity at point A, i.e. where congestion begins. This is the level at which traffic may flow freely without being impeded by other vehicles.

The fact that capacity can be defined in these different ways suggests of itself that there are dangers in drawing the conclusion that resources should be devoted to expansion when capacity is fully utilised. These dangers are particularly acute in the case of capacity definitions which have implicit in them a high quality standard, e.g. the definition of highway capacity which sets it at A. If capacity in this sense is used as a guide to further investment, the danger is that the definition used, which in fact contains a very strong value judgement on the distribution of resources, will be taken to have as much force as the statement that a bottle will only hold a pint of water. The following paragraphs give further reasons why the notion of capacity may be a poor guide to investment.

Capacity is an elastic concept. Production plants are often quoted as having a certain capacity. This may be expressed by a rising cost curve, which gradually becomes vertical at the capacity point. But this may be misleading as a guide to the output which may in fact be achieved at fairly low additional cost, e.g. extra storage or handling facilities may be added, some items pre-processed, and in these ways the effective capacity of the plant may be increased. Thus it is important in practice, if it is argued that capacity is being approached and more facilities must be provided, to examine what constraints on the production process may be lifted by small amounts of extra investment, or better management of the existing assets.

Another related and important aspect is the unit at which capacity is defined; for example, road capacities are expressed in hourly or annual terms. It is very rare that an annual capacity is defined as 8,760 times the hourly capacity, because it is clearly unlikely that the maximum hourly rate could be maintained the whole year through. This is partly a matter of costs and maintenance; the capacity of a steelworks in annual terms has to allow for close-downs for maintenance. But in the case of many facilities, capacity is quoted to allow for other factors such as the variation in usage through the year and through the day. Thus the capacity of a road may be defined in annual terms by a calculation which runs from peak hour to peak day, (e.g. 10 times peak hour) from peak day to peak month and peak month to the year, by various factors which allow for intertemporal variation.

This procedure is realistic, if it is aimed at estimating how many people may use a given facility in a year, and how much money they may bring in through parking fees. But it may be a poor guide to the allocation of investment and additional resources. Suppose that it is estimated that a given number of visits to the countryside will be made, then the annual capacity figure for the existing open spaces may be used to provide an estimate of the need for additional capacity. But an estimate of this kind is inadequate in the three basic respects. First, it ignores the cost of providing the extra facilities. Second, it assumes away the need to estimate the value of additional facilities. Third, it ignores the use of pricing or other management measures. These in effect alter the capacity of the facilities concerned if they encourage patterns of use which allow higher utilisation rates, e.g. by diverting users to off-peak times.

A large number of services or facilities with which land-use planning is concerned, including most kinds of infrastructure, are frequently analysed in terms of their available capacity. The discussion above is directly relevant to them. In transport planning, policies on the utilisation of the network, not merely its expansion, are now commonplace. For other services the issue is more easily seen as one of quality of service than congestion. For example, if users are added to the water-supply system of given physical capacity, two consequences may follow. First, there may be a decline in the quality of the waterways into which effluent is put and second, the risk of water-supply failures due to drought may also arise, since the margin of space capacity, e.g. storage to meet peak demands, is reduced, and can only be restored by more expenditure. To use a rigid capacity concept is equivalent to maintaining a specific standard of service. The issues are therefore identical to those discussed in the previous section.

8.3 Distributional Considerations

For many services, common standards are laid down or aimed for on grounds of equity between income or other groups. These might concern public open space, refuse collection and many other services provided by public authorities. Standards of this kind have a strong egalitarian appeal and where the services concerned – refuse collection is a good example – are usually regarded by individuals as essential and would result in external costs to other members of society if they were not in fact supplied to all individuals, then there is a strong case for uniform levels of service. There is little or no conflict between efficiency and distributional considerations.

More difficult issues arise where standards are laid down for services for which some members of society, not necessarily the poor alone, would not wish to pay. For example, it might seem equitable for everyone to be provided with the same amount of open space. But it would not necessarily be a sound distributive policy if some sections of the population would prefer to lower the standards of public open space they enjoy in return for improved social facilities. In such a case what may appear to be an equitable policy may be exactly the converse since its effect may be to provide services to some groups using resources which they would value more highly in other uses. We have noted above that as incomes rise, demand for some items, i.e. those which are income elastic, tends to rise rapidly. In private markets in the absence of external effects this presents no problem, since markets for different qualities can be effectively separated. But in the case of public goods it does, since it implies that different income groups will place different weight, in relation to other goods and services, on extra units of provision. Thus in coming to a decision on provision which affects everyone, there is an important distributional issue involved which centres on the correct set of relative weights to be given to the expected benefits. This point is further discussed in Chapter 13.

The issue can be seen by considering the case where a planning authority is faced with the choice between provision of a park in a poor area and one in a rich area. It would not be surprising that willingness to pay should be higher in the latter case. We might, in a case like this, want to weight benefits to individuals equally no matter what their income was, i.e. attach the same importance to time spent in a park no matter who spent the time, or we might want to go further and provide the road or park in the poor area, even if the number of people likely to benefit from it, e.g. the number of visits to the park, would be lower there.

We must not, however, reject 'willingness to pay' evidence too rapidly even in the context of specifically distributional policies. The basic issue posed in the first section of the chapter remains: whose preferences are relevant? If it has been decided to build a park because that is the best way of helping a particular area, we need to know how 'best' is defined. It may be defined paternalistically or it may be defined by reference to what the inhabitants of the area concerned might wish to have, given that a sum of money is to be spent on it. In this case, willingness to pay, in the sense defined above – i.e. as an index of intensity of preference – is clearly relevant. It is a means of ranking alternatives once the decision to exercise a distributional policy has been taken. It may be, as in the example mentioned above, that the people concerned would prefer social facilities or environmental improvement.

We can put this issue another way: once agreement has been reached at a political level to redistribute welfare through public expenditures, then the funds concerned acquire a special kind of opportunity cost.

The choice is no longer one between a park in a rich area and a park in a poor area, but between a park in the poor area and some other facility there, such as a social centre. The consumers, or users, are clearly identified, so the issue is precisely that posed in section 9.1 above: which scheme offers the greatest consumer surplus? How this issue should be decided – whether by political processes within the area concerned, or by 'technical' procedures aimed at measuring the area under the demand curve, is another matter. The only point to be made here is that it would be senseless to insist on open space on the grounds that this was equitable or to reject 'willingness to pay' evidence on the grounds that it was irrelevant.

A similar point arises in cases, of which housing is one, where expenditure in the public sector requires complementary expenditure by the individual; the house needs furniture and running costs, the sports centre requires users to bring personal equipment, if only the less expensive items. We have already noted the paternalistic assumptions often implicit in the use of standards for housing provision. These may have particularly unfortunate consequences where complementary expenditure is required. A famous example is the installation of central heating in houses for people for whom central heating is not a requirement because their incomes do not extend so far. The result in some cases has been simply abortive expenditure with the facilities not being used; in others the more serious one of chronic damp problems which could only be removed by constant running of the central heating installations. The assumption implicit in the design concerned was that incomes would be high enough to support central heating and that the people who were to live in them would wish to spend their money in the same way as those with higher incomes. In this situation, even paternalistic motives have to reckon with individual preference, since failure to do so means that the intentions of paternalistic policies are themselves frustrated. In this example, the tenants suffer from chronic damp and are unable to use all the rooms in their flats.

A rather different set of issues is posed by transport or other major items of infrastructure, which cause disruption and loss of benefit to some while leading to increased benefit to others. Some losers may be only partially compensated or not compensated at all; should willingness to pay to avoid losses in such cases be treated as being the same as willingness to pay to enjoy benefits? In other words, can we measure gains and losses of consumer surplus in the same way? Even where incomes are initially identical, there are grounds for arguing that this is unreasonable: a small loss or gain may be treated as equivalent, e.g. my time-saving of one and a half minutes may be deemed to outweigh your loss of one minute (provided that all such gains do not accrue to me and all such losses to you). But such a straightforward cancelling out may seem unreasonable in other circumstances, e.g. if the time-savings are enjoyed at the expense of severe noise nuisance to a few individuals willingness to pay for time savings might exceed willingness to pay to avoid noise. But if the noise effects were serious, the assumption of diminishing marginal utility of income might be invoked to modify this result, i.e. a unit loss measured in pounds and pence might be given more weight than a unit gain.

Thus there are strong arguments on distributional grounds for modifying the measure of consumer surplus introduced in the first section of this chapter. But the evidence it would provide on relativities may nevertheless still remain valuable. This is clearly true when policies are overtly redistributive and even true where policies are paternalistic. In both cases, if the policies are to have their best possible effect, the relevance of the preferences of those affected by the decisions remains.

So far we have been discussing the criteria relevant to assessing merit of alternative policies. But there are problems associated with predicting the distributional aspects of public expenditure very similar to those arising from market regulation discussed in Chapter 6. They need to be considered here since where distributional considerations are not deemed relevant many of these difficulties can be ignored. From an analytic point of view, the major problem, as before, is that of determining what the actual incidence of costs and benefits is. Enough has already been said to indicate that prediction of who benefits and who loses from a given policy is by no means a straightforward matter in many of the situations with which land-use planners are concerned. Let us recall our simple urban model and consider the effects of a transport improvement which leads to more rapid journeys from the periphery to the centre. If the city is physically free to expand, then the model would tend to suggest that people would seek to live further from the centre and in doing so have larger dwellings situated in larger plots, since land will tend to be cheaper, the further away from the centre it is situated. However, the very fact of the transport improvement will tend to make this peripheral land of more value, so although the first-comers might find they can buy accommodation which is cheaper and better (in terms of accessibility) than they had before, as the price is bid up, this will cease to be true. In this way, benefits from the transport improvement will tend to accrue to the peripheral landowner.

Most examples are somewhat more complicated than the one we

have briefly considered. Consider the case of a transport improvement which cuts transport times from an inner area to the city centre, a kind of project which is sometimes proposed to help those with poor job opportunities. But projects like this can be damaging to the objectives they are trying to promote. If they so improve the accessibility of an area that it becomes attractive to higher-income groups, then a process of 'gentrification' may occur, i.e. higher-income groups move in which would result in increased housing stress in the area concerned, as its inhabitants made way for newcomers, prepared to outbid them.

But suppose this effect did not happen, because there was only public housing in the area concerned. This would not mean necessarily that low income-earners would benefit. If they find it easier to travel into work in the central area then two main effects will tend to occur; first, they will tend to displace other workers, who now have relatively poor accessibility and second, to the extent that they do not, they will tend to make employers slightly less eager to bid up wages or improve working conditions to attract labour, since the supply is improved by the better transport. Thus the workers in the area concerned may gain, at the expense of others. There may be a slight increase in employment in the central area, since labour is easier to attract, though on a much smaller scale than the increase in numbers employed in the area with which we are concerned.

In many cases, the incidence of expenditure will be straightforward enough. But in those land-use planning contexts which involve major investment by public authorities, the opposite will be true and the ramifications of the projects concerned virtually impossible to unravel. The analytic problems stem in part from the nature of market processes, particularly urban land markets, which as we saw in Chapter 3 reflect, more or less closely, events in other sectors. In part it reflects the nature of the goods provided by the public sector. Transport itself will be analysed more closely in a separate chapter but other facilities such as open space have similar effects on land values in the neighbourhoods enjoying it and consequently on the spatial pattern of development activity.

8.4 Concluding Comment

We set out in the introduction to the chapter the basic rule for the allocation of resources within the public sector, the equi-marginal rule. This is the rule which the rational planning authority as outlined in Chapter 5 would follow. It is particularly relevant when changes in resource availability occur. At any point in time services will be supplied at given quantities and given qualities or standards. If the available budget is reduced, the application of the rule requires that both the scale and the quality of service should be modified. Use of the notion of capacity, fixed needs or predetermined standards restricts the operation of the rule, since each of them tends to be taken to imply that no adjustment is possible to the level of service. In some cases, e.g. the purity of the water supplied to domestic consumers, this may well be true, in that such standards do come close to being absolute constraints. But in other cases this is not true and serious welfare losses may be sustained by failing to make adjustments in quality or quantity of service where they can best be made. This loss arises because the maintenance of standards or the rigid interpretation of needs prevents resources being shifted from valuable to more valuable uses.

The importance of this point to the individual land-use planning authority depends on the range of services for which it is responsible. For a purely regulatory authority the discussion of this chapter is not relevant. But to UK local planning authorities with a wide range of services under their control this discussion is of central importance. The immediate concerns of land-use planning, such as transport and the physical environment, form only a small part of the claims on the public sector. Other claims arise less directly; for example, proposals for new areas of development require the provision of education and other facilities, sometimes making existing facilities obsolete. In these cases, the claims of the physical environment can only be met at the expense of other claims.

What is required, therefore, is a balancing of commitments under the various expenditure heads. This involves a check on the levels of output and the quality of output to see whether or not these can be modified in such a way as to bring about an increase in the welfare enjoyed from the given budget. Here the points made about standards and needs and the interpretation of capacity are relevant. All these terms have their use. But the danger with them all is that they are easily taken as having a validity independent of available resources.

9 PRICING IN THE PUBLIC SECTOR

The previous chapter discussed the issues involved in determining the scale of public provision in the absence of suitable demand information. In the first part of this chapter we will consider a closely related issue: how publicly provided services which are subject to a financial régime should be charged for. Private firms must set prices for their products which are sufficient to cover costs and make profits. If, as assumed throughout the book so far, the firms are small and in close competition with each other, then they have very little freedom of manoeuvre in respect of the pricing policies they employ. Some public sector firms are in the same position. Many, however, by virtue of their monopoly powers have considerable discretion in the pricing policies they employ. They may charge the same prices to all users, regardless of any differences in the costs of provision, or they may differentiate their charges spatially, or according to time of day. Where they have a large amount of overhead cost they may distribute the burden by various sets of criteria. Earlier chapters have brought out the role of prices in determining the allocation of resources in terms of both efficiency and distribution. If public agencies can exercise discretion in the pricing policies, then the question arises, how, from a social viewpoint, should their policies be framed?

We do not need in the present context to consider all the issues which arise when considering the pricing policies of public enterprises. These would take us far from the concerns of land-use planning. In this chapter we will pursue the more limited objective of considering how, from the point of the allocation of resources to physical development, the various services which make up the development process should be charged for and the issues which arise when prices and costs are not closely related. Pricing failure in this sense was identified in Chapter 4 as one type of market failure and the point applies to public as much as to private enterprises. Although the opening paragraphs of this chapter will consider the characteristics of an ideal pricing system, the main aim of the first section of the chapter is to bring out the significance for land-use planning of the fact that typically prices are not set ideally. There may be scope for greater use of pricing measures in the public sector and for improved pricing structures, but in many cases administrative and political considerations will rule them out. Nevertheless the effects of inefficient prices remain and consequently a case for intervention on grounds of pricing failure, as discussed in Chapter 4, exists.

Many services provided by planning authorities do not command a price at all, or the prices they command are not related at all to the total costs of provision. In these circumstances a different set of problems arises; that of determining the best means of allocating the use of a limited supply of facilities, be it housing, open space or sports facilities, if demand exceeds supply when the service is made available free of charge. In these circumstances we are looking for mechanisms which carry out the same functions as price in financial markets but do not actually involve monetary transactions. These are considered in section 9.2. The final section considers some of the distributional implications of the various policies discussed in the first two sections of the chapter.

9.1 Pricing Policies

The rule that resources should not be devoted to a good or service beyond the point where the marginal social costs exceed the marginal social benefit has already been discussed. Chapter 6, in considering how divergences between marginal private and marginal social costs could be removed showed how taxes might be used to ensure that production took place at the point where marginal social cost and benefit were equal. In this section the case for using the same rule in setting prices for the services of an agency supplying infrastructure services to private development will be illustrated.

We assume that decisions on where to develop and at what density are left to the private sector and that the cost conditions in the servicing agency are those illustrated in Diagram 20. This shows marginal costs to be above average costs so that as the surface area of the city concerned grows, the average and marginal costs of providing capacity rise also. The demand curve for development cuts the MC curve at point B and the average curve at point C. If the price P_1 is set, then the correct amount of resources is devoted to supplying the services concerned. At price P_2, too many resources are used in this way and the city spreads out over a larger surface area than is justified, since beyond Q_1 the value gained from using resources in this way is below their value in alternative uses. This analysis illustrates the case, in terms of economic efficiency, against urban sprawl. Sprawl will tend to occur when the prices facing developers systematically understate the total social costs of development. These prices go to determine, as Chapter 3 showed, the developers' decisions on the appropriate scale and location of development. If they are set too low at the extensive margin of the city, then the balance between inner and outer area development is distorted.

Diagram 20

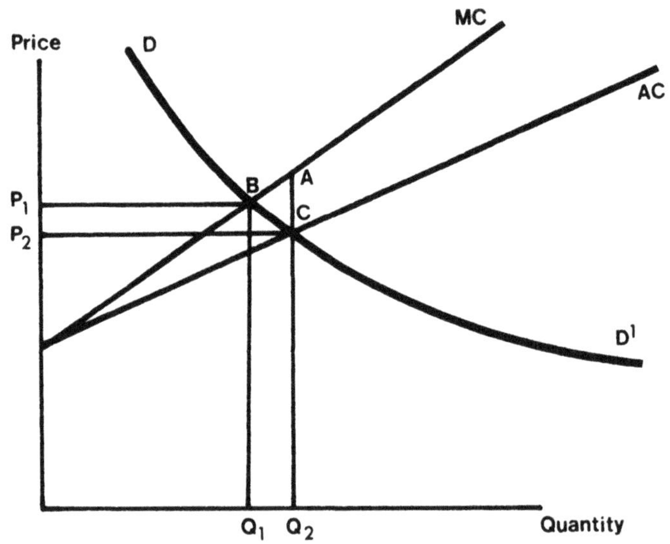

A similar issue arises if marginal costs vary from one part of the city to another and according to the density of development. If charges reflected these variations, then developers would be guided, other things being equal, to go for locations where costs to the agency were lowest and to build at densities which reflect these costs. Factors other than public service costs would enter into the decision where and how to develop but unless the marginal costs concerned are brought home to whoever is responsible for making the relevant decisions, then the supplying authority will tend to find itself committed to wasteful expenditure. That is, it will find itself servicing developments which would have taken place elsewhere or on a different scale, had the servicing costs been brought home properly.

The assumption made above of a single supplier of infrastructure is of course a simplification of reality in most circumstances. In practice, outside certain new town developments, a large number of different agencies are involved, operating under different pricing rules and using different investment criteria. Some agencies in both public and private sectors are concerned to see that each individual development is profitable to them; others charge prices unrelated, or related only very imperfectly, to specific costs of provision concerned. Others do not charge for their services at all. The upshot of this is that it is difficult to discern simply from information on prices or charges where development is best located and what form it should take.

Let us bring out the general problem by means of a simplified example using hypothetical data, which involves the choice between two possible sites for a public housing project. Both sites must be serviced by two agencies, one agency is responsible for all transport services and the other for all other services including water, drainage and power. Both agencies charge at average cost, even though the cost of providing both services varies a great deal from site to site. The hypothetical costs are shown in Table 1, together with the prices based on average costs over the whole of the operations of the agencies concerned. As the figures have been selected to show, the comparison of average costs suggests that there is nothing to choose between the two sites, even though the real cost differences, disguised by the averaging, show one site to be much cheaper.

Table 1

		Site 1	Site 2
Agency 1	Average Costs	100	100
	Marginal Costs	25	25
Agency 2	Average Costs	50	50
	Marginal Costs	25	60

This problem does not arise simply because a number of suppliers are involved. A development process could be imagined which involved a number of suppliers, but in which charges for all services were linked to costs of provision in alternative circumstances and alternative locations. The result would not be a single price but rather a schedule of prices according to variation in such factors as terrain and building density which influence costs. In such a process, whoever was responsible for development could decide in the light of this information where it should be located. Such a judgement would also involve estimating relative benefits as well, so it would not always follow that the cheapest sites should be chosen. As we saw within the simple urban model, where sites had particular advantages due to accessibility or amenity, then developers – and ultimately their customers – would be prepared to pay more for them. In the case of a development directly controlled by a planning authority, e.g. a New Town corporation, the judgement required would be the same, i.e. which sites yielded the greatest net benefit, but the evidence used on differential benefits and the processes of decision might well be different from that involved in private markets.

The case for attempting to give a closer relationship between charges and cost depends on the scale of the cost variation experienced and on this the amount of empirical evidence is limited. If there were significant variations resulting from long-term factors such as topography or short-term conditions such as spare capacity, then the case for attempting a closer relationship between prices and costs would be strong. We can discuss one important case here.

It is a characteristic of nearly all urban areas that populations or densities are falling, with the consequence in some cases that new development can often be accommodated at no extra cost in terms of infrastructure. If this holds, then it would be important to reflect this fact to developers, public or private, when they are making decisions on whether to expand at the periphery or within the existing urban areas. Failure to reflect social opportunity costs in these conditions can have serious consequences. The decline in private housing investment in the inner parts of urban areas is an international phenomenon. In part (and only in part) this is due to the failure of infrastructure charging policies which, by averaging costs over all users, irrespective of location, undercharges these areas where new capacity is being installed and overcharges developments within the existing fabric. This point is considered further in Chapter 11.

Despite this analysis, a correct pricing structure may be ineffective when land supply is rationed in the way analysed in Chapter 7. Within the simple urban model, the bids which developers made for land depend on their expectation of net profit. If the costs of developing one particular site were higher than another, but the selling prices of buildings the same, then they would have a clear preference for the second site. When land is rationed and a surplus accrues to its release by virtue of its artificial scarcity, the main effect of differentiating infrastructure charges would be to affect the surplus made by different landowners. That is, developers would modify their bid prices by the extent of the differences in charges. If no other developed use was in competition for the land, the result would be a lower price for the landowner.

The significance of this point depends on the nature of the market for land in the area concerned. If housing were the only user of land, then the consequences of differential charging would be slight. But if housing and other uses were in competition, or if charges were related to different kinds of housing according to their expected level of usage, then the bids made by developers would have an allocative function, since they would lead to land being allocated away from high-cost towards low-cost uses.

If a pricing solution of the kind outlined was ruled out, then an alternative approach would be to put the whole development process within a single organisation. The issues involved in this go much wider than the present discussion as they involve fundamental political choices which cannot be examined here. However, it is worth noting that the information which this single agency would require if it was to make best use of the resources available to it would be precisely the same as that needed by individual suppliers to base their prices on. That is, the overall authority would, if rational, wish to avoid high-cost areas unless they offered exceptional benefits and vice versa. This serves to emphasise the point made in Chapter 3 that the basic economic issues arise irrespective of the institutional framework.

Where neither of these solutions is possible, then alternative policies may have to be developed to influence the pattern of development in the direction of areas where costs are low. Many planning policies, both of a general and a locational nature are geared to this end. The problems with this kind of control in relation to housing are discussed in Chapter 11.

The consequences of pricing failure do not show themselves solely in undesirable spatial patterns of development as the example of water supply shows. Water supply has an increasing marginal cost curve, since, like mining, the easiest and cheapest sources of supply are used up first. As the demand for water grows, less accessible and hence more expensive sites in engineering and also frequently in environmental terms have to be developed. We can assume the demand curve for water to be a conventional kind, i.e. the first units consumed are of great, if not infinite, value and additional units are of decreasing importance. The left-hand part of the demand curve expresses the need for water used to support life itself, moving down through washing and cooking uses, to watering the garden and washing the car to the right. Not all users of course have precisely this order of priorities.

If users are charged some average figure, unrelated to the use they make of the water supplied, then as Diagram 20 shows, the amount Q_2 is demanded. At a price equal to marginal cost, only Q_1 would be demanded. The result of the failure to charge marginal cost is that resources are required, equal to the area BAQ_2Q_1 to expand production from Q_1 to Q_2. This produces an addition to consumer surplus of only P_1BCP_2, an amount below their value in alternative uses (on the assumption that this value is correctly represented in the cost curve). The result is that resources are devoted to expanding capacity to meet low-value needs. This may have wider implications if the expansion of capacity entails reservoir and pipe-work which has environmental consequences such as loss of amenity.

The marginal cost rule also applies to a situation where marginal costs are below average costs. These conditions may occur with a facility, such as a unique historic site on which money has been spent to ensure its continued preservation. The cost of allowing users to visit it is low, involving only a small amount of routine upkeep, and these costs do not vary significantly with the number using the site. In this situation, if a charge is levied which is higher than marginal costs, then users are deterred unnecessarily from visiting it. Extra consumer surplus could be generated as long as the demand curve lies above the marginal cost curve. What people would be willing to pay is in excess of cost of provision.

It might be argued that if a lot of money had been spent on the site then users should be charged a sum which recouped these expenditures involved. However, when considering the use of resources, we are always looking forward and not backward in time. If the expenditure has been carried out, then it is a sunk cost, and we can apply the rule: bygones are bygones. To understand this rule, we need to distinguish between the financial motive and the economic or allocational motive for charging. What is important for the allocation of resources is that the decisions people make are guided by prices which reflect the resource implications of those decisions. If marginal costs are low, then a charge which is higher will tend to dissuade them from making visits and will encourage them to go elsewhere. Equally, however, it would be correct for prices to be raised on the historic site as congestion built up, even though this would result in revenue much in excess of the costs currently being incurred. The case for doing this has already been discussed in section 6.2.

A central problem with marginal cost pricing is that it may produce too little revenue or too much. If marginal costs are rising the supplying organisation would make large profits and if they are falling, large losses. For various reasons this may not be considered to be right. It is often argued that activities should be self-supporting: that the financial constraints which the need to cover costs provides is a guide to good management and a check on bad management or that there should be no price differentiation between different user groups. Most people would consider it gross exploitation that a public enterprise should make large surpluses. If these arguments prevail as they have done in relation to most public enterprises in Britain and elsewhere, then the pattern of charges which emerges may be unsatisfactory from the allocational point of view, especially where, as in most developments, a number of agencies are involved in any given development. In other words, they do little or nothing to encourage development in the most economic manner or location.

A second major difficulty stems from the fact that the right price for publicly provided services cannot be considered in isolation from prices charged elsewhere in the economy. If these other sectors do not charge prices which equal marginal costs – as frequently they do not – then determination of the right policy for the public sector may become very complex. A simple example will bring out some of the issues. Let us take two facilities, one publicly and one privately owned. The latter has to make a profit if it is to survive. The former, however, may be subject to any pricing policy desired. Following the discussion above, a marginal cost-pricing policy might be adopted in conditions where marginal cost was greater than average cost. If demand for the two facilities was closely related such that a fall in the price led to a large demand for the other (so the cross-elasticity was high) this could have the effect of putting the private firm out of business. In due course the public facility would fill up, become congested and prices would rise in line with the rules discussed above. If demand continued to rise, then further public investment would be required. There is an obvious nonsense about this situation – intuitively average cost would have been a better pricing policy for the public facility, as this would have allowed the private sector facility to continue.

Typically, however, the situation may be more complicated and no 'intuitively obvious' solutions available. For example, the cross-elasticity of demand between the two facilities might be low so that it might be possible to get a better utilisation of the public facility without diminishing supply in the private sector. In the real world, there is likely to be a wide range of facilities so that the demand interrelationships between them would be particularly hard to estimate. Equally relevant would be the supply elasticities in the private sector. If supply were inelastic, i.e. if the level of supply was unresponsive to revenue received, then again the public sector could have relative freedom in the prices it set, since even if the private sector lost business it would still keep its facilities open. The major issue here would be the distributional one: whether or not it was fair to reduce the return to the private supplier. On the other hand, if supply was very responsive to price, the greater the probability that the opposite would hold. No single set of pricing rules can fit all possible circumstances. The only general point to be made is that pricing policy in the public sector must be considered in relation to both public and private sectors, where the cross-elasticities of demand are significantly large.

Even if it is considered to be politically necessary that activities should cover their costs and no more, then within that constraint, price structures may be devised which do have a useful allocational function. The relative pattern of charges might be set as to discourage expensive provision and vice versa. That is, if costs vary sharply from one location to another, charges might reflect this in part: electricity boards, for example, have higher connection charges in some areas than others. More important perhaps are variations of charges with time: demand for most public sector services varies sharply between different times of day. Total costs tend to be determined by the need to meet peak demand, hence if demand peaks can be flattened by charging higher prices at peak than at off-peak, demand can be diverted in such a way as to make it cheaper to meet. Electricity, telephones and to some extent transport have adopted this kind of charging structure and it is used in some recreational facilities.

The case for a charging pattern of this kind is based on the analysis of congestion costs, introduced in Chapter 6. In the case of a unique countryside facility or an ancient monument, the economic aim of a differential charge is to obtain an improved use of a given facility. The charge discourages users at peak times, while at the same time encourages use at off-peak times. Those deterred by the higher charge may decide to go off-peak and others will not use the facility at all. In the case of facilities such as transport or power, the economic objectives of such a pricing system are similar, but not identical. For in these cases further investment is practical. If investment is required purely to meet demand at peak times, the marginal costs of the peak will be high. If demand is diverted by a high peak charge to off-peak, then investment resources are saved which otherwise would have been used uneconomically – i.e. to provide the service concerned below its cost of provision. If demand is not diverted significantly by a peak charge then this suggests that users attach such weight to having the service available at these times that the commitment of resources to providing services is justified. A similar problem arose in the discussion of capacity in the previous chapter. If prices are set at a level which only covers running costs, or if no charges are made at all, then facilities may be heavily used, above the 'capacity' level, but the case for new investment may nevertheless be weak. This would be so if the effect of raising charges to reflect congestion costs was sufficient to reduce demand to a level much within the capacity of the existing facilities. Eventually of course, if demand continues to build up, then further investment would be required. But if prices are not charged which reflect the fact that marginal cost rises with increased levels of usage, then the case for investment will always be premature.

9.2 Alternative Methods of Allocation

For both economic and political reasons, pricing solutions may not be feasible. They may be expensive to administer or politically unacceptable. But the *function* of pricing, nevertheless, must be carried out. This section, therefore, looks at alternative means of regulating the use of facilities such as public housing or recreational areas for which the use of pricing is modified by distributional or other considerations. To illustrate the problem, take the case of a countryside pleasure spot, the demand for which would exceed the physical capacity of the site if no prices were charged. How should visits be regulated?

To bring out the characteristics of the pricing solution, consider Diagram 21 with price set at P_1 : those whose demand is less intense, i.e. those to the right of point A on the demand curve, will be disinclined to pay the charge and will take their purchasing power elsewhere, where they could get what they considered better value for money. Those whose desire to visit this particular spot is more intense remain, and have to pay for the benefits they hope to enjoy, reducing their expenditure elsewhere.

Suppose that all concerned were of equal income and we had no desire to see some particular group among the potential users enjoy the facility in question. Then the pricing solution is attractive, provided that the actual imposition of the charging system is not itself costly. It has the important characteristic of allowing those who value this particular countryside facility most to gain access to it and to enjoy it in relatively uncongested circumstances.

Now take an alternative means, that of allocating the right of admission by an arbitrary system; each would-be visitor has to pull a ball out of a bag and if it is the right colour he gains admission. Consider this procedure in the light of the simple diagram above; if the visitors

Diagram 21

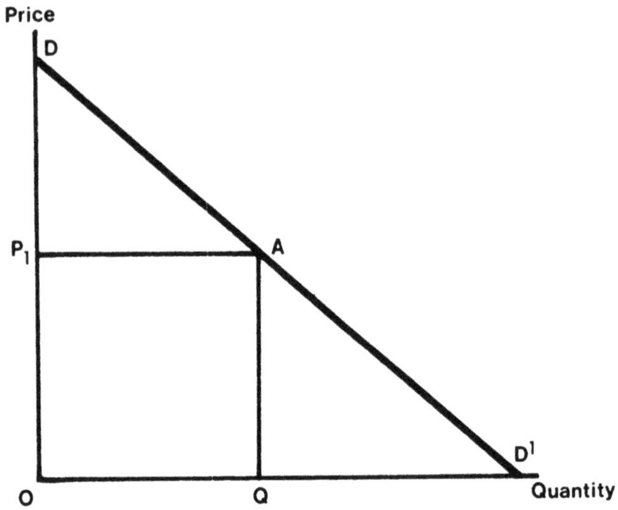

are selected at random, then the chances of getting a keen visitor and an indifferent visitor are equal. On average, some of each would be chosen. The average consumer surplus enjoyed would be half the difference between the maximum (to the left of the demand curve) and the minimum (to the right). This is less than could be obtained by a charging solution, because the random selection procedure fails to sort out the keen from the less keen. The diagram has been drawn to illustrate the point. It has been assumed that half the potential users can be allowed in, i.e. OQ. If a pricing solution is adopted, total benefits enjoyed from visiting the park equals DAQO. If the random number procedure is followed, it will be on average P_1AQO, since the changes of selecting a user to the right of A are assumed equal to the chances of users being equal to the left.

An alternative policy, and one more likely to be put into practice, is to let queues form. There are many examples: from allotments to home-helps to recreational facilities, although the time spent in such queues is clearly of varying length. A housing queue may take years to move through, others may be a matter of minutes. In what senses may queuing be a bad or a good way of dealing with the allocation problem?

Queues prevent the rich from gaining precedence over the poor, and in doing so fulfil a major distributional objective. Nevertheless, queues may be both inefficient and undesirable on distributional grounds, as the following points show. First, a queue as such does little to select those within a given social economic or 'need' group whose 'need' or potential demand for the service in question is greater than others. Some may be discouraged by the length of a queue and will not put their names on it. These may be the less enthusiastic and the less needy, but it may be precisely those whose need is greatest who will be discouraged and forced to look elsewhere. For example, individuals in severest housing need may be forced, if a simple queue is in operation, to go to the most expensive parts of the private sector, as they have no alternative. Second, once entry has been obtained into the facility whose use is rationed by a queue, there is no incentive for the individuals concerned to reconsider this position and vacate it. For example, if use of a facility were charged for on a time basis, those initially allowed to enjoy it would be continually reminded of the relevant costs and might decide after a while to cease to use it. But if they are not charged in this way they may continue to use the facility concerned, even though it has little value to them. This point is clearly more important for facilities such as housing than it is for parks, since the possible period of use is so much longer.

Queues may, however, be operated in ways which overcome some of these problems. UK public housing authorities award 'points' to families or individuals in different situations, while accepting an absolute obligation to offer some form of accommodation to certain groups, e.g. those they have themselves displaced through road construction. Queues used in this way are in a sense a construction of need as opposed to a demand curve, i.e. the position on the curve AB above is judged by the authority itself applying judgement to the importance of the various factors relevant to the definition of housing need. Such a system does not allow direct expression by the individuals themselves or their own preferences; indeed it is one of the objects of systems of this kind to prevent personal circumstances – other than those deemed relevant to the definition of need – from entering into the allocation decisions.

This kind of improvement on a simple queue, though important, suffers from three basic weaknesses. First, once a system of this kind has selected entrants to the facility in short supply, it does not cope with change in need over time. Second, a queue, modified or otherwise, is not by itself a good ground for justifying further investment. If a facility is allocated by administrative means, such as a points system, then the authority concerned loses the kind of information which a pricing solution offers about the strength of demand and leaves the case open for further investment in the facility concerned. If prices are low in relation to costs of provision, or zero, then people 'put their names down' even though they would value the facility, e.g. an allotment, very slightly. The mere fact of a queue is itself poor evidence that further allotments – or any other kind of facility – should be provided.

Third, unless the points system is highly efficient, queues can have undesirable distributional consequences. An important example of this has already been analysed in Chapter 7. When land supply to a particular use is rationed, the effect is to create a queue for permission to use land in that way. In Diagram 16 the length of the queue would be Q_1-Q_2, i.e. the number who at a price would like to devote more land to the use in question. As the analysis in Chapter 7 shows, the effect of allowing a small number of individuals the right to change of use is to give them a large windfall profit, which in the absence of a suitable fiscal system may be regarded as inequitable. In the absence of suitable tax measures, the only way in which such an outcome can be avoided is to sell the permissions concerned or tap the exceptional profit by the means discussed in Chapter 6. This is an extreme case, but the point is a general one. Queuing, of its nature, offers a windfall gain to those who are successful. Unless the selection methods are efficient, this will lead to inequity. Gross inequity between rich and poor may be removed. It is less easy to remove inequity between those in similar income circumstances.

In any particular situation a great deal will turn on the facts of usage. In the case of a crowded recreational facility, it may seem fair to allow people in on a first-come-first-served basis. This would, however, impose costs on those who had a high value of time and who would therefore prefer to pay more rather than queue. These might be the richer members of the community or people from any sector of society with large families and hence a limited amount of completely free time. If a pricing solution is adopted, then clearly this would tell against the poorer members of society and hence be regarded as unfair. But the weight to be attached to this point depends very much on the pattern of usage at the facility concerned; a large number of recreational facilities are used by people in the upper-income groups, with the result that they receive an unjustified distribution of income in their favour.

9.3 Distributional Considerations

Distributional considerations are at the heart of many of the arguments which reject pricing solutions in favour of other methods of allocation.

But it should be apparent by now that we cannot simply identify pricing solutions as being undesirable from a distributional viewpoint and non-pricing solutions as being desirable. It may be helpful to bring together the various points which have emerged from the earlier discussion.

First, principles of equity themselves conflict. Some will argue that people should pay for the costs they give rise to. This might lead, for example, to prices being set at marginal cost, and a highly differentiated charging structure. Others will argue that the same services should, as a matter of equity, be charged the same to everyone, no matter where he lives and no matter what the variation in the costs of provision. Such arguments usually have little to do with concern about income distribution between broad classes of the population, but are based on notions of horizontal equity, i.e. between individuals in similar economic circumstances. In the land-use planning context, there is a case on efficiency grounds for differentiating charges for basic services between various parts of an urban area, but this might conflict not only with feelings about horizontal equity but also with expectations. It might be considered unfair to introduce differentiation, once people have made decisions on another basis.

But equity, like other 'goods', has its own opportunity cost. In trying to make charges uniform, resources may be wasted for the reasons we have described. Individuals are encouraged to use services where costs are high but value low and to take decisions, e.g. on where to locate development, which have expensive consequences for the public sector. Similarly, rigid pursuit of equity in the allocation of public sector housing may conflict with the need to allocate such housing to key workers required for the maintenance of essential services.

Third, where prices are set low, or at zero level, the net effect may not be to distribute welfare in favour of those with low incomes. As noted above, the effect zero charges will have depends very much on the pattern of usage of the facilities concerned. It is often argued that it is socially undesirable to price countryside amenities, yet as noted above, analysis of the pattern of use, young people apart, suggests that users, especially of remote facilities, are primarily from the upper-income groups. Fourth, non-pricing methods of allocation are not themselves necessarily equitable. They can be inefficient at picking out those in most need, as the analysis of queues showed.

Finally, some brief comments on finance, in relation both to this chapter and the previous one. This cannot be ignored when considering the distributional implications of either investment or pricing policies.

We have not been specific about the nature of the means available to the planning authority for raising finance from its citizens. In the case of a zero-priced facility, the whole of the cost must be raised in this way. The distributional implications of this therefore could only be fully assessed by considering the incidence of the relevant taxes, which would obviously depend on whether an income, a sales or a property-based tax was involved. There is not space to analyse these alternatives here, but the discussion in Chapter 7 of incidence effects shows how difficult this would be.

In the case of an authority receiving central government finance, the problem could be yet more complicated, depending on the precise nature of the financial system. But perhaps the most severe problems lie within the authority's own budget. Let us assume that it is considering what policy to take on charging for public parking or public transport facilities. It might, on distributional grounds, want to keep charges down. However, to do so, if it felt unable to raise more finance from its residents, it would have to cut down on other items in its budget. If it already had a pattern of spending which favoured lower-income groups, then the distributional effects of low charges for the additional facility could be unfavourable. For example, it might have to reduce its housing programme in order to provide free recreational facilities. This serves to emphasise a point which has emerged several times before, that the distributional effects of policies are hard to disentangle and are by no means self-evident. Given this, it is foolish to rule out any particular solution to the allocation problem and to the pricing of public services without examining the wider implications of the alternatives.

PART 2: ANALYSING THE EFFECTS OF POLICIES

10 LAND-USE CONTROLS AND ECONOMIC ACTIVITY

So far we have taken the economic activity within the urban economy for granted. It has simply been 'there', providing jobs at the centre of our notional city and spreading out as peripheral locations appeared more attractive. There are, however, significant interactions between policies towards the control of land use and the process by which personal incomes are generated from economic activity. Economic activity, be it in manufacturing industry or commerce, will, for example, give rise to external effects which impose costs on other parts of the urban economy and which the planning authority may be concerned to alleviate. Alternatively, some sections of the urban economy may not work well as markets, i.e. they may make bad investment decisions because of poor information or failure to co-ordinate individual expansion plans.

The two cases are worth distinguishing. In the second there is no conflict between the interests of producers and the interests of other parts of the urban economy. If the authority is efficient at providing information about the future, then individual firms should make better investment and locational decisions than they otherwise would. Provision of facilities within the public sector where there is a public good problem may also add to the efficiency of the local economy. So does intervention where private provision would be feasible but inefficient. In these contexts there is no conflict between the enjoyment of money income gained from employment and the other items which affect individuals' utility. In terms of Diagram 12, the effect of policy intervention is to shift both the private and the social production possibility curve outwards to the right.

In the first case, the intervention designed to reduce the impact of external costs arising from economic activity will tend, as we saw in Chapter 6, to increase production costs in the industry affected. This will tend to lead to higher prices for the goods or services concerned as firms are forced by regulation or induced by tax or subsidy to adopt production methods which, from their point of view, are not the most efficient. Thus a conflict arises between the interests of individuals as recipients of money income and their enjoyment of unpriced goods, such as freedom from pollution. It is the task of the planning authority to balance such costs with the gains to be enjoyed from the effects of the regulation, in the way analysed in Chapter 6.

A planning authority may wish to modify the behaviour of the urban economy in various ways. For example, it may seek to influence the spatial pattern of economic activity in an area through its control of planning permission for new developments. In areas of high demand pressures, authorities may seek to limit growth in demand for the local labour force, to prevent 'overheating'. In other cases it may seek to control what it considers wasteful levels of investment in, for example, shopping facilities. In yet others, it may seek to forbid certain developments entirely because of the external costs associated with them – e.g. the introduction of large-scale industry to areas of scenic beauty.

These various possible aims of policy set the analyst two principal tasks. The first is to consider in what circumstances the instruments available to the planning authority are likely to be effective in achieving the declared aims of policy. The second is to identify all the relevant effects which intervention is likely to induce, including both efficiency and distributional considerations. This chapter, therefore, will consider a selection of land-use policies which authorities frequently pursue, to identify their consequences as their effects work through the urban economy and to bring out the constraints under which the authority must work in attempting to influence these outcomes.

10.1 Controls over the Intensity of Commercial Development: Plot Ratios

The plot ratio is the ratio of total floor-space to the area of a site. In residential areas it may be fixed as a fraction, i.e. the buildings or extensions are not allowed to cover the total site or it may, in commercial cases, be a fairly high figure, where tall building is allowed. Plot-ratio control has recently been described as

> basically a local matter introduced for local environmental control and designed to prevent over-development of sites with bulky buildings which damage their neighbours' amenities and the pleasantness of the neighbourhood.

Where plot ratios are a local matter, the costs and benefits of a development are easy to identify. On the one hand are the advantages accruing through having more space. These are expressed in the potential profit stream of the developer, i.e. the increased rental value of the site, which in turn reflects the higher efficiency and increased profitability of the ultimate user of the site. On the other hand are the external costs thought likely to arise, e.g. the amenity of the immediate neighbours which might be harmed by new building or that of anyone concerned with the visual appearance of the city who might wish to see an old building preserved. Although such costs and benefits will normally be easy enough to identify, their quantification and measurement will not be straightforward in practice. But if plot ratio controls are pursued as a general policy, the implications are less easy to see. Consequently the nature of the trade-offs involved are hard to identify, as the following example brings out.

At a strategic level, plot ratios have traditionally had two main justifications: first, by limiting the amount of development in an area some check is placed on the volume of employment and trip-making. If the transport system in an area is congested, so that marginal social cost exceeds marginal private cost, then there is clearly a case for attempting to limit any further increases in transport demand. The second argument is that by limiting the scale of the redevelopment expenditure on any one site, the funds available for investment are spread around. According to one planning department – San Francisco –

> overloading of individual sites can create unwarranted monopolies in building space, to the detriment of development potentials in the remainder of the district. The result would be a paradox of high bulk and high value accompanied by sterilisation of undeveloped sites.

These two lines of argument are best considered separately.

The case for plot-ratio controls of the first kind is illustrated in Diagram 22, which uses the distinction developed in Chapter 4 between private and social costs. The former, curve MPC, represents the costs to the developer of building higher: the curve MSC embodies these costs, plus the costs of congestion which the development is expected to generate and for which it is assumed those making the trips concerned do not pay. The line MR shows the revenue which the developer expects: for simplicity the rental has been assumed not to vary with the amount of space provided. At point B he would make his maximum profit, to the right of point A where the social cost curve (MSC) intersects with his revenue curve. This is the point where the plot ratio should be set, where private and public interest are properly balanced against each other.

This analysis takes in only a single commercial development but if

Diagram 22

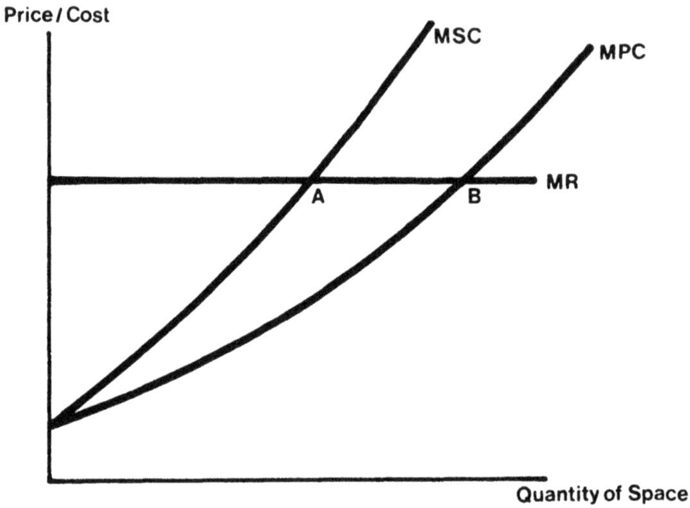

plot ratio is to be assessed as a strategic control it must be assessed on the assumption that it is being applied everywhere else. When the wider effects are taken into account it may be shown, as Evans has done, that the effect of plot-ratio control can be counter-productive. The main lines of his analysis will be followed through in the rest of this section.

The first point to be considered is whether or not the control will tend to promote the very effect which it is aimed at curbing. The ratio between floor-space and employment is not constant but can vary. For example, if space costs are high then uses of space which can be economised on will tend to be reduced. If the effect of the plot-ratio control over a wide area is to increase the price of commercial space in that area – which, since it involves a limitation in the amount supplied it is likely to do – then the market is likely to respond by moving out uses which can readily be decentralised, e.g. routine clerical operations. This is an effect which the control is aimed to promote. But firms may also react by moving out such space-intensive uses as show, display, store and filing rooms, and replacing these with employees, an effect diametrically opposed to the one intended.

Secondly, the decentralisation of activities may generate extra trips between the decentralised offices and the centre or between firms formerly supplying the central area with services which find it better to move away and move their supplies in by vehicle. It cannot be said *a priori* whether the net effect of all these reactions to the control would be favourable or not. In the case of the transport movement there may be some advantage if peak hour commuting trips are replaced by off-peak delivery trips, as the latter are likely to be cheaper in both private and social terms.

Third, plot-ratio control is likely to make the commercial sector spread out over a greater area or, as we have noted, to decentralise entirely. Both effects lead to an increase of trips between buildings as opposed to trips made within buildings, i.e. a net increase in the use of the road system. For example, meetings would involve bringing staff to one central location from various outlying ones.

Fourth, if control leads to an expansion of the central business district in spatial terms, but not in terms of numbers employed, then it may be less easy to serve it by public transport, which does best when destinations are concentrated. If office activities decentralise completely then there will tend to be a move to private transport, since peripheral locations are normally difficult to serve by public transport because the requisite densities of traffic are not available. Thus, as far as traffic congestion is concerned, the main effect of plot-ratio controls appears to be to shift congestion around while providing very little incentive to reduce it.

If the planning authority has the requisite powers, there is no doubt that a plot-ratio control is feasible. The main issue, therefore, in any particular situation, is its desirability. Because of the wider ramifications of a general policy towards the use of plot ratios, it is much less easy than in the simplest case to draw up a balance sheet of costs and benefits. A policy of this kind, if suddenly imposed upon a city which previously had not been subject to any such restrictions, could, in time, be radically altered by it. Consequently the problem of prediction would be severe, so that it would not be easy to estimate whether some effects would be negative or positive. In general, however, the main categories of effect would be similar to the simple case:

(a) changes in building costs – including both capital and maintenance;
(b) changes in movement costs;
(c) changes in the efficiency of office operation;
(d) changes in visual amenity.

But in addition there would be:

(e) various effects due to changes in location of the facilities affected by the control.

If we suppose that the control was aimed primarily at offices, then item (a) would require estimation of the change in costs (including running costs accruing over the lives of the assets concerned), resulting from a different pattern of construction. The scale of these changes will depend very much on the nature of the production function for offices. If construction and maintenance of offices enjoyed economies of scale with respect to height of building, then such costs would tend to be considerable. Supposing that the cost of adding further storeys was as shown in Table 2, then if the top five storeys were forbidden and replaced by a separate building, the additional costs would be £0.22m. If the opposite were true, plot-ratio control might reduce the resources devoted to office-building at the cost of increases in (c). One important reaction could occur within the existing stock. The control would tend to lead to internal restructuring of space and other means (e.g. exploiting tolerances) for getting more usable space out of the existing stock of buildings. The significance of this depends on the costs involved but the presumption can be that as long as such activities are only profitable under control, they are less efficient than other means of providing extra capacity.

Table 2

	Construction Costs (£000's)										
	Storeys										
	1	2	3	4	5	6	7	8	9	10	Total Costs
Scheme 1 (Single Building)	100	100	100	90	80	70	60	50	40	30	720
Scheme 2	100	100	100	90	80						470
(Two Buildings)	100	100	100	90	80						470

The effects of (b), as the earlier discussion has shown, are complex to estimate, even if effects on trip-making to and from the office alone are taken into account. There can be no general presumption that the effects on movement costs will be favourable or unfavourable. The estimation of (c) would also be difficult. If the control prevented the building of very large offices then those firms which found it advantageous to be in a single building would lose a certain amount of efficiency. Similarly, if the control made the commercial core spread out, then the peculiar advantages – external economies – of very close proximity might be lost. In principle the losses might be measured by the differences in rents which would be paid in the two situations or by direct measurements of operating efficiency in different working conditions. Neither would be easy.

In the case of item (d) there will tend to be little difficulty in identifying it, although there may be difficulty in valuing it. The catch-all item (e) presents severe forecasting problems. The imposition of a plot-ratio control would alter the relative profitability of all sites capable of being transferred to the use affected. This would not only change the pattern of activity in building for that use, but it would affect the supply of land to other users. For example, it might increase the pressure on non-commercial uses near the commercial core. Large houses would tend to be taken for office purposes or sites cleared for new construction. Whether those effects are favourable or unfavourable will depend on the circumstances prevailing in the area concerned. The pressure on housing may be welcome for reasons noted in Chapter 4, provided it was not sudden. Equally, it might impose hardships on particularly vulnerable groups of the population.

This discussion has been inconclusive, but it has brought out one main point; that when the reactions to this particular control are analysed there is a *prima facie* case that it fails to achieve the desired objective and imposes costs on the urban economy in attempting to do so. The obvious inference is that either the control should not be used at all or alternatives devised which bear directly on the problem in hand – in this case measures designed to influence traffic movement directly.

The second kind of effect to be considered is that on the pattern of development through the influence plot ratios may have on the spatial allocation of the funds available for financing it. In a city where no controls existed – and hence there were no special premiums to be enjoyed from providing commercial space – then buildings would be put up at a plot ratio chosen to maximise the profit of the developer on a particular site – as shown in Diagram 22 above. His decisions on what to redevelop might not be optimal, traffic arguments apart, if a social value were attached to redevelopment as such. For example, old buildings which are poorly maintained impose losses of visual amenity.

Unless these were internalised by a tax, then society's valuation of redevelopment would be greater than the developer's or owner's. As a consequence, the pace of redevelopment would be too slow from a social viewpoint. (The converse possibility is ignored here.)

From the private point of view, intense development might tend to be preferred because it economises on demolition costs – the site has to be cleared no matter what is to be built on it – but only to the extent that building high is not subject to sharply rising marginal costs. If they do so rise, then the costs of plot-ratio control will not in any case be significant because there would be no incentive to build high. But if they build below the point where diseconomies set in, then the costs to the private sector might be considerable as the illustrative figures given above have suggested. This, if policy is designed to reduce the externalities due to a too slow pace of development, there would be a clear trade-off between extra construction costs and environmental benefit. The measurement issues would be identical to those already discussed.

Even if desirable, plot-ratio control may fail to meet its second objective. First, if it is applied too severely, then no development may take place at all, or its scale may be considerably reduced. Whether this will follow will depend on the profitability of different kinds and scales of development. At the prevailing structure of land values, no central area development may be worthwhile unless it is very intensive in nature. This would be so if acquisition and clearance costs were such that only a large-scale development would allow them to be recouped. In these circumstances two kinds of reaction are likely. First, developers may refurbish, rather than redevelop, existing properties. The effect of this might be entirely in line with the objectives of the control, i.e. there would be a gradual upgrading of the quality of the capital stock. A second reaction would not be so favourable. If plot-ratio control is rigidly applied in a central location, the balance of advantage between periphery and centre will be altered. Development activity may therefore be diverted spatially away from the centre, a reaction which would run counter to the objectives of the policy, if it leads to neglect of the centre entirely.

The implications of this very brief discussion are considerable. It brings out how the success of the authority depends on the precise nature of the reactions of the urban economy to its policies. These in turn depend on the strength of the pressures for development in that economy on the one hand, and the relative advantage of particular parts of it on the other. In one set of circumstances the policy fails; in the other it succeeds. To establish, *ex ante*, which was the more likely outcome would require a large number of difficult forecasts and judgements.

To attempt such forecasts may not however be the right approach for the authority to take. Before instituting a policy of this kind it would be important to establish why developers preferred concentrated to dispersed schemes. They may prefer to develop on several sites but find the land assembly problems too difficult. In these circumstances, plot-ratio control would be ineffective unless the authority stepped in with land purchase, in which case it may not be necessary.

Concentration of development might occur for other reasons. The nature of the development control process itself might encourage it. If it imposed long delays and costly preparation of preliminary material and works, which were put at risk if permission was not granted, then developers might be unwilling to make more than a limited number of applications and place all their efforts on them. Alternatively, the development process may be much less competitive than was assumed in the simple urban model. There are indications, for example, that the London office boom during the fifties and sixties was uncompetitive partly because perception of the available opportunities and knowledge of how to realise them were confined to a relatively small group of people. Whatever the obstacles are to more dispersed development, the correct approach is for the authority to identify them and devise policies appropriate to them. The general point which emerges here is that to give the desired effect it may be both unnecessary and inefficient simply to define the desired end-product, i.e. a given pattern of investment. It may be more productive to promote the conditions in which market activity will itself tend to create that pattern.

10.2 Controls over the Scale of Development: The Case of Offices

The previous section analysed how plot-ratio controls might be used as a way of limiting the total amount of development on a particular site so as to encourage a pattern of total development which is better from the overall point of view. However, in some situations, planning authorities may wish to regulate the total volume of investment in office space, taking into account only the office market itself. Such policies have, in part, at least,been encouraged by the fact that a number of office buildings have remained empty for some time after construction, with the implication that resources were being wasted which might be put to better use elsewhere. Over the last few years there is evidence from New York that the office market there has over-provided accommodation and that prices have fallen to levels which will not repay the initial cost of construction. This suggests that this particular market has some sort of tendency to 'over-supply'. *Prima facie*, therefore, a case may exist for regulating the level of investment.

The office market, like any other, can be analysed using demand and supply curves. Diagram 11 in Chapter 4 shows a supply curve which is fairly flat – i.e. supply is assumed to be very responsive to changes in the price which accommodation can fetch. Three demand curves are shown, which are fairly steep, i.e. inelastic over the range we are considering. If demand shifts from DD_1 to DD_2, then the amount supplied will tend to increase to Q_2. However, let us assume that the supply response is lagged by a year. When demand increases, supply does not in the first instance do so. Consequently, the price of accommodation will rise to P_2, i.e. the point which brings into equilibrium demand and supply with supply constant. In real life not all prices would react in this way because of the length of most leasing agreements and other agreements. Such restrictions on the freedom of prices to adjust will tend to exaggerate the effect of shifts in demand on the price of those properties which do come into the market in the time period before supply is expanded, because the whole of the shift in demand will tend to be concentrated on to them. Although by no means the whole story, this analysis in part explains why central London rents for some categories of accommodation rose so rapidly during the boom of 1971-3.

If in time period 1 suppliers see that prices are at P_2, they will attempt to react by increasing supply to Q_3, which we will assume they manage to bring on to the market in the following year. But the price at which they can let Q_3 amount of space is only P_3, a price which is much below their costs of construction. However, because there is in the short run at least, and certainly not without extra expenditure, no alternative use for the office space they have built, they will tend, perhaps with some delay, to lower their prices in the direction of P_3, so that at least they can get some return for their investment. Gradually, as over time demand increases they realise a price which compensates them for their initial investment. How well they do overall will depend on whether or not demand increases yet further. If it does, then the same kind of effect might appear again and a cyclical pattern of prices result. Suppliers will hold back as long as they see prices depressed and will not attempt to bring any more space on to the market, but if demand rises rapidly then profitable supply again seems possible and the cycle can be repeated.

The analysis can be complicated by allowing for the fact that offices take time to plan and produce. For example, the production lag for office space may be several years. Only where conversion of existing low-quality space into a higher price bracket is concerned is it likely to be as little as one year. In analysing a specific situation, it would be useful to look at qualities of accommodation, location, etc., since possible substitution effects between these might modify the nature of the cycle and tend to damp it down. For example, if over-supply in one category of space could easily be shifted into another, then demand and supply would equilibriate very quickly, even if supply lags were long for the provision of new space. In other words, the greater the elasticity of supply, the less the risk is of wasteful over-investment or under-supply. The greater the lags and the lower the substitution possibilities, the greater such risks are.

This analysis shows how conditions of under- and over-supply may occur. But this does not in itself indicate that a case for intervention exists. This must rest on an understanding of why, in a particular situation, incorrect investment decisions are likely and a reasonable expectation that intervention could lead to better ones. As a starting point, it would be necessary to consider how developers formed expectations about future demand levels and on what information they were based. One interesting point about the New York office boom was that it got under way at a time when total office employment in Manhattan had begun to fall, although this was not appreciated at the time. If the risk of over-investment is due largely to imperfect information about the future, and if that information can be supplied by a planning authority, then, as we saw in Chapter 6, there is a clear case for intervention of this minimum kind. However, it seems clear, from the history of the UK as well as the New York office market, that information on the part of both developers and planning authorities has been highly imperfect over the last fifteen years, and the scale location and timing of the growth in demand for space have not been accurately foreseen. In London, for example, the forces making for decentralisation of offices from the central area appear to have been underestimated by nearly all concerned.

Even if information about current trends is perfect, however, and expectations exact, problems may still arise in a market like that for office space due to the nature of supply. If supply is slow to react, because of the need to obtain planning permission, site availability, financing problems or any other factor and if space is provided in large units to exploit economies of scale then there will tend to be periods when there is too little space and too much. This kind of effect is observable in other capital goods industries such as steel, which are highly organised and often subject to control of investment by governments. Such problems may be inherent in a market of this kind and hence intervention may have little or no impact on them. Demand and supply will be in balance only infrequently, i.e. it will only rarely happen that the price obtaining is no more and no less than that needed to produce a satisfactory rate of profit on the investment carried out. The implication for policy is that if planning control on the amount of space supplied is applied so as to restrict increases in supply in periods of boom, then this will tend to be at the price of having too little capacity at a time when demand does pick up. In other words, if demand is variable over time, but subject to an increasing, if irregular upward trend, if supply is unresponsive in the short run to increases in demand through unavoidable lags, and if capacity is installed in large lumps because of economies of scale, then shortages and excesses of supply will inevitably occur. Furthermore, the price of trying to eliminate one may be to exaggerate the other, i.e. if supply is held up in the upswing, this will tend to exaggerate the shortage in the following boom.

These words shortage and excess of supply are worth examining further. Statements are often made about office and industrial floorspace to the effect that there is a shortage or over-supply. If demand increases for space in a given location, and if neither price nor quantity react, there will be a shortage of space. Existing tenants will sit tight and new tenants may not be able to get any space at all. However, if the market is working, then price will tend to go up and some users will have to reduce the amount of space they employ. Shortages are frequently defined, however, without any reference to price: for example, it is common to read that the City of London, or some other centre, is short of 1m square feet of space. This statement may reflect the scale of enquiries passing through estate agents, but these do not reflect the scale of demand at prices which would be necessary to induce the necessary supply. In this sense all that estate agents may be observing is a failure of price and not quantity to adjust, or some mixture of the two. Use of the word shortage implies that only an adjustment in quantity is required. Similarly, where there is an excess of supply in the sense that there is empty space available and unlet, it may not be clear whether this is due to unreasonable expectations about rents on behalf of suppliers or whether there is a need to reduce the quantity of space on the market because the price obtaining at that level of supply is too low to justify any more being provided.

The essential diagnostic need is to determine whether or not shortages or surpluses should be regarded as problems for public policy to solve, or as temporary phenomena with which the market itself can cope, either by price or quantity adjustments. If intervention does seem potentially useful, several issues arise. The first is the cost which intervention can impose: any quantitative control over new investment can only prevent, not induce, investment. Thus such controls may avoid the costs of over-capacity by increasing the risks of under-capacity when demand increases, since it cannot stimulate investment ahead of the perceived need for it.

There is no inherent reason why a more regulated system should not achieve a better phasing of investment than a completely free market. But for the benefits of greater control to outweigh its potential costs would require an accurate monitoring and management of the development process. For example, in the upswing the authority would have to determine the point where new investment should be allowed to proceed again. If it misestimated this, then its efforts would be counterproductive, i.e. it would produce a period of under-supply. But to have a reasonable chance of improving on the free market outcome would require the authority itself acquiring the kind of knowledge of the market on which developers would base their own investment decisions – trends in demand costs, in brief of the economics of the development process itself.

Whether it would be sensible for the authority to attempt to gain this expertise depends to some extent on the reasons why the private market had been failing. Evidence of over-investment in the past, for example, may reflect a widespread misestimation of the growth in demand, not confined to developers alone. If the planning authority is in a better position than the individual developer to estimate demand, then the obvious form of intervention would be to make its estimates public and leave developers to make their own decisions in the light of them. As noted already in section 6.1, the circumstances in which a planning authority is likely to be better informed than developers are limited, but they may have this advantage where the underlying factors are local ones or where the development process as a whole is under their close direction, e.g. in a New Town situation.

Finally, the authority's case for intervention may be based on other considerations. If a commercial development is unsuccessful, it may impose external costs on the public at large. The issues which arise in this case are discussed below in relation to the supply of shopping space.

10.3 Controls over the Scale of Development: Shopping Floor-Space

Planning authorities are typically concerned with both the spatial distribution of shopping floor-space and its total amount. Although these concerns relate, we shall examine the former in Chapter 13. The total amount of space is of interest to the planning authority looking ahead because it wishes to know how much land might be required. Thus it is common to see estimates of floor-space needed based on estimates of population and income growth, modified by such factors as competing locations, tourism, etc. Some average sales per square foot provided can then be used to provide an estimate in physical terms.

Clearly such a forecasting procedure is unlikely to be reliable because each of its components is liable to considerable error, from the basic demographic income estimates to the assumptions implied about the 'technology' of retail distribution, and hence the amount of space likely to be used in future years to market a given quantity of goods. It is not our concern here to criticise forecasting procedures as such nor to imply that there are better ways of estimating how much space will be in use in the future, but we must be clear about the actual ability of authorities to forecast before we can know what significance to attach to 'needs' so defined. If the process of forecasting is something like that sketched out, then it contains the important, if unavoidable, weakness that it does not allow any interaction between the demand for space and the likely price of that space. It is difficult to suggest convincing methods by which this interaction could be incorporated in a forecast but given that it is not done, then such estimates must be treated with due caution when interpreting them as estimates of what actually is likely to be demanded by retailers. This emphasises the point already made in Chapters 4 and 8 that forecasts of needs must not be treated normatively as requirements.

The importance of these points becomes clearer in considering the kind of policies which authorities actually pursue. Apart from concern about the arrangements of shops, the case is often put for limiting the amount of space available for retailing purposes to prevent their becoming 'over-shopped'. If the provision of space were left to the free market, then retailers or would-be retailers would, by their investment decisions, determine the volume of space available. Like other economic units they have to risk capital either directly in their capacity as retailers or as providers of retail space (i.e. as developers). They will only supply extra space if they consider that they can earn money on their investment. They may of course be wrong and wasteful investment may therefore ensue as in any other economic activity. Examples of this in town centre schemes and shopping redevelopments are not infrequent, but they occur also on a minor and less dramatic scale. Whatever the size of the effect, its nature is the same; an opportunity cost attaches itself to the resources embodied in the under-used or unused capacity. One reaction to this possibility is to regulate the amount of space provided to prevent areas becoming 'over-shopped'. What effects is such a policy likely to have?

If the inflow of capital is restricted, and if demand for retail services grows in a given area (assumed for convenience to be self-contained) then, other things equal, the rents or capital values of the stock of existing shops will rise. Ground landlords will be able to extract more rent from their customers; shopkeepers owning their own freehold enjoy a capital gain and increased current income. All this follows the analysis of Chapter 7. Further consequences follow: the turnover per square foot rises; retailers will rearrange the pattern of their activities, perhaps holding lower stocks to create more selling space. They may employ more assistants in a given space to handle the increased custom. If the planning regulations allow it, they may rebuild or extend by exploiting their existing rights to the full.

There are long-term consequences. Those activities which find it difficult to maintain a high throughput, such as specialist suppliers, will tend to be removed as they will not be able to pay the high level of rents which the restriction generates. This may be the small corner shop selling to low-income customers; it may be a greengrocer who finds it difficult to increase throughput or it might be a specialist hardware shop. The net result is a loss of variety and restriction on choice. This may be still further reduced because the entry of new shops is made more difficult, especially for those independents not backed like multiples by ample capital. The risk of a new venture is increased because of the high level of rents. Both the short-run and the long-run costs tend to increase the costs of goods to the consumer as well as lead to a reduction in service levels. These are the consequences of an area being 'under-shopped'.

Where as much capacity is provided as the market demands, then one would expect that more floor-space would be provided than under regulation, that the costs of retailing would be lower and entry of new firms easier. If we assume that free entry will allow new methods of retailing to develop and if these require new premises (or conversion out of other uses), then some of the existing stock of shops may become 'redundant'. It would be dangerous to assume, however, that this itself is necessarily wasteful. Such relatively cheap premises allow the free entry of new uses at fairly low risk. It would also be important to establish the extent to which any space made redundant, or apparently redundant, in the short run would remain so for long. It may be possible to divert it to other uses, e.g. the provision of services which are not normally considered to be a part of retailing activity. Furthermore, there are dangers in attempting to protect investment which has clearly been wrong, e.g. if space is persistently difficult to let. A policy which restricts the development of new space, e.g. in other centres, in order to make such space profitable is potentially a very expensive one in terms of its effect on the urban economy as a whole. It may be better simply to write off the investment, let the space off for social purposes and allow new investment in a better location or of a more suitable type. No matter whose judgement is involved, the 'wrong' amount of space may be provided in the wrong locations and hence wasteful investment might result which may give rise to the social costs resulting from the visual disamenity of empty shops, etc.

What criteria might be used to determine the right volume of investment? To consider this it will be useful to go back to the simple urban model. In that model, land was allocated to retail and other uses under free competition and we later saw that there might be reasons for imposing general land-use control, e.g. on peripheral expansion which raised the price of land to all users. If there are no reasons for treating retailing as a special case, the price of land to retailing should be the same as land in other developed uses. If this is so, then the point at which control should be aimed is one where land values under shopping uses are similar, for equivalent sites, to land values under other uses. If this is not so, then the implication is that external effects arise from retailing uses which it is appropriate to bring home to the retailer in the form of a higher land price. In other words, if the disamenity resulting from having a certain amount of unused capacity were (dis)valued highly then a restrictive policy on shopping space would be appropriate. But the costs of pursuing this objective would be the consequences listed above.

Ordinary market processes would equalise land values but they would only do so as a general tendency. For example, if a large amount of new space were provided by a peripheral supermarket, which proved attractive enough to divert customers away from a central area, then rents in these central areas would fall, although the first effect would probably be felt on profits. That is, firms in the centre may have reduced turnover, but some costs remained fixed due to long-term rental agreements and they may have to lower their prices in order to compete. If the assets they were using were enjoying a monopoly rent, i.e. if they produced values much above the value of land in other uses, then the implication is that new investment in retailing space is justified. That is, no space need go out of use, but the space might be used in different ways, i.e. users may appear in the centre at lower rents, with different kinds of business. These might be service rather than retail establishments, but in either case, no waste of investment resources would have occurred. If problems do arise, they stem essentially from the *scale* of addition to capacity (cf. the discussion of offices) and if these offer significant cost advantages, then the price in terms of underused provision may have to be paid.

In conclusion, let us consider the two basic issues of feasibility and desirability. If a planning authority has the power to refuse permission for new investment in retailing on grounds relating to the capacity available, the question of feasibility may appear not to arise. It does, however, in this sense: that unless the authority can control the nature of goods sold and the efficiency with which existing space is used, then it will be unable, in some circumstances, to prevent spare capacity emerging or capacity going out of use. These effects would emerge from changes in the use of the existing capacity as well as from additions to it, particularly if there was rapid progress occurring in retailing techniques or decline in sales volume.

The analysis of this section cannot prove, one way or other, that control over the supply of new space is desirable. Whether it is or not will depend on the magnitude of the effects identified and the relative weight attached to them. For example, if very great weight is attached to the visual disamenity resulting from over-investment, then the case for limiting additions to capacity is the stronger. But to do this does, as the section has shown, impose costs of other kinds: higher prices as a direct result and possibly other undesirable long-term effects such as loss of variety. The latter point is worth taking a little further as one argument for restricting capacity is to maintain variety, i.e. to prevent certain kinds of shop being driven out of business. It can be shown that both restrictive and non-restrictive policies may lead to loss of variety, depending on the circumstances obtaining. These will of course vary from place to place and from time to time. The following discussion can only indicate the kinds of consideration which are relevant to deciding the issue.

Suppose that the set of shopping facilities judged to provide variety exists at a point in time and that no additional space is allowed. Clearly in this circumstance the entry of new users of space – which can only occur because they hid away existing space from existing users – must upset the desired balance. In these circumstances, the issue is: would the benefits from variety as defined be greater or less than the benefits of having a smaller range of shops competing more closely with each other and offering improvements in terms of some aspect of service quality not available before? Clearly this is in part a distributional issue and in part an efficiency issue. The new shops may employ fewer people and make better use of the existing floor-space – primarily efficiency effects: but they may offer advantages, e.g. lower prices and bulk bargains which are valued relatively more by some sections of the community than others. The price of variety for the one group may be higher prices for the other.

Relax the assumption that the supply of space is fixed. The same result could still follow, if the new firms could so undercut the existing firms that they could not survive at all. However an alternative possibility is that the new firms would create new space for their own requirements and that the existing space would fall in price, sufficient to allow the existing firms to carry on, if at reduced levels of business. Furthermore, as already noted, in these conditions new firms are more likely to be able to come in to extend choice in directions hitherto neglected.

Thus the link between control and variety is a complex one. Two points are worth noting: first, the initial effects of entry of new competition may be misleading; the longer-term position may be different from the short-term. The initial effects of increased competition may be to remove certain kinds of retailer, the longer-run effects may be to encourage the entry of others. Second, prediction of how the market is likely to react depends on an understanding of the general cost conditions under which different kinds of retailer operate, e.g. the scale of the cost advantage offered by new firms and the likely level of demand for different kinds of specialist service. Without this, it is difficult to discriminate between the different possibilities sketched out above.

10.4 The Labour Market

The planning authority may be concerned with the level of demand for labour for the reasons noted in the introduction. In some cases the nature of the choice they may be faced with is clear, e.g. where they are faced with an application for open-cast mining in a site of outstanding natural beauty. In other cases the nature of the issues facing an authority may be less clear. Authorities sometimes pursue policies aimed at broadening the range of job opportunities, at getting the right mix of jobs or policies which aim at damping down the demand for particular kinds of labour, sometimes only in specific locations (the transport reasons for this we consider in Chapter 13). In London, for example, one of the reasons for trying to restrict the growth of office space in the central area was put in terms of excessive labour demand and later on, when demand by employers was tending to fall, policies were put forward which were expressed in the opposite terms. These policy aims raise two kinds of issue; the first is concerned with the practicality of controlling the demand and supply of labour in the way implied above; the second is the underlying logic of policies of this kind. We discuss these issues in turn.

We have already considered in several places the general effects of effective restrictions on the supply of land in general or of land in particular uses. It has been assumed that the authority has been able to impose such policies, i.e. that they have been feasible although not necessarily desirable. Authorities may wish, however, to see given amounts of space provided. For example, they may forecast that jobs in a given sector will increase by x per cent and this implies a y per cent increase in space. Such forecasts, if accurate, would be helpful in decisions within the urban economy on the scale and siting of main services.

Such forecasts may take the form of targets, i.e. desired amounts of space. The prime issue which such normative forecasts raise is that of feasibility: can an authority influence the amount of space to be provided by the private sector, using only the instruments of regulatory planning control? In some conditions it may be able to do so. For example, if there is excess demand for space then some of the pressure might be diverted into channels which the authority favoured. In other words, where firms are very eager to find space and choice is limited, they would be prepared to look at locations which were not ideal from their point of view. The high profits they hope to win would compensate for the disadvantages they perceive. But if the firms concerned have a choice of location, then a policy which limits the extent to which they may choose their most preferred location will not necessarily lead to them going to the locations which suit the planning authority. They may go elsewhere or the existing space may be used much more intensively. Thus, in considering how effective a control can be, the main need is to identify the options open to firms or individuals on which policy is intended to bite.

This is just one instance of a general point about the abilities of a planning authority armed only with powers over the use and allocation of land to manage the economic system within its area. Most of the economic agents are independent decision-makers with considerable freedom of manoeuvre. Their freedom is determined by the alternatives open to them. In choosing what they do they will be responsive to a wide range of phenomena such as production costs, demand and labour supply, only a small fraction of which are controlled by the planning authority. The authority may react to this by making its policies more restrictive in those aıeas where it is able to do so. But this raises two risks: first of increasing the costs of the policy without compensating increase to its effectiveness. Second, it may exacerbate the conflict with other policy objectives. As pointed out in Chapter 7, highly restrictive policies may have undesirable distributional consequences. This conflict will be intensified by more rigorous implementation of restriction.

These points lead us to the second issue, the logic of policies of this kind. There are two assumptions we must examine, first that significant social costs arise, and second that intervention in the market for land can reduce them. There can be no doubt that in some circumstances significant costs do arise. The persistent low level of demand for labour in some parts of most countries indicate this. The costs of the opposite condition are more difficult to identify. The central government typically has an interest in the level of demand for labour in the economy as a whole as part of its concern with national economic management. In this role, it may be concerned about the pressure of demand in particular regions of the country. The local planning authority has a narrower focus and with different considerations in mind. What exactly should these be?

In the simple urban model, any increase in demand for labour in one part of the urban area would lead to a series of reactions. Employers in that sector would have to bid up labour prices, if they wanted to continue; workers living near to the centre of demand working in other locations would tend to change their place of work and those living in the area not actually in the labour market would tend to move out and be replaced by others. These adjustments may range very much from being rapid to being very long-term, but whatever their speed, we can at least point to a large number of adjustment mechanisms within the various markets making up the urban economy.

Despite this, it may not alway be correct to assume that adjustment mechanisms are working. It is often asserted, in relation to parts of the south-east region in the UK or the Paris region of France, that they are persistently overheated. What kind of costs does this sort of situation imply? Where labour markets are very tight, in the sense that there are few registered unemployed, then the price of labour may tend to rise. It may do so in money terms, or through improvements in conditions and hours of work, or such factors as the amount of working space and other inducements. Firms which cannot adjust in these ways will tend to go out of business, because they cannot afford the higher price of labour. This may well give rise to transitional difficulties which are not likely to be serious in conditions of high labour demand. Some firms may find it difficult to adjust for other reasons, e.g. public sector organisations with wage agreements and standardised service conditions which make it difficult for them to apply the adjustment mechanism which the private sector might use. This, if true, will tend to lead to shortages in those industries and reduced levels of service, to which high costs may be attached. These may be more than in proportion to the simple loss of manpower, i.e. a 5 per cent shortfall in labour requirements may lead to a 10 per cent decrease in service levels. This is probably true of transport services.

These two cases must be distinguished. In the case of those firms which are able to adjust their wage or employment policies in the face of pressure on labour supply, the costs are essentially transitional, i.e. the problems they encounter are no more than arise from any change in the relative prices of factors of production. Shortages of labour encourage the substitution of capital and other means of cutting down on labour requirements. Organisations such as nationalised industries may not be able to respond so easily to differences in local conditions, particularly if they are subject to national wage agreements. If this is so, then overheating will impose costs in those areas where it occurs.

The above suggests that when an actual or potential problem of uneven demand for labour is diagnosed, it may be approached in three steps. First, are adjustment processes within the urban economy itself likely to reduce, or diminish, the impact of shortages or over-supply? In other words, are such problems likely to be short-lived, or perhaps never to emerge at all? The importance of this should be seen against some of the procedures which are often used to define a condition of labour shortage, or an emergent shortage. For example, in many planning situations forecasts are made of growth in the demand for labour based on past trends, estimates of labour supply within easy commuting distance taking into account possible changes in participation rates and then an estimate made of the 'gap' with some presumption that this gap ought to be filled. These procedures are very similar to the methods described above for estimating required shopping space. Like them they ignore the likely response of demand to the available supply, and the role of prices – in this case wage levels – in bringing demand and supply into balance.

Because estimates of this kind ignore the existence of any adjustment mechanism within the labour market of the kind referred to, they may lead to diagnoses of the current situation which suggest the existence of non-existent problems. For example, in the London case mentioned above, the pressure on labour costs induced by high levels of demand in turn induced, along with other influences, changes in the location of employment away from the central area. It is not easy to make better forecasts; the need therefore is to avoid misinterpreting the figures which are produced by the procedures outlined above.

The second step is to consider whether the efficiency of the existing adjustment processes can be improved, e.g. by increasing mobility through the housing stock or by increasing occupational mobility. Improvements in either of these would obviously tend to increase the efficiency of the kind of processes which were discussed above in relation to the simple urban model. Thirdly, if a problem seems likely to remain, the final question to consider is the contribution of spatial planning policies to their solution. This question is too large to go into in detail here. The problems identified at regional level or in the inner parts of the conurbations stem from a wide variety of causes, including trends in the national economy, educational provision and racial and other forms of discrimination. Problems within labour markets are likely to require action on all these and other fronts. In the light of the discussion above, it seems obvious that while policies affecting the spatial distribution of demand for and supply of labour may be required, the contribution of policy instruments based on regulation of land supply seems likely to be small. As the Layfield Panel commented on GLC policy:

> not sufficient is known about the relationship of labour demand and supply in the future, nor about the effects of floor space controls on employment, to enable any person to say whether such policies are reasonable, realistic, or would have predictable results.

11 LAND-USE CONTROLS AND HOUSING

This chapter will consider some of the interrelationships between land-use planning and housing. These are so extensive that there is not sufficient space to consider all of them, nor can a book primarily devoted to land-use planning consider housing policy itself very deeply. There is simply too much of it. This chapter, therefore, will analyse only some of the ways in which policy on land-use influences the housing sector and shapes the conditions within which housing policy must operate. Following the pattern set earlier, it will assume a planning authority whose powers do not correspond to that in any particular institutional setting, but examples will be used to indicate the relevance of the analysis to actual policy situations. We must begin, however, by indicating the significance of housing within the urban economy.

People value houses not simply because of the shelter or accommodation they provide but also because of such factors as accessibility to schools, shops and jobs, the quality of the physical environment in its immediate vicinity, the proximity of other dwellings, the extent of traffic noise, the general appearance of the surroundings. Land-use planning has in general more influence on these factors than on the housing structures themselves on which, particularly in the public sector, housing policies have the greatest influence. In the private sector, however, the distinction is, as we shall see, not so easy to draw.

Housing does not give rise solely to benefits. It also imposes external costs, primarily through the losses of amenity which housing in undeveloped areas gives rise to, with which land-use planning must deal. But there may also be problems in relation to urban infrastructure due to pricing failures of the kind analysed in Chapters 4 and 9. If this is at or near capacity, additional development may impose congestion costs and reduce existing service standards.

In the UK in particular, planning controls have been directed towards avoiding or reducing the external costs which developers and their clients would impose if housing could be located freely. Restrictions on building in many agricultural areas, National Parks, and areas of outstanding natural beauty clearly come into this category. The issues here are typically very straightforward. Because the open country is not a marketed commodity, there are no market disincentives to discourage building operations within it. Developers do not, therefore, have to meet the full costs of what they do.

This chapter will examine a number of other ways in which the interests of suppliers of housing services may diverge from the social interest. The first part of the chapter considers policies towards the intensity or density on development, which directly concern the use of land. We start with the problem of design control, beginning with the individual housing development and the development of new estates. The following section goes on to consider strategic controls over housing within both private and public sector. Finally, the influence of land-use controls over the process of urban renewal is analysed. The aim here is to relate the description of the urban renewal process in Chapter 3 with the observed problems in real life.

11.1 The Supply of New Housing

Planning authorities may exercise very detailed control over the design and precise siting of new or redeveloped housing. For example, it is common to find in-fill development required to abide by building and site lines, or to adopt external features which fit in with the appearance of the existing buildings, even in areas which are not the subject of conservation orders. Typically the density at which a site may be used is specified or controlled within a range. Controls over new estate development are frequently of the same kind, but may go further by specifying the kind of housing and its layout as well as its external appearance. In addition, some authorities exercise very broad strategic controls over the intensity with which land may be used for housing, e.g. by specifying plot ratios or density limits, both in the form of maxima and minima which apply to large tracts of the area for which they are responsible.

The justification for controls of these kinds may be expressed in various terms: to promote good design or to prevent the wasteful use of land and infrastructure. This section will analyse examples of these policies using the concepts introduced in the earlier chapters with the aim, as in the previous chapter, of bringing out the economic issues which underlie them and which are typically implicit rather than explicit when such policies are exercised. We begin with a very simple case and then proceed to examples of policies with a rather wider application up to the level of the urban area as a whole.

Under British planning legislation, the individual householder wishing to modify his house, for example by building an extension, requires permission to do so from the planning authority, unless it is less than a certain size. The issues in a single case of this kind are clear and straightforward. They centre round the possibility that the proposed development will give rise to external costs to neighbours and passers-by. These costs, such as loss of daylight, visual disamenity, loss of view, will normally be uncompensated, since the applicant will rarely provide compensation for any loss of amenity he causes. In principle, as we saw in Chapter 6, it might be possible to devise a system under which compensation was paid to immediate neighbours. Each neighbour affected by the extension could be individually compensated on the basis of a bilateral bargain, which would leave no party feeling worse off after the extension had been built. If such a procedure were practical in relation to neighbours – and there clearly would be problems in defining who was a relevant neighbour – it would not cope with the interests of passers-by. They, being in advance an unknown quantity, would not be able to claim compensation for any loss. The planning authority in this instance must stand proxy for such passers-by and weigh up the potential benefit to the individual from his extension against the losses they may experience.

The same kind of analysis underlies other cases; for example, a new development may be expected to give rise to extra traffic, which might impose delays on existing flows. These external costs, like those of loss of visual amenity, would also not be met by those giving rise to them. This divergence between social and private costs arises because of pricing failures and when these are uncorrected, the private and social interest persistently diverge. The implications, however, go somewhat wider than the individual application for planning permission. If the planning authority operates a discretionary control on a case-by-case system, it is faced in each case with the need to make a very difficult judgement. Although the effects may be easy to see, in any individual case it must weigh together very disparate items of private and social cost and benefit, including some, such as loss of visual amenity, which are very difficult to value. A more fundamental problem remains. However efficiently it does this task, it can only decide the cases which are put to it. It cannot, unless the authority is itself responsible for all the development process, provide for housing to be put where the private and social interest conflict least, i.e. where the net social benefit from additional housing is greatest.

We assume a demand for additional housing space which arises from the preferences of individuals and their income level. The total social costs of meeting this demand will vary. If building costs do not vary with location, then developers will seek out those sites where the price obtainable for extra housing units is greatest, i.e. those sites which have the right balance between accessibility and amenity for the part of the market being served. These locations may not, however, coincide with those locations where external costs to existing house-owners and to the public at large are at a minimum and will persistently tend not to in the absence of a fiscal system of the kind outlined in Chapter 7. If such a system were in force, it would alter the locational choice of developers, i.e. if they had to pay a disamenity tax in one area and not in another, they may be persuaded by this tax to go to the latter area. The authority may nevertheless still allow housing to take place in the first area on the legitimate ground that the costs of doing so are outweighed by the benefits. But these would not be the sites where the net social benefit was greatest.

There is an important implication. If we assume that the authority is behaving rationally in the sense defined in Chapter 5 and allowing housing development up to the point where marginal costs and marginal social benefit are equal, then it follows that, in the circumstances just analysed, housing supply is restricted below what it need be. The private benefit is greater in the first area than in the second. However, the social benefit position is the converse. If the developer makes an application for development in what is to him the best area he will be allowed fewer units than could be allowed in the second while still observing the marginal rules.

The case just considered is one example of the point made in Chapter 7, that regulatory controls may be successful in ruling out extreme outcomes, i.e. development where social cost outweighs social benefit, but they will not necessarily lead development in the best overall direction since they do not alter the motivation of developers or the information on which developers work. The costs, i.e. the benefits lost because of this weakness, are the difference between the outcome in the situation which actually results and that which could in principle have been reached if better policy instruments had been available.

The next kind of case we will consider, which also centres on divergence between private and social cost, is that of design guides. These may be laid down to achieve two kinds of objective: first, to modify the external costs of development and second, to regulate the provision of such public goods as road and verge spaces. The economic issues in the latter case are straightforward enough. The developer may be able to recoup in terms of higher prices for his houses some of the costs of road space or open space provision, but this will not be possible in respect of benefits enjoyed by non-residents. The practical problem is to determine the point where costs of provision exceed benefits and hence where any regulatory control should be set.

The basic issue involved in the treatment of external costs has already been discussed in earlier chapters – whether the standard is set at the level which achieves the right balance between private interest – in this case those paying for the houses – and the social interest – all those who may be involved as visitors or passers-by. Quality controls only have point if they raise the level above what it would otherwise have been, i.e. if they impose costs on house purchasers. To the extent that such controls bite on external features and aspects of layout, they cannot rest on the kinds of arguments considered in Chapter 6 for building regulations, i.e. the lack of technical competence of most house purchasers and the cost of acquiring that competence, since these items may be readily appreciated, and they are much more questions of taste than such fundamentals as damp courses. Such controls may be founded on rather different arguments, such as the need to consider future generations by building to standards which will last, or the need to protect the interests of current house purchasers from too low a quality product. These are all paternalistic justifications.

Here we are not concerned with assessing the strength of the arguments for specific regulations but rather with the general implications of controls of this kind. By laying down rules on the kinds of housing which may be supplied (or at least the external features of that housing) and the detailed densities at which it may be built, planning authorities may, if their influence is general in this respect, have an important influence on the housing market as a whole. By influencing the kind of new housing which may be added to the stock and in particular the price at which it may be supplied, they influence indirectly the demands placed upon the existing stock of housing. For example, if only 'high-quality' developments are permitted, those unable to afford them will be diverted to the existing stock of housing. The result of this depends on the situation in the area concerned, but it is easy to envisage circumstances where the indirect costs of such a policy were serious, for example, where the resulting pressure on the housing stock led to increased housing costs for the rest of the population. Clearly the importance of these effects depends on the scale of the costs which design standards impose and the rigour with which certain kinds of housing are excluded. In many cases their effects may be trivial. But there is evidence from American studies that their effects may be considerable and that they have unfavourable distributional consequences by ruling out certain groups from home ownership.

A number of recent studies have examined the implications of the zoning policies of some American planning authorities by which large areas of land are zoned for low-density dwellings and little land or no new land zoned for higher-density units. Under certain housing demand conditions the effect of this kind of policy can be to increase housing costs for those wanting small or relatively cheap housing, a group which includes the poorer sections of the community. Typically the low-density plots will only be built on with dwellings of which the structures themselves are expensive and hence out of reach of most of the population. The result is that the effective demand for housing of the remainder of the population is concentrated on those parcels of land on which higher-density dwellings can be built. The outcome is higher land prices than those obtaining for the richer members of the community, a result which would not occur under free market conditions.

Within the simple urban model, it will be recalled, land would have the same value to any use category, because there were no obstacles to it being moved from one land use to another. The same would hold for housing uses, for any given location. No studies comparable to the American work have been done in the UK, but nevertheless it is common in many situations for the land value even within housing use to depend on the nature of the permission which is given. In the simple urban model, the developer would know what he could sell a given category of house for, and on the basis of his expected construction and financing costs he would make a bid for a piece of land becoming ripe for development. He would be successful (a) if he was more efficient than his competitors and hence his costs were lower – in this case he would enjoy a supernormal profit, and (b) if the type of building he was proposing was the one which earned the highest return. If he was proposing to build the wrong kind of dwelling, then his bid would be exceeded by some other builder who had made a better estimate of the nature of the demand for new housing and had estimated correctly which dwellings were in short supply.

The building industry may not behave precisely in line with these assumptions. Nevertheless, if different values emerge for different kinds of housing use, and if this is sustained over a long period of time by virtue of the policies of a planning authority, then the implication would be that the planning authority was making available more land for one type of house than the market would ideally want and less of another. This does not by itself indicate one way or another that the policy is incorrect, but it suggests a *prima facie* case that it is not. There are however circumstances where a differential would be justified.

To see why, let us again go back to the simple urban model and recall the analysis in Chapter 7 of the effects of average cost pricing among statutory undertakers and other suppliers of services complementary to housing. Let us assume – and the evidence does suggest this – that the costs of providing these services at different densities are U-shaped, i.e. the costs are very high per unit at lower densities, fall at average densities and then rise again. In the absence of price signals to the developer about the significance of these costs there would be no presumption that the right balance between private benefit and public costs was reached. Let us assume, contrary to the example above, that the bulk of demand was for low-density dwellings. In the absencc of improved pricing to developers there would in this case be an argument for restricting land supply to low-density uses, until the price differential between low- and medium-density land equalled the differential cost of infrastructure, for at that point those still willing to pay the higher price would be indicating that they would be prepared to meet the full public costs of their choice. The distributional implications – i.e. the increased surplus is reaped by some landowners as a result of the restriction on land supply – may not be welcome. But they may be no less desirable than the situation, typical in many parts of the US, where low-density development has been taken much beyond the point where costs of servicing are at a minimum. This kind of argument would also apply to any other costs which were correlated with density and which were not reflected in prices paid by developers and their clients.

We now turn to a rather broader issue of urban planning centred on density of housing. In some large metropolitan areas, density zones have been established. In some cases this policy suffers from the same problems as the zoning practices just analysed, i.e. it represents an *a priori* judgement of the scale of the housing to be supplied in different size and price brackets which is unrelated to the likely scale and pattern of effective demand for that housing. The result may be differences in land prices between different categories of use which have no policy justification. In London, a rather different approach was adopted of a more flexible nature which suggested three concentric rings which set maximum densities, according to distance from the core. In other words, the plan proposal followed broadly the pattern which would be expected from the simple urban model, although the limits were not set on the basis of any such model empirically calibrated for the London situation. Consequently there would be no reason to expect that the pattern of housing provision allowed would bear a close relationship to what people might be prepared to pay for.

Chapter 3 showed how in the simple urban model, developers would decide densities in relation to the costs of building on the one hand and the revenue to be earned on the other. Such calculations might not, as noted already, take into account all the relevant costs falling on the public sector and on individuals and if such costs increased rapidly with density, or there was a local shortage of infrastructure, then a case for control could be made similar to that already discussed, i.e. in terms of external costs and pricing failure.

In the context of a changing metropolitan area, however, a rather different argument may be relevant. Decisions on density may be taken at a point in time but have implications for subsequent periods. The right density to build at, as we saw earlier, is a function of expected changes in land values and preferences for different kinds of housing, so that a correct decision depends on having the right set of expectations about the future. Thus it might be argued that there was a need for a limit at both the upper and lower bounds to ensure that developers did not take wrong decisions which subsequently became a liability to the individuals in the buildings concerned. Intervention of this kind might be justified on two grounds. First, the developer might be thought to be less well informed about the future than the planning authority. Second, it could be argued that the developer's time horizon is much shorter than the authority's, so he disregards certain future costs which the authority would wish to take into account.

If these arguments were not applied, then in the absence of other externality problems there is no ground for modifying a development proposal on grounds of excessive density. If it proved to be excessive as far as purchasers were concerned, its capital value would fall and the developer or his client would bear the consequences. The argument is clearly different in the public sector, since tenants in the public sector exercise less freedom of choice than do house- or flat-buyers in the private. Although the assumption made in the simple urban model that housing satisfaction decreases with density does reflect the bulk of the empirical evidence, this does not rule out the possibility that some people prefer high to low density or that there are people who, while preferring low density, nevertheless are prepared to trade it off against reduced travel costs which a high-density inner-city location can offer them in a large metropolitan area. Thus, any density limit applied generally to housing in the inner parts of such an area would impose costs on such people if it reduced the effective supply of high accessibility accommodation. These costs would have to be weighed against the potential benefits under any of the heads considered above.

The arguments for a minimum density may be expressed in terms of land saving. What this means, in the framework of the arguments used here, is that a decision to develop below the set limit would be proved wrong. The grounds for this view would be, first, an expectation that land within the area would grow relatively in value as population and/or income grow and with it the effective demand for space and, second, that the developers concerned were not allowing for this properly. A good example is the low-density suburban developments common in England between the wars which were carried out at densities close to American or Australian levels and which now seem to have been prodigal of land. Some of these within those parts of south-east England where land pressures have been most severe have already been demolished or their gardens given over to new housing. If foresight had been perfect, it may have been beneficial not to have permitted such developments and thus saved the high costs of demolition and rebuilding of houses which were structurally sound. Even so, the case is not clear-cut since the earlier low-density development provided benefits to the occupiers some thirty to forty years before being redeveloped.

Finally, the question of the definition of density must be considered. Various definitions have been suggested and are in common use: dwelling units per acre, habitable rooms per acre, bedspaces per acre, square footage of building or total cube. None of these measures are of direct significance in themselves. They are important only when they correlate with features which relate to the arguments used above. Empirically very little work has been done to establish such relationships and *prima facie* it is not very easy to see which way they might go.

Taking purely the externality argument for control, it is clear that each of the various definitions has some validity because they each might be correlated with some externality. Square footage or cube is correlated with bulk and hence with visual amenity in the broad sense – clearly it says nothing about detailed design. Number of dwellings will be correlated with persons living on a site and accordingly with the use of infrastructure and other facilities. However it is obvious that the correlation may be highly imperfect. Suppose for example that the use of infrastructure is related to income and that income is inversely related to density. Then it is possible that more strain may be put on local facilities by a site developed at low rather than high density.

Quite generally, it is clear that the relationship between density, however defined, and external costs is unlikely to be close. First, because different costs will be related to the different measures in different ways, and second because the nature and scale of these costs will vary over time as the use to which the buildings are put alters. They may be taken over by different income or socio-economic groups and as a result the numbers of individuals and their behaviour radically alter. There is no way in which a system of control which applies only at the point of construction can deal with changes of this kind.

The case for intervention in the low-density case like this rests on the assumption that the planning authority is better placed than the developer or his client to make judgements about the future in respect both of individual preferences and the price of land. The same is true of the last kind of planning control to be considered in the present section, that of the control over the release of land to be developed from agricultural use. Such controls may take the form of Green Belts, which have been adopted in a number of parts of the UK and many other cities, or it may simply take the form of restrictive land release policies which ensure that the price of urbanised land is much higher than non-urbanised land.

We have already seen that a control of this kind may be used as a proxy for pricing failure for infrastructure services. If these services were charged for properly, then the price of development land would fall in those areas where costs of provision were above average cost prices and vice versa. Developers would reflect these costs in their bid for land and the residual land price would be squeezed in the former case and allowed to increase in the latter. We have also noted some other reasons why the price of land for housing might be kept above agricultural value, e.g. the fact that the countryside is a public good, which cannot be valued directly. In other words housing in general, or in particular cases, might be attributed an external cost. If this is so, then the aim of policy must be, as with quality regulations, to get the balance right between benefits experienced through housing services and benefits experienced through countryside. As we note in more detail below, the implicit price placed on these latter benefits can be very high. In much of England, for example, land prices are much in excess of the level which can be justified in terms of infrastructure alone.

In particular cities, especially those with Green Belts, the arguments for restrictive land release policies are more complex than this. In some cases such policies are justified in terms of scale of the outward spread of the urban area concerned and the resultant distancing of the population from countryside. In other cases the argument is put in terms of the impact of development on the nature of the city concerned, e.g. a university town like Oxford or rural communities. These are all examples of externality-type arguments and pricing failure, i.e. the individual seeking to live at the edge of one of these areas is not in a position to take into account the consequences of his actions for those already living in them. Marginal social cost is in excess of marginal private cost.

If the objectives of a restrictive land release policy are accepted then the analytic task is to identify what costs are associated with pursuing them. Consider the implications of a policy of this kind. The most obvious effect is an increase in the price of land to developed uses – among them housing – which would, as the analysis of Chapter 7 has already demonstrated, set off the expected economising reactions. It is London and the south-east of England, for example, where land values and densities are highest and where the pressures for infill and redevelopment of low-density sites are greatest.

Other uses of land would also be affected. The price of locally produced services would tend to rise as a direct result of higher land prices and as an indirect effect of the implications of the restrictive policy for the labour market. The extent of the latter effects would depend critically on the behaviour of employers. If, in spite of pressures on land and labour costs, the attractions of the area concerned as a job location remained, then the costs of the restrictive policy could be very high. The unwillingness of firms to relocate would mean that the demand for labour in the area was highly inelastic and hence that the labour market did not tend to adjust in a way favourable to avoiding the burden of the restriction. In this case, the adjustments would have to take place in housing markets with the consequences already mentioned: higher occupancy rates and higher densities and longer commuting trips of workers brought in from outlying areas. Some costs, particularly those arising from generally higher price levels, would tend to fall hardest on those whose incomes did not, for institutional or other reasons, adjust to the particular local situation obtaining. Such groups would suffer a loss of real income since they would face higher prices, but not enjoy higher money incomes.

The precise chain of consequences can only be unravelled in a particular situation and then only with difficulty. To try to examine them in detail would take us too far from the purposes of this chapter. But one more issue does need examining: how, if a restrictive land release policy is in operation, should it be used in conjunction with density controls within the area concerned?

The economic issue involved is this: how can an efficient combination of these controls be defined? As noted, density controls within the urban economy impose costs in order to attain certain benefits. If densities are reduced below what the market would produce given the price set by the control on peripheral development, then there is a *prima facie* case that the controls were mutually inconsistent. If upper-density limits were enforced rigidly, and if these limits did bite, then the inconsistency would be clear. The right balance between relaxing the density control or relaxing more peripheral land should be determined by considering the social benefits attached to each policy and the costs consequent on achieving them. Thus it would be irrational to impose large costs on housing via restrictive land release policies and at the same time restrict the supply of housing within the development area for benefits of a much lower order. If policy is in equilibrium, benefits of more land release at the periphery will equal the social costs of releasing it. The same should be true at the intensive margin, i.e. within the urban area itself.

11.2 Urban Renewal

Within the simple urban economy developed in Chapter 3, the process of renewal is straightforward. As structures grow old and their physical quality declines, they are renewed as soon as there is a net profit to be gained from doing so. If none of the factors such as income, building and transport costs which determine the nature of the city structure changed, then the urban fabric would be renewed and replaced in essentially the same form, in the way that a bus or lorry operator will need from time to time to replace his vehicles as they grow old and need increasing amounts of repairs. For example, in the urban economy the gradual renewal and replacement of buildings in the commercial core is seen in most urban areas. Where cities have grown and where conditions have changed, then the scale and rate of physical renewal will be modified. A change in retailing techniques and the price of labour relative to other prices will tend to lead to substitution of capital for labour in the retailing process through the building of large self-service units. Changes in office technology and the need with rising incomes to give workers better working conditions leads to refitting of old offices and the building of new. A change in the relative attractiveness of the older locations in relation to the new will influence the form of redevelopment. If demand has risen, densities will tend to rise to take advantage of the changed demand conditions and vice versa.

Within the simple urban model, the same kind of changes and additions to the housing stock would also take place. If incomes, preferences and technology remained constant, the housing stock would be renewed and replaced as it wore out, like the rest of the urban capital stock. If, however, some of the factors had changed since the original buildings were put up, then they would not be simply replaced like for like. Suppose that the urban economy had grown faster than anticipated in spatial extent because developers as a whole had underestimated the rate at which with rising incomes people would prefer to have more space. If this occurred, the capital stock in the inner parts of the city would be inappropriate to the new urban structure. The rents to be earned from it would fall rapidly, more rapidly than anticipated when the buildings were originally built. They would tend to be replaced by housing which in terms of the new income and preference combination was more profitable or they would be rehabilitated to the same effect. Alternatively, suppose that the city had grown faster than anticipated in terms of central employment and that this had created much greater than anticipated pressure on inner urban land. The value of the accessibility of the near-in sites would, in these circumstances, rise to unanticipated levels and there would be a tendency for buildings to be replaced or added to in order to make better use of the sites. Thus in these conditions, the conversion of large units into numerous small units would be common, buildings on low-density sites would be demolished while still physically fit to allow their land area to be better utilised and, where appropriate, buildings would have storeys added to them. Other combinations of circumstances could produce similar results. For example, the outward expansion of some cities – London and Sydney are two examples – has been such that the balance of attractiveness of peripheral and central locations has altered sufficiently for some groups of the population for them to be induced to return to inner locations – the so-called gentrification phenomenon.

This brief discussion is simply an elaboration of the discussion in Chapter 3 of the behaviour of developers and workers to allow for the fact that the relative value attached to different geographical parts of the urban economy will change through time as the income and technology used within it changes. The processes described are typical market adjustment processes, responding to the changes in relative prices which result from the underlying economic factors described. Within the model, the price of land is the main 'signal' to developers as to the kind of redevelopment appropriate for sites within the existing urban fabric. But as we noted in Chapter 9, other price signals would also be relevant, in particular the price of infrastructure. Thus if inner-area sites fell in relative value in accessibility terms they might retain advantages in terms of ancillary infrastructure development costs. In any case the land price would fall until some user was found for the sites concerned. Developers in this situation could offer a variety of housing types, e.g. low cost at moderate density suitable for single-person households or high-cost units involving the privatisation of open space on the lines discussed in Chapter 6.

These various reactions within the simple urban economy do reflect activities which are observable in the housing stock of most large cities. Nevertheless, the process of urban renewal is scarcely as smooth or effective as the discussion has tended to suggest. Typically, it is the part of the urban economy which commands most attention from public policy. Here we will try to bring out, using the analysis developed earlier, some of the reasons why the process of housing renewal may not take place smoothly or may not take place at all.

The main focus of the discussion will be on the information facing the developers, or householder, considering whether or not to invest in a redevelopment or renewal scheme. The relevant information is of two kinds: first, a set of expectations about the future development of the urban area as a whole and the particular part of it where the development concerned may take place and second, the prices of land, services, etc., which are needed for a calculation of profitability.

Take, for example, a piece of old industrial land near to the city centre, which has become derelict as the demand for industrial activity in such a location has disappeared. Within the assumptions of the simple urban model this land, assuming away possible extensions of the commercial core, would be used for housing, by virtue of the accessibility advantages to be derived from it. However, it is a commonplace observation that this frequently does not take place. There are various reasons why this should be so.

One point we have already noted – the possibility that the pricing of ancillary services such as main services and other items of infrastructure may distort the choice facing the developer. If, to take the extreme case, the inner-area site required no further expenditure of this kind, but all new sites did, and if such costs did not fall upon the developer, then it would not be surprising to find some sites not being developed at all. The same kind of result could obtain where charges were averaged and failed to reflect local variations in cost; for example, suppose that it required very little additional expenditure to service the inner-area sites, e.g. some minor renewals, then the choice of site would be biased in the same way.

The next point arises from the nature of the derelict site itself. Typically, even if it does not require services, it will require clearance. Where pressures on land are intense, then these costs can be met and a profitable development still take place. But where pressures on land are less urgent, and hence the appropriate scale of development less rather than more dense, then the cost of clearance will weigh heavily in the balance of financial advantage. It will be a fixed overhead to be spread over a small number of units. Where the costs of clearance are high enough land values may be negative, i.e. developers would have to be paid to build on them.

In terms of our earlier analysis, this situation arises from a pricing failure. When planning permissions are given for quarrying or mining, conditions may be attached which require the restoration of the land to its pre-use condition. The effect of a condition of this kind is to make the activity bear the full costs it gives rise to, in this case the loss of countryside amenity. Typically, however, industrial operations have not been subject to conditions of this kind so that the firms concerned, when they move, or go out of business, are able to impose costs on society as a whole.

This pricing failure has wider implications as it affects neighbouring sites as well, with the familiar result that areas of cities exist where no development in the private sector will take place, because other sites will be available which offer greater returns. Only in extreme cases will the benefits of accessibility be such as to outweigh the adverse environmental conditions. Some parts of inner East London, for example, have attracted private investment capital, but such examples are rare, particularly in the larger provincial cities. The reason is obvious: that in nearly all cases a better combination of environment and accessibility can be provided peripherally or through redevelopment further out at the prices obtaining. This is likely to be true in all but the largest cities, in which, for some people at least, the accessibility advantages may be sufficient inducement to locate in the inner city.

In addition to pricing failures, there are problems of information. One simple example is that of the individual considering whether or not to improve his house in an area of relatively old housing which requires expenditure if it is not to become completely dilapidated. Let us assume that all the houses are owner-occupied. The individual may be very attached to his house and to the area and he may decide therefore to go ahead, make improvements and to paint and renovate the exterior of his dwelling. He may feel, however, that it is not worth his while to do so because others will not follow suit. If they do not follow, then the area will continue to decline in value and his investment will be wasted. He is in the prisoner's dilemma introduced in Chapter 4. If he does take the risk, others may join in and the total area may be renewed by its own efforts without policy intervention. But equally he might not.

His decision will be affected by the behaviour of the planning authority itself. In areas of renewal, the authority may itself be active, but it may not make its intentions clear. The result may be planning blight, i.e. individuals who may consider investing in such areas will be unwilling to do so because the uncertainty attached to the investment is too great. The phenomenon of planning blight reflects a situation where the information being given by the authority is, in terms of market response, counter-productive. As noted in Chapter 4, where uncertainty is acute, markets will tend not to respond to such price signals as do exist. Individuals will 'wait and see' and those whose capital is spatially mobile will go elsewhere, unless the gains they anticipate are too enormous to make them risk making a wrong investment decision. The bulk of housing renewal will not present this kind of opportunity. Thus to obtain a market response – from individuals or firms – a clear-cut set of expectations either of a specific intervention by the authority or a complete withdrawal from intervention is likely to be most productive.

A large number of policy instruments have been used by government to influence the urban renewal process, including direct intervention by means of public housing schemes. The full range of these cannot be examined here, but some of the policy implications of the analysis above are worth bringing out. First, we should note the influence of land release policy on the balance of advantage between inner and outer locations. As noted above, where the inner area is subject to Green Belt or similar controls, land values will tend to be higher than those produced by a free land market and the rent or land value structure of the urban area, its densities, etc., will tend to be different. As noted already, the price of land which emerges at the margin from such controls could in principle be set to express the full social costs of further land release, not simply loss of amenity and agricultural land but also the public sector costs associated with making the land available.

Second, there is a clear role for a planning authority in the provision of information, or a set of expectations about the future which will allow private markets to work efficiently. The interesting question is how such information is to be conveyed in a manner which is sufficiently convincing to induce the required response, i.e. does not have a blighting effect because it is convincing enough to be partly believed, but not convincing enough to be acted on. Chapter 6 pointed out that individuals may have an advantage over the planning authority in some matters. In this context they are more likely to trust their own immediate perception of what is going on in their area than a broad analysis of the forces at work in the urban area concerned, or general statements of policy intent about the need for an inner-area renewal, the speed and the form of which will affect crucially the balance of advantage to individuals. Hence they require, if their confidence is to be created, statements which relate to their particular area.

The most tangible way of giving information about the future is to make investments which imply a belief that the area concerned does have a reasonable expectation of further effective life. This implies a concentration on those items of physical environment of a public goods nature which individual initiative is unable to supply but which is complementary to it. How important this is depends very much on the form of the private activity. For example, in some circumstances private developers will 'bring their environment with them' by privatising such amenities as open space, in the way described in Chapter 4. In others, it would be necessary to spend on environmental features to attract private investment.

Recent UK approaches to urban renewal in the private sector have tended to favour an area approach, in which local authority action in terms of subsidy and environmental treatment is concentrated into particular parts of the areas needing rehabilitation. Such an approach may have cost advantages, e.g. there may be economies of scale in the execution of the physical works involved, but the prime justification for this approach is that it provides a clear framework of expectations for individuals living in the areas concerned that the investment they make will have a reasonable opportunity of yielding a return. The 1974 Housing Act which embodies this approach has a large number of features which cannot be examined here. Leaving aside its particular provisions, it is worth considering the issues involved in this kind of concentration in terms of the earlier analysis. The key issue is whether the gain from firming up expectations in the particular areas concerned outweigh the losses which might occur in other areas which were not subject to that treatment. Various possibilities exist. At one extreme, there might exist a given number of people prepared to invest in renewal, whose locational decisions would be affected by an area-based policy, i.e. they would seek to locate in the areas concerned because of the relative security they offered over and above any special financial advantages which might be offered. The net effect would be a spatial redirection of the same basic level of activity, plus the loss of any effects their actions may have had to other areas. Suppose, for example, that in an unconstrained situation they would have carried out improvements in various parts of the urban area concerned. In some circumstances they may all have perished as lonely pioneers, but in others they might have induced a much wider response through taking the risks inherent in the prisoner's dilemma situation.

In the former set of circumstances, a policy of concentration might produce an additional response. In the latter, it would reduce the level of activity below what would have occurred anyway. To discriminate between these possibilities requires an understanding of the determinants of improvement activity in the area concerned, and of the response of individuals to different patterns of market behaviour, and to different policy instruments. Without these, the contribution of policy remains uncertain, both in advance and after its introduction. In the latter case, recalling the point first made in Chapter 5, the base-line against which policy is to be judged cannot confidently be estimated.

The general issue which underlies this discussion is that within the mixed economy framework, the most appropriate policy instruments depend on the nature of the market forces at work within the area concerned. How these operate is affected by the land-use policies applying in the area, but these are unlikely to constrain developers' choices, whether these are individuals or companies, very precisely. Consequently, the degree to which the authority can influence their pattern of activity is limited. Further, the previous paragraph has suggested that even when policies appear effective, their main result may have been to redistribute spatially a level of activity which would in any case have taken place. The net benefits of intervention in these circumstances would be small or negative. This does not in itself prove that intervention cannot improve the renewal process but it does suggest that care is required in attributing benefits to it.

11.3 Density Controls: The London Case

The recent enquiry on the Greater London Development Plan is one of the few recent examples of an explicit consideration at strategic level of the case for specific density limits – minimum and maximum. The draft Written Statement stated that:

> Except in special circumstances, the net density of new developments designed for family living should fall within the range 70-140 habitable rooms per acre and the desire of families for a house with its own private garden space should be met as far as possible. For other types of new development not intended for family living, higher densities may be suitable particularly in Central London and at strategic centres and other exceptional sites where the accessibility

> of transport and other local facilities is specially advantageous. Special care should be taken wherever net densities exceed 140 habitable rooms per acre to see that the types of dwelling are suitable, that shops, open space and other necessities are close at hand, and that traffic conditions and access arrangements allow for the services that will be needed.

As the Layfield Panel commented, the GLC did not explain the technical basis on which this very wide range was chosen, but nevertheless the committee went on to propose a narrower band allowing exceptions in a number of circumstances, i.e. where

> (a) the site is close to transport interchanges, transport nodal points, or termini with appropriate capacity, or to growth centres or concentrations of employment;
> (b) full regard has been taken to the good design of the development, the character of the surroundings, and especially the presence of permanent open space;
> (c) the characteristics of the proposed inhabitants of the development are such that they will not suffer from poor living conditions;
> (d) families with children are to be housed in the development, good living conditions, including open space integral to the dwellings or the scheme proposed, can be provided.

The lower limit had similarly to be subject to certain exceptions, in the following circumstances:

> (a) those where there are exceptionally strong environmental reasons for lower densities, e.g. to preserve the appearance of the wooded slopes of Sydenham Hill;
> (b) those where the authority has taken a clear decision that the land is to be developed for private housing, and is convinced that there is no market for housing at a density of 70 rooms per acre, so that if it insists on such a density, the land will not be developed;
> (c) those where the size and characteristics of the site are such that to insist on a density of 70 rooms per acre would mean either an environmentally unattractive or very expensive scheme.

As a final point, it should be noted that the Panel thought that the old concentric circles of density rings should be abandoned and a uniform density applied, subject to the above exceptions.

These recommendations have been the subject of extensive comment and it is not proposed here to rehearse all the relevant arguments in full, but merely to bring out some of the points relating to our earlier discussion. Several are worth noting. First, although the policy is put forward in the form of defined upper and lower limits, i.e. in the forms of constraints or standards, a fairly detailed attempt is made to indicate where exceptions should be allowed according to the local circumstances. These have the effect of diminishing the strategic recommendation and placing the emphasis on the considerations to be taken into account at the level of the individual application for planning permission.

Second,at several points, acknowledgement is made that the dwellings supplied to the rules suggested have to be sold in markets and hence if the rules do not allow the product to be marketed, they must be adapted to allow it.

Third, the measure of density, e.g. habitable rooms per acre, is clearly linked in a very loose fashion to the kinds of considerations set out in the report. Demands on local services and infrastructure will vary greatly at a point in time and also through time. No account is taken of changing family size and the changing social composition.

Fourth, no distinction is made between the private and the public sector. As far as the former is concerned, all the arguments above relating to minimum and maximum densities are clearly relevant. But if the line of argument developed earlier was accepted, then the reformulation should have run: in the private sector there is no upper limit provided the external costs are not 'excessive'. Whether or not they are excessive would be decided on a case-by-case basis.

In the public sector the argument must run differently, as the average council tenant cannot choose where he lives: hence, an upper-density limit (the only one of the two likely to be operative in the public sector) cannot be set in the same terms. However the public sector does make on behalf of its users essentially the same kind of choices, i.e. in the inner boroughs, where in general accessibility to the central area job market is good, there is a trade-off between better environmental quality – which is the main concern of the report – accessibility and costs. The effect of imposing a maximum lower than currently in use is to reduce the capacity of the inner areas to absorb population, thus furthering the environmental objective, but at the cost of placing others in less attractive locations from an accessibility point of view. The only additional point to make there is that this trade-off is not discussed in the context of the general policy although it is in the particular case of locations near transport centres. But if the logic of the latter is followed through then one would expect that the inner areas would have higher average densities than the outer even in new developments, since there are more jobs close in. The recommendations, in other words, are inconsistent. The committee did, however, follow its logic through to arguing that if the standards meant that the capacity of London to absorb population was reduced by what they proposed, then measures should be taken to house population elsewhere. In this way the trade-off between increasing urban environmental quality and taking more land from country uses was made explicit. The other trade-offs, including those with cost, were not.

12 TRANSPORT

Transport is involved in nearly every land-use planning issue. At the tactical level the provision of new transport facilities may bring with it undesirable external effects such as noise or visual intrusion which have to be weighed against the benefits of shorter journey times. At the strategic level a large number of policies concerning the use of land – individual plots or large zones – are justified in part at least in terms of their transport implications. Within the simple urban model, and the real world, the standard of transport service determines the spatial extent of the city and through that real income levels and housing standards. In the appraisal therefore of any transport policy, the implications of transport changes for land-use planning policy may be relevant and in any land-use decision the transport implications may have to be taken into account. Before either can be done a suitable analytic framework is required; it is the aim of this chapter to provide one.

The task of harmonising transport and the arrangement of land uses is perhaps the central and most difficult problem for land-use planning. It is not made easier by the effective separation of responsibility within many planning authorities, but even where formally responsibilities are combined, there remains the deeper problem that the way in which people tend to think about transport tends to depend on whether they start primarily with transport considerations in mind, or with planning objectives set primarily in non-transport terms.

This chapter will start at the transport end and go on to relate the discussion to our primary concern with the pattern of land use. In section 12.1 a simple theory of transport behaviour will be set out. The following sections show how this theory can be used to develop an investment criterion for transport facilities. The fourth section of the chapter relates the earlier analysis to objectives set primarily in land-use terms by showing how the investment criterion may be re-expressed in land-use terms. The fifth section considers a practical problem which starts with the need to change the pattern of land use in a specific area. The final section briefly sets out some of the issues involved in the pricing of transport services.

12.1 A Simple Model of Travel Behaviour

A start in developing a theory of transport behaviour has already been made within the simple urban model. Within this simple city, when all employment is located at the centre, the worker must decide where to locate. He is faced with a choice influenced by three factors: housing costs, travel cost and travel time. Within the model the individual is faced with trade-off between high accessibility and better housing. The price of the latter is made up not only of the rent, or equivalent capital sum, but of the extra travel costs involved in living at the edge of a city. Travel costs consist of two elements, time and money, which we shall call the *generalised* cost of travel. In the rest of this chapter, unless indicated otherwise, the cost of travel will be taken to refer to both components.

If all workers had identical preferences and identical incomes then it would be a matter of chance where they located. But if one individual disliked travel and another had a strong preference for housing, then the former would tend to live near the centre of the city and the latter near the periphery. Each must trade off the factors concerned, until he finds the 'mix' which suits him most and if the relative prices of housing transport changed, then we would expect to find an adjustment of location would follow.

If the individual worker has decided where to live, i.e. has a fixed place of residence, we can use the generalised cost concept to develop a model of transport behaviour which closely follows the pattern of that for consumer expenditures outlined in Chapter 2. The task facing the individual can be redefined as that of maximising his utility subject not only to the constraint set by his income but also that set by the availability of time, the constraint set by nature. Within our model of consumer behaviour, two types of activity can be distinguished, those which bring the individual money – primarily work – and those which cost money – primarily purchases of goods. But all goods or services will have a time and money price; time must be spent going to work or in buying goods and in some activities such as recreation, the time price may be more significant than the money costs involved.

The task facing the individual may now be put as follows. Given his initial location – which in the long run may of course be varied – he is faced with various opportunities for earning income and also various ways of spending it and using the time he has left over from earning. Opportunities for spending time and money are scattered round at various distances from him; so are work opportunities. Any time or money spent on travel reduces his time on other activities – either earning income or enjoying activities or commodities which contribute directly to his utility. Thus in considering whether to go to a further destination in preference to a nearer one, he is forced to balance any advantages which that location may offer in terms of higher income, or greater enjoyment, against the costs, in terms of extra time and money outlay, spent in doing so. For example, in deciding whether to work at the centre of the city or at the periphery he may have to balance the extra income at the centre against the extra time and costs of travel, as well as such factors as job satisfaction which may also feature in his choice. The notion of opportunity cost expressed in money terms is already familiar. In this model of travel behaviour, we are effectively treating time in the same way and assuming that it too has an opportunity cost, because it may always be deployed in an alternative activity which would bring positive utility. If time and money are freely interchangeable, as they are when the individual can vary his hours of work, then time is in any case equivalent to money for the individual concerned.

If a transport improvement takes place, which reduces the time of all the trips made by a given individual, two kinds of consequence may be defined. The first of these is an *income* effect since the (generalised) price of all the commodities he wishes to buy have fallen. If the money prices of all goods have fallen then his real purchasing power or income must simultaneously rise. In the case of time he may increase his utility either by using the time gained earning more money or more directly by spending the extra time on activities which involve time alone, such as leisure, or some combination of the two. The balance between these various reactions will depend on the strength of the individual's preferences for activities or commodities involving a larger outlay of money and lower of time and vice versa.

The second category is a *price* effect. If all transport times are reduced by the same proportionate amount, then the relative prices of goods and services are altered, because those which are furthest away – and more 'travel intensive' – fall more in price than those which are nearer. Following the theory of consumer behaviour set out in Chapter 2, we would expect that the consumer would shift his pattern of time and money expenditures in favour of those activities which had fallen most relatively in cost to him. That is, he will tend to change his travel pattern in favour of activities which are at greater distance from his home, away from activities which he formerly carried out at or near his home.

In considering these changes it is important to distinguish two kinds of reaction. The first of these involves a change in the destination of a trip: for example, the transport change might induce our individual to go further afield in his shopping expeditions, balancing the advantages of greater choice against the extra costs involved. As he was already making shopping trips, he would be said in this case to be *redistributing* his trips. In some cases however he may make entirely new trips, that is he may make an extra outing to the country, in place of messing around in his garden. In this case we would say that the trip was *generated*, an entirely new trip. As we have so far assumed only one mode of travel, we have not considered mode change or *modal choice,* but in practice a large amount of the extra trip-making observed as car ownership is increased represents only extra trips by vehicle – i.e. shorter trips were already being made by foot to local parks, or shops. In general the most important category of reaction to a change in transport costs is redistribution of trips, rather than generation. This model of transport behaviour can be combined with the analysis developed in Chapter 8 to develop a consumer surplus measure of the benefits of transport improvements. Before this is done, some important limitations must be mentioned. For example, because our prime concern is not transport as such we will not go very far into conditions of travel such as comfort, or such other factors as travel reliability. All problems which factors like these present to assessing the value of transport projects will be assumed away. Such problems as the degree to which time savings may in any particular circumstances be used will be ignored. We will assume perfect flexibility in converting any time or money saved in travel to profitable use.

12.2 The Measurement of Transport Benefits

To define a measure of benefit to the individual of a change in transport costs, we will use Diagram 23, in which the vertical axis is expressed in terms of generalised cost, rather than money price, while the horizontal axis measures the number of vehicle miles of travel. The demand curve $D_1 D_1$ plots the relationship between the amount of travel which would be demanded by the individual to various levels of generalised cost per mile. We assume for convenience that this cost is constant over all journeys and that it does not vary with the distance of travel.

Two levels of generalised cost are shown in the Diagram as C_1 and C_2. The first represents the cost of travel to the individual before a change in transport conditions and the second the cost after the change. This change leads to an increase in the number of miles he travels from Q_1 to Q_2. The measure of benefit resulting from this change is shown by the shaded area $C_1 ACBC_2$. We now indicate the significance of this area and show how it relates to the earlier theoretical discussion in Chapter 2.

Diagram 23

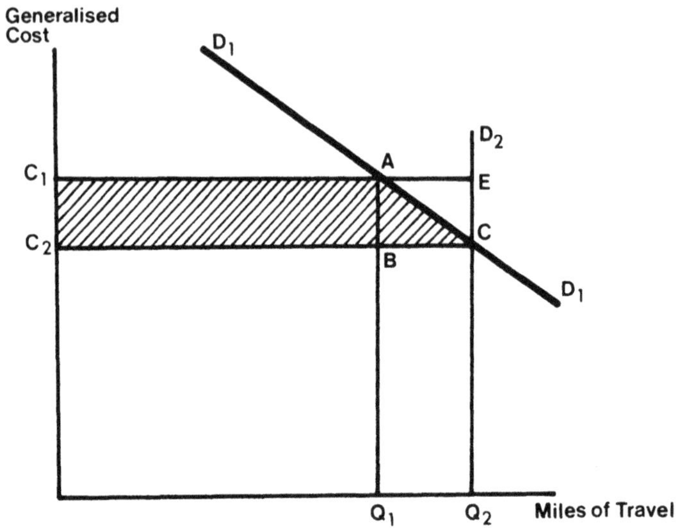

To do this, it will be useful to divide the area into two parts, the first consisting of the rectangle C_1ABC_2 and the second of the triangle ABC. The first of these areas is a cost reduction. It corresponds to a fall in the generalised price of all the activities or commodities previously purchased, and thus directly increases the income of the individual in the ways described in the previous section. If demand for transport were perfectly inelastic then this measure of cost reduction would comprise the whole of the benefit. But if demand is at all elastic, then the second area of benefit ABC cannot be ignored.

This area reflects the second category of the response of the traveller to the change in the relative price of goods and activities which a change in transport costs brings about. It thus reflects the various kinds of behavioural reaction described above, i.e. changes in the length of trip, changes in destination, changes in the frequency of trips to particular destinations, or overall changes in the number of trips generated. Each of these changes brings about a benefit to the traveller – otherwise he would not make it – but the amount of benefit varies. Just to the right of point A in Diagram 23 the extra miles of travel induced by a fall in costs leads to a benefit per mile very similar to that on the miles of travel to the left of A. This implies that the traveller was very near to making some trips at the level of cost C_1 and hence needed only a small change to induce him to carry out the extra travel. For example his choice between two recreational areas at different distances may have been very finely balanced at the old set of prices, but at the new, the balance may be struck very sharply in favour of one of them. In these circumstances, the gain from changing destination is very close to the total transport change. We can show this in Diagram 24 where the two columns on the left indicate the amount of benefit the traveller enjoys from the destinations concerned. Before the change he prefers destination 1 by a small amount, so that when he diverts to destination 2 after the change, he loses only a small amount of benefit at the recreational destination itself.

Diagram 24

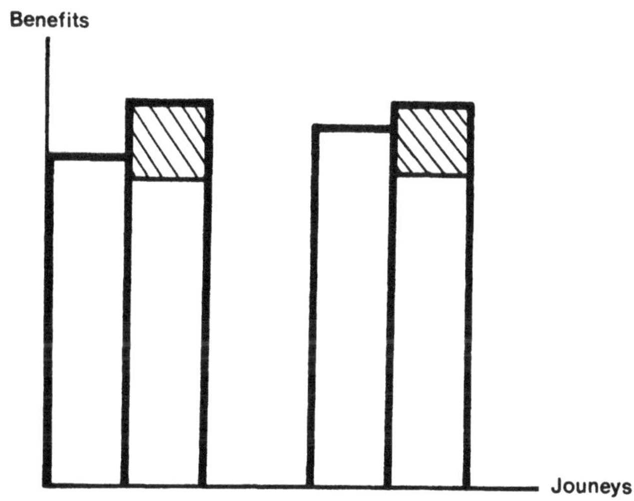

The second part of the diagram shows the opposite situation where before the change the destination was not at all competitive, but where, after it, destination 2 is just preferred to destination 1. These are the miles of travel just to the left of point C, where the extra benefits are shown to be very small, reducing towards zero at point C itself. At this point, the consumer is in equilibrium, i.e. he can no longer adjust his pattern of trip-making and in so doing increase his utility.

Now suppose that we do not have the benefit of Diagram 23, but that it is possible to predict that after a change in transport costs Q_2-Q_1 extra miles of travel will take place. Then on the basis of the discussion above the average benefit on those extra miles of travel can be taken to be half that on the existing miles of travel Q_1. This assumption which we shall call the 'rule of half' is equivalent to assuming that the demand curve is straight – as it is drawn in the diagram. Over fairly small changes this may be regarded as a useful approximation.

The assumptions underlying use of the rule of half for the individual traveller are those involved in our discussion in section 2.1 of the rational consumer, i.e. that he is aware of the benefits of the alternatives facing him and that if he changes his pattern of expenditures he does so in order to improve his total utility. However, the same kind of artgument may be used if more than one individual is concerned. For example the demand curve in Diagram 23 can be taken to refer to a large number of travellers on a particular trip or length of road, or going to a particular destination. We would define those users to the left of Q_1 as *stayers*, i.e. their demand for this particular trip was completely inelastic. Those, on the other hand, whose demand was elastic we may call *switchers*. Some travellers need only a small change to induce them to change – their demand is highly elastic – others need almost the full change to make them change – their demand is nearly as inelastic as the stayers'.

The diagram may also be used to describe business travel. In this case the generalised cost of travel refers to the costs which firms would have to pay for transport (which would include the working time of drivers and others) and the volume for transport. The firm would, like the individual, be expected to increase its use of transport as its cost fell, e.g. by making more frequent deliveries to customers, by sending its goods further afield, or by concentrating production and bringing in supplies from a wider area.

The diagram and the analysis underlying it may be elaborated to include situations where there is more than one mode of travel, where conditions other than time and cost change and so on. These extensions of the basic analysis cannot be considered here. Instead some general points may be brought out of the analysis developed so far, which are directly relevant to other parts of this book.

First, provided that the upper and lower bounds of a transport change may be ascertained for an individual or for any number of individuals and provided that their response to this can be measured, then an approximate measure of the benefits they enjoy may be derived, *purely by looking at conditions on the transport network*. Provided the travel response can be predicted, the details of the changes in behaviour underlying the changes in travel need not be known. Thus if it is expected that a new rapid transit system will generate some new trips to the central area it is not necessary to know whether the travellers will be shopping, eating out, or changing their job, because none of this is relevant to the estimation of the benefit concerned. But this conclusion only holds if the assumptions used in Chapter 2 also hold, i.e. that the prices facing the individual reflect the relevant private and social costs. They often do not and so many of the problems discussed in Chapter 3 arise, such as the presence of externalities. We will consider below the extent to which the transport benefit measure must be modified to take these effects into account.

The second general point is that the amount of travel an individual may wish to enjoy will vary with the conditions facing him on the network; or put another way, he is able to adjust to changing transport conditions in a large variety of ways. This simple statement has two important consequences which we will examine later in more detail. First, in considering the benefits of a transport system or in trying to define a layout of land uses, it makes no sense to attempt to minimise transport costs. It is only sensible to minimise transport costs if the pattern of transport can be assumed to be invariant to whatever is proposed, i.e. demand is perfectly inelastic.

The second consequence is that in considering the costs in transport terms of land-use policies, it is essential to take into account the adjustments which may be expected to occur to changes in those costs. For example, a land-use proposal may be expected to generate new traffic which would impose costs on existing users of the transport system. Unless there is spare capacity in the transport system, their travel costs will be increased, i.e. the opposite of the movement in costs we have been considering so far. This is shown by a shift in the cost curve from C_1 to C_2. If it is assumed that the demand of existing users is perfectly inelastic (demand curve D_2), then the measure of loss would be given by the area in Diagram 23. However, if demand is at all responsive, then this is a clear overstatement. In the diagram the loss imposed on existing users is equal only to the amount C_1ACC_2 because the diagram implies, through the slope of the demand curve, that individuals would prefer to reduce their travel from Q_1 to Q_2 when their travel costs are increased by the amount P_1-P_2. The significance of these two points when policies are being evaluated is brought out in Chapter 13.

12.3 Further Analysis of the Benefit Measure

The benefit measure discussed so far is clearly not a full account of the effects of a transport policy. For a complete evaluation, it would be necessary to take into account the environmental externalities which changes in traffic would bring about and also the costs to the public sector of the measures in question. The measure described is confined to measuring user benefits and in discussing it, the word used has been employed in its obvious meaning to refer to those actually making a trip. However, although this may seem straightforward, it is nevertheless misleading. To see why, we will consider the effects of a transport change within the simple urban model.

We have been inexplicit about the nature of the transport system within our model city, but let us assume for the purposes of this section that it consists purely of a public transport mode and that this mode operates radially. The pattern of rents will reflect the pattern of accessibility and hence will be higher nearer the centre and near to the radial routes themselves. If an improved link is brought into this situation, which speeds up journeys on one side of the city, but leaves the others unaffected, then under the assumptions which have been made rents would rise along that corridor in line with the change in relative accessibility. But the increases could not exceed the gain in terms of reduced transport costs, since it would be of no advantage to pay more in increased rental than the extra accessibility advantage was worth.

Exactly who benefits in a situation like this is difficult to unravel for the reasons discussed in Chapter 7 which make the incidence of a tax or any other policy measure hard to estimate. Existing users of the service in the corridor affected by the improvement will experience a direct gain through the time/cost reductions they enjoy. These are the *stayers*. But if they rent their housing then under the free market conditions we have assumed, these rents would adjust, to the point where they would be no better off. Those holding the freeholds clearly would be. However, if an existing user owned his house but decided to move, for reasons unconnected with the change in transport conditions, then he would be able to sell his house for a much higher amount than otherwise. In this way he would take the benefit with him when he want, while the user who replaced him while enjoying a quicker trip would have paid for it through his higher house price. If the accommodation was rent-controlled then sitting tenants would benefit, and if any moved out then incomers would enjoy the full extent of the gain. Unless the analysis is concerned with the welfare of particular groups of people, these complications may be ignored. The only rule to follow is to be careful to avoid double counting by taking either the changes in transport costs as a benefit or the changes in land values.

This case may seem fairly straightforward, but the concept of user benefit must be unpacked still further before we can be sure that double counting is eliminated. Consider the case of a change in the level of transport service to the central area part of a large city. This would have the effect of encouraging some people to commute out of this area who otherwise would not do so. This in turn would help to retain some firms in the central area. Some people would move into the area, because of its changed level of accessibility. Some local employers might have to give up because they could not compete and some employers would not move in because the area might be thought too competitive with the centre. The effects of all these changes are clearly very varied. Some individuals may enjoy a better combination of housing and travel costs than they otherwise would. Some change to jobs they prefer. Some employers make slightly larger profits and some smaller. But following the lines of the earlier discussion, the gain to each of all these changes must be related to the extent of the transport change involved. The individuals we are concerned with are the switchers; some of them will gain fairly large amounts, some very small. The benefits they gain are of various kinds but ultimately they may be linked back to the change in accessibility which gave rise to them.

In making this assertion, however, we must recall the assumptions which underlie it. These are, as noted above, that the individual decision-maker perceives his own interest correctly, at least on average (i.e. for all those who underestimate benefit there are some who do the reverse) and that the prices facing the individual reflect the full social opportunity costs of his actions. If these assumptions do not hold, then there is a presumption that the benefit measure may be misleading, though there is no presumption in which direction. Bearing these assumptions in mind we will consider in the next section some alternative ways of expressing the benefits of transport improvements, which arise from considering the *effects* of transport changes, but not necessarily the benefits arising from them. However these effects – of the kind described above – are often highly important for land-use policies. For this reason the expression 'planning benefits' will be used in what follows.

12.4 Transport Benefits and Spatial Planning Objectives

We have seen how transport benefits may be 'converted' into benefits of different kinds, sometimes in parts of the urban system far from the initial impact of the transport change concerned. One implication of this is that transport may not be a very selective instrument of policy, since its effects in detail are not easy to predict and the longer-term effects may be in conflict with the short term. This was true even within the limits of the simple urban model. Within a large metropolitan area, provided market forces are working, the actual complexities will of course be much greater.

Two examples will illustrate this point. The first of these is an investment proposal aimed at increasing the accessibility of the poorer sections of the population living near to the centre of the city, where most of the employment is located. Following the earlier analysis this will tend to increase the attractiveness of these areas for people of all income groups. The result will be an increase in rent or property values. If the transport change is sufficiently large there will be further repercussions, e.g. pressures for redevelopment and provision of more expensive accommodation, at perhaps lower densities if the incomers have higher incomes. The result then will be a complex shuffling round in the use and adaptation of use of the existing housing stock. One possible outcome is that the original inhabitants of the area are faced with the choice of living at higher densities in the parts of the city still devoted to lower-income housing or moving further away from the centre – at the price of reduced accessibility.

As noted already in Chapter 8, there could be effects in job as well as housing markets. To the extent that the population which it is intended to benefit is in fact aided, this will mean that its competitiveness in the labour market is increased, i.e. as employers find it easier to recruit labour at the central location, they will not need to bid up its price to the level it would have reached without the improvement. The main sufferers from this increased competitiveness will be those classes of labour which are closest in terms of skill, age, etc. Thus some of the gains concerned will be redistributed within the socio-economic groups which it is aimed to benefit and some will go to people in general if the price of goods or services is reduced. The final result will probably be a mixture of all these outcomes and the original hoped-for effect. Even where the housing concerned is in the public sector, similar kinds of effect may occur, for example, if the attractiveness of an estate is increased through improved accessibility, its social composition would also tend to change.

The second example is a cheap fares policy aimed at an objective similar to the one above, i.e. increasing accessibility of all lower-income groups to labour markets. If free fares are enjoyed by all, then within our simple urban economy one would expect that housing would tend to spread out further from the centre, and, if the transport system is radial, that the central employment area would tend to remain competitive and perhaps expand its share of total employment. If the centre was the only source of employment then it would be able to pay lower wages in order to attract the same volume of labour. This would affect all categories of labour, but the countervailing effect of increased demand for labour would depend on the elasticity of demand for the class of labour concerned. All this implies that some sections of the labour force might be advantaged and some not, i.e. that some would find that their wages fell, and also their transport costs and their price of accommodation, though to a lesser extent. Others would find the opposite. Much of the total gain would be enjoyed in the form of increased rent to those holding land in the area affected.

The change just considered is a very thorough-going one and it should not surprise us that its effects are difficult to disentangle. We now consider one or two simpler cases where transport projects may contribute to planning objectives in ways not expressed in the transport benefit diagram discussed above. These cases arise because the basic assumption that the individual is presented with price information which reflects the social opportunity costs concerned is violated. Suppose, as in the first example, that there are benefits from expanding shopping centres beyond a certain size and that these economies do not accrue to each individual retailer, i.e. he does not enjoy economies of scale, but the centre as a whole provides increasing benefits of choice as it expands. In other words, it is an *external economy*. In these circumstances the cost to the shopper of using a centre may be above the social cost of him doing so, since his visit brings with it certain benefits to others (as well as certain disbenefits of crowding). A gain ensues if a transport change induces an increase in usage, by shifting the private cost curve down to the level of the social cost curve. The simple transport measure would not reflect it.

A second case is provided by a situation in which an area is being developed privately but, because of the way in which the costs of services are charged for, the response by private developers is not adequate. If, as in the examples in Chapter 9, all services are charged on an average cost basis, but this particular area has below-average costs, and if the areas from which the people concerned are expected to come have above-average costs, then a gain would ensue if the transport change altered these relative costs in a way which would help to restore the true balance. Land-use planners may for this reason be interested in the specific spatial impact of a transport policy which may not concern the transport planner at all. Consider the development costs in two alternative locations presented in Table 1 on page 153. From the developer's viewpoint the sites are equally attractive, but site 1 is preferable from a social viewpoint. A transport improvement could alter the balance of financial advantage in favour of the site whose resource costs are lowest if it were to enhance the price which people would be prepared to pay for the houses concerned.

A third example is given from the situation where there are price rigidities and spatial immobility within labour and housing markets. This may result, within a large metropolitan area, in there being, simultaneously, shortages of labour and excess of supply. A transport improvement might reduce the imbalance by bringing labour from the latter areas to the former. The firm in the area of excess demand, by definition, is not getting enough labour at the price it is paying – which may be fixed by convention or through labour agreements. Therefore it would be willing to pay for the extra labour more than the wage – i.e. an amount extra equivalent to the difference between the wage and the demand curve for labour at the existing level of employment. If a change in transport reduces the cost of access to the jobs concerned and shifts the supply curve of labour to the left, then employment of labour will shift to the right. The gain from this will exceed the amount paid to the labour concerned. This benefit could not be reflected in the benefit measure described.

These cases could easily be multiplied from other real-world examples but their significance must be assessed against two points. First, examples of this kind can easily be matched by examples which would produce transport benefits lower than the measure suggests, so that there can be no general presumption that the benefit measure we have described systematically understates, or overstates, benefits. Second, we have not questioned the assumption that if these spatial objectives are to be pursued, then transport is the right means of doing so. In any real policy context, it would of course be desirable to look to alternatives, and consider their relative efficiency, taking all costs and benefits into account in achieving these objectives. Transport would be a wasteful means of achieving the kind of spatial planning objectives considered in the second example, if an attractive and hence expensive facility had to be provided, which would be far in excess of actual usage requirements.

To illustrate this point consider a case where a transport improvement is judged to be vital to the revitalisation of an area, which we will take to be a run-down section in the inner part of a large city. Various plans have been prepared for this area, embodying various types and intensities of land use. These plans suggest different levels of transport demands, but in none of them would sufficient demand be forthcoming to justify, in terms of the criteria we have discussed, the provision of major new infrastructure, such as a railway, because in no case is the level of demand and the size of the travel time savings large enough. However, it may be argued that some of the plans would only succeed if a railway were provided. This assumption we will not question. Our problem is to see how a case for a railway might be made out in those circumstances where demand levels are low and the amount of extra traffic which would be generated by the rail link itself also low.

We can start to consider this problem in terms of 'willingness to pay', and suppose for simplicity that there were four plans, each specialising in a particular land use and that for each land use a combined 'bid' could be made for all the sites concerned which would reflect the benefits attainable. These bids would be made taking into account only the costs which the uses themselves would incur if they took over the site. They are shown in Table 3. Against each use, the public sector would have various costs to meet, but we will assume that these are purely transport costs – shown in column 1. Column 2 shows what the bid would be if the high level of transport was not provided; and column 3 the bid if it was. We can see from the table that land use A is highly dependent on the existence of the rail link. Its bid increases by 60 if the link is provided. This is not true of land use B. Its bid is below A if the link is there, but above if it is not. Land uses C and D are below A if the link is provided but above B: below B if it is not, and above A.

Table 3

		Benefits		
	Cost of Link	Without Link	With Link	Net Gain With Link
Land Uses A	50	20	80	30
B	50	40	60	10
C	50	25	70	20
D	50	30	65	15

In these circumstances, land use B is the preferred use, since it produces a surplus of 40 in the absence of the link, which is greater than the surplus produced by any other use, with or without it. However, if the bid made by land use A – if the link was provided – was increased by 20 to 100, then the surplus would rise to 50 and the link would be justified. If, despite this, its measured transport benefit were less than its costs, then the implication would be that this land use derived special advantages from the site which were not expressed in the evaluation of the rail link.

In a real case, the arguments would not of course be conducted in these terms, but the principles would be the same, that is, the aim would be to assess the specific advantages derived from one pattern of land use and set it against the costs incurred in attaining it. Thus, if it was considered that the transport link was vital to some specific use, such as upper-income group housing, then the objective of any analysis would be to show what special advantages this use would derive from the redevelopment. In this case, market evidence may be available – whereas it would not be for public sector housing. Costs would be available for producing public sector housing in other locations, so a judgement could be made as to whether the incremental costs due to rail link were worth paying in return for public housing in this particular location.

12.5 Pricing in the Transport Sector – A Brief Note

We do not need to consider in this chapter the full range of pricing problems which arise in the transport sector. Many of the issues concerned have been discussed in Chapter 9. We do need however to consider briefly ways in which pricing in the transport sector is deficient from a land-use planning viewpoint. Ideally, the charges faced by transport users should reflect the marginal social costs of the alternatives facing them. For example, a land use generating a large amount of traffic in a congested area should have to meet a larger transport bill than if it located in an area where the transport system had spare capacity. In practice transport charges do not reflect costs in this way. Failures of this kind arise from a variety of causes.

One group of causes stems from the nature of the transport sector itself. First, there is the variability of costs by time of day, place and time of year, and the large gap between short-run variable costs and the total costs of transport provision. This means that any charging mechanism, if it is to reflect costs accurately, must be extremely flexible and versatile. Ideally charging mechanisms should reflect the fact of congestion in the way discussed in Chapter 6. This may arise not only on roads, the context in which it is commonly discussed, but also on public transport networks, since the addition of extra trains may reduce the performance of others, in respect of time-keeping if not in respect of speed. Yet further difficulties arise through the existence of costs, such as overheads, which cannot be identified precisely with particular services.

The second group of causes arises from the intervention of public authorities. Most transport prices reflect taxes such as fuel duty or subsidies, e.g. to public transport services. Others reflect the desire of policy-makers to keep charges uniform between parts of an urban area or over different times of the day. Further, the organisation of the transport sector is, typically, asymmetrical. On the one hand, public transport operators are subject to financial constraints which require them to charge prices which cover some, if not all, of their costs. Prices tend, therefore, to reflect average rather than marginal costs. On the other, individual car-users pay for their vehicles themselves and for their own time and are able to consider only the marginal costs of each trip. Roads are charged for (if fuel and vehicle tax can be considered charges) in a manner which relates only roughly to the marginal social costs of road use.

These imperfections in charging mechanisms have several consequences. The relative cost of different modes is rarely accurately reflected in the charges users pay. Just as important, the true costs of alternative destinations and locations are also poorly reflected. In the absence of specific policy to the contrary, central destinations tend to be underpriced because charges for the use of central area roads are not adequate to cover the total social costs, including congestion, which the trips concerned give rise to. Similarly, firms locating in the centre do not have brought home to them the costs they impose, by attracting extra commuters, on the agencies supplying public transport services. Finally, there is the question of costs external to the transport sector. If road-users impose environmental costs, there is no charging mechanism which brings home the costs to them. This is true even where compensation is paid for dislocation and injurious affection. This does not bite on the particular road-users concerned, as they do not have to pay it.

Because, for all these reasons, prices in the transport sector do not reflect the relevant social costs, a great deal of interest has been shown in recent years in attempting to get better pricing into urban transport systems – for example, through the imposition of parking fees. There have been investigations of other mechanisms, such as road pricing and supplementary licensing, but they are still untried in practice and even if introduced are unlikely to bring private and social costs perfectly into line. This means that there would still be no general presumption that individual locational decisions (particularly those made by firms, since these affect employees' journeys to work) were correct from a social point of view. In the short term, the main interest in getting transport prices right focuses on the transport sector itself, i.e. getting higher speeds or giving priority to public transport. But in the longer term, as we saw within the simple urban model, the level of transport prices (i.e. what users have to pay as opposed to cost of provision) will determine the physical extent of the city. If prices at the periphery are below cost, then there will be a tendency for the area to over-expand. If transport costs are expected to rise in relation to other prices, then there may be a case for the authority to modify densities against this expectation. Accordingly, planning authorities would still be obliged to take transport implications of development into account directly by considering the congestion implications of any development proposed.

13 THE ARRANGEMENT OF LAND USES

A large number of planning policies are concerned with the spatial arrangement of activities. These range from the very small-scale micro-issue of whether a commercial activity should be allowed in a private housing estate, to the national issue of whether the major conurbations should be allowed to expand and other parts of the country allowed to run down and decline. In between these two extremes lie a large number of difficult but common problems: the '*best*' arrangement of shopping facilities, the '*right*' location for a public facility, the '*proper*' distribution of jobs.

The task of finding the optimal arrangement of land uses is at the core of the land-use planning problem. Changes in the arrangement of land uses have transport implications and changes in transport have implications for the arrangement of land use. Further, as we have seen in the previous chapters, transport and other infrastructure prices frequently do not reflect the marginal social costs of different locations. But perhaps the main reason is that the individual household or firm cannot possibly take into account the implications of his actions for others, since the essence of a good or a bad arrangement of uses, where transport is concerned, cannot be defined unilaterally; it is a mutual thing. If I am not well placed with regard to A, A is not well placed with regard to me – although the importance we may attach to these facts may differ a great deal. I cannot change my position, if I am dissatisfied with it, without also changing his position in relation to me. It is precisely in situations of mutual dependence that the case for intervention based on better information is strongest.

Planning policies may be concerned with trying to produce the best arrangement at a point in time, and in a New Town situation there may be a large measure of control over the pattern which will be initially laid down. But in established urban areas there are typically very powerful forces making for changes in the spatial arrangement of land uses of the kind discussed in Chapter 3. Income growth leads to demand for better standards of accommodation, technical change alters the relative attractiveness of different kinds of location, changes in tastes lead to demands for new kinds of economic activity. Planning authorities have, therefore, the difficult problem of devising policies which allow for change and dealing with the consequences of change in some sectors of the urban economy on other sectors.

The chapter is concerned primarily with two things: first, the relationship between the transport sector and the advantages to be gained from different arrangements of land uses; second, the use of policies towards the arrangement of land uses designed to reduce external costs resulting from commercial and industrial activities. The first section analyses the factors to be taken into account in determining the best location or locations for land uses such as public services or shopping facilities. We saw in Chapter 12 how the pattern of travel is determined by the pattern of land uses. However, because the amount of travel varies with the quality of the transport sector, the objective of policies towards the arrangement of land uses cannot be expressed purely in terms of minimising the costs of travel. The first section of this chapter, therefore, will look at the implications of this for land-use policy.

The following section goes on to consider the additional complication brought about by external costs. Most land-use planning authorities have adopted policies designed to segregate uses such as heavy industry which give rise to external costs, from uses such as housing which might suffer from them. Policies of this kind also have transport consequences, i.e. transport costs might be imposed on residents in order that they may enjoy environmental benefits. This section will consider, therefore, the nature of this trade-off and the efficiency of such policies in relation to other measures which might be taken to achieve the same objectives. The chapter goes on to consider other reasons why land-use policies might be concerned with the spatial pattern of employment, in particular the problems arising from changes in the pattern of employment and the externalities this may give rise to. Using a London example, the chapter concludes by assessing the case for using fiscal measures in order to correct for these externalities, following the analysis developed in Chapter 6.

This chapter, like the previous one, will examine the rationale for various kinds of policy with the aim, not of justifying any particular policy line, but of exposing the underlying logic and indicating the kind of consideration which would be relevant to an assessment of the costs and benefits of such policies in a real-life situation.

13.1 Single and Multiple Locations

A characteristic of many kinds of land use, except in the smallest towns, is that they occur in more than one location. They comprise what is sometimes called a 'system'. The parts are distinct and have an identity of their own, but they are best regarded, in recognition of their interaction, as a whole. Examples occur in both public and private sectors. In the private sector retailing is the best example. Typically, shops occur in several different locations within an urban area, and shoppers may go regularly to a number of them, for each location does not provide identical services. The same is true within the public sector for such services as libraries or amenities such as open space.

The general problem with this kind of land use is that of deciding what the best spatial arrangement for such facilities is. Technically most could be provided in a single location or in several. How is the balance to be struck? As we shall see, although the uses concerned in choices of this kind are very diverse, the same few basic concepts can be used to analyse them.

To simplify the problem initially, let us first take a facility in the public sector for which the demand is completely *inelastic* (i.e. a fixed number of units of the service concerned will be consumed no matter what the price) and consider the problem of finding the best location for a single unit of the facility. From the user point of view the best location would be the one which minimised the cost of access to it. The cost concerned would be the generalised cost of access defined, as in Chapter 12, to include both time and money costs of travel. In all probability such a location would be found in the centre of the urban area where accessibility was greatest. The most accessible locations are, however, likely to be the most expensive. The authority would, therefore, have to consider whether a less central site should be chosen. The problem can be expressed in Diagram 25 which assumes that land costs fall with distance from the centre, while accessibility cost rises. The best site is given in the diagram by the point at which the two curves combined reach a minimum. If costs of provision also varied with the site chosen, then another curve could be added to the diagram to take account of this.

The decision becomes more complex if we relax the assumption that demand is fixed. If the facility is moved to a peripheral location, the volume of usage is likely to go down in response to the increase in generalised cost, since some users will not find the trip worthwhile. A more complicated calculation is therefore required which involves estimating the extra social benefit from the higher costs of provision. If a peripheral site is used as a base-line, then the decision the authority must make is whether the extra cost of provision at a more central point creates sufficient extra benefit to justify it. The peripheral site is shown on the right of Diagram 25. As we move to the left towards a more central location, user benefit rises both through reduced transport costs and extra use of the facility, but costs of provision also rise. In this case, benefits are assumed to exceed costs of provision only at a central location. In all others, the effect of increased access costs is to reduce user benefit below cost of provision. In practice there may be several points where the benefits of provision exceeded the costs. If this were so, then the correct location would be that where the difference between costs and benefits, i.e. the net surplus, was greatest.

Diagram 25

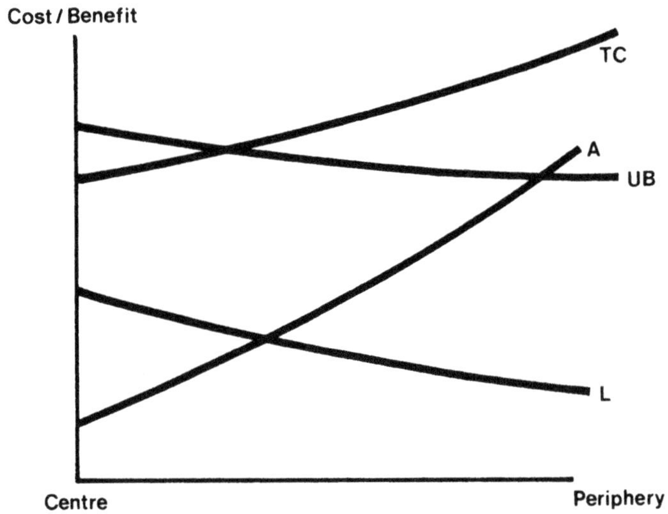

It may be possible for the authority to supply the service concerned at different locations, and in this way avoid some of the generalised costs imposed on individuals while saving the costs of a central site. To see the nature of the choices this presents, the costs involved in providing the service concerned must be considered under the initial assumption that the quality of the service is held constant. If economies of scale were marked, it would pay, as far as minimising costs of supply are concerned, to have all production located in one place. This ignores costs of access. When these are added in, the issue is the same as that considered already. It may be worthwhile to sacrifice some of the costs which might be saved by concentrating production in order to reduce the costs to users. But the case for doing this is the weaker, the greater the economies of scale in providing the service concerned. On the contrary, if such economies are exhausted at very low levels of output, the case for concentration is very weak. The overall level of demand could be best supplied by a large number of small units, each located near its market.

If the assumption of fixed demand is relaxed, then the best solution is found further along the road towards decentralisation, since this reduces user costs, induces a greater amount of use, and hence leads to greater benefits. The more responsive demand, the greater the case for multiple provision. In considering how many locations to provide the rule to follow is the familiar one, i.e. to increase provision costs until marginal social and marginal private costs are equal. In this case the rule implies that locations should be increased in number as long as each addition brings with it sufficient additional benefit to justify itself. One important implication of this analysis when comparing the merits of alternative spatial policies is this: that, for reasons noted in Chapter 12, if the level of user demand varies, it is not correct to make a simple comparison between transport costs. Existing or inelastic users must be distinguished from new generated users. If we know or can estimate the level of use at one site, or set of sites, then any locational change can be costed on the transport network for those users who do not change their behaviour. But any users who change their behaviour – who are discouraged or encouraged to make use of the facilities concerned – must not be treated in this way, since for the reasons discussed in section 12.2 their gains or losses will not be equal to the transport cost difference. In particular, the extra travel should be treated as an indicator of benefit, not as an extra cost.

We have so far ignored the quality factor. In most services, e.g. libraries, the quality of the service varies with the scale. Choice tends to increase with size and specialised services can be provided where demand is sufficient to justify it. Thus for some purposes the small branch libraries may be as good as the central libraries, e.g. for those categories of book for which the level of demand is high, such as popular fiction, but it will not be for reference works. In terms of the diagram we may express the quality factor by a shift in the position of the benefit curve, i.e. there will be a difference not only in the number of books borrowed, but in the benefit enjoyed on average on each book, where the standard of service is higher.

Finally, we must consider the distributional implications of the alternatives considered. The best library system must involve some judgement between people who use one kind of book and those who use another; the library which puts greater weight on the reference section might be less willing to decentralise than one which puts greater weight on getting the maximum number of books issued. These judgements may be made paternalistically or an attempt may be made to estimate the relative valuations of users themselves. But of more general importance in the land-use planning field is that the location of facilities will, to some large extent, determine *who* uses them.

This is especially important for those facilities which do require a fairly high degree of expenditure on access, e.g. countryside recreation. Given the general nature of the trade-offs described in the paragraphs above, the point of optimal 'production' will depend on the preferences of the users concerned and these preferences are likely to vary between income groups. Their relative valuation of time, money and recreational experience will differ. Thus, if a given amount of space were to be allocated to a poorer area, it might be better provided from the users' point of view in small parcels even though this meant that the advantages of large areas of space were lost – since such an arrangement would reduce travel expenditures. But other parts of the population who placed less weight on access costs because they were not reliant on public transport and had higher incomes might get a better deal by having a small number of facilities concentrated in certain locations. This would be so if they valued the benefits of scale more than the extra costs of travel.

The discussion so far has stressed three basic points: first, that the best solution is not that which minimises costs to the authority providing the service nor, where quality or level of usage varies, which minimises costs overall. It is the one where any increase in benefit is outweighed by an increase in costs, i.e. marginal social costs equals marginal social benefit. Second, the best pattern of provision does not necessarily involve that which, from some professional viewpoint, is 'best', usually the large-scale facility, but that which gets the best correct balance between public expenditure, user benefits and user costs. Third, the arrangement of facilities necessarily has distributional implications. For most facilities, there cannot be one spatial pattern for those with high incomes and one for those with low. The pattern chosen will therefore benefit some groups more than others.

The analysis developed above can now be applied to a private sector use, shopping, or retail distribution. If they were free to locate, where would retail facilities tend to be found, and would this be socially optimal? We cannot begin to answer this question even within the simple urban model without considering the costs of providing retail services. If we assume that they enjoy very considerable economies of scale, then there would be a tendency for them to be found in one location, probably where transport facilities were best. If, however, there were few scale economies, shops would tend to be found all over the city. This would follow from the fact that users must pay in terms of generalised cost to reach shopping facilities, so that, unless the single source offers very considerable price advantages – possible only if costs were low – then access costs will very soon outweigh them and people will prefer local facilities. Thus, even where there are economies of scale in retailing, facilities will tend to be small and of about the same size if catchment areas are not concentrated. All this mirrors the analysis of the location of public services.

In the real world there are many goods and competitive ways of providing the same physical commodities. Some shops are generalised, some highly specialised. Local shops tend to stock standard goods, while central area shops will stock these items plus items or ranges of choice not found in the local shops, because there is insufficient custom to make it worthwhile. The larger the catchment area the more specialised retailing facilities will appear.

The way in which shopping (and related facilities) congregate with different degrees of speciality has been categorised, mainly by geographers, into various 'orders'. These categorisations have not been geared to determining what the most desirable of shopping facilities would be, although they have influenced views on this, but have reflected the state of affairs as it has turned out. Might there be reasons for thinking that 'what turns out' is not desirable from a social viewpoint?

Let us first consider reasons within the retail sector itself excluding such externalities as traffic congestion, but retaining the assumption that facilities are provided by a competitive private market. In the simple urban model, facilities would begin by being located at the centre, and then, as the city expanded, facilities would tend to move away from the centre, as soon as it was possible to achieve a viable level of custom at peripheral locations. If only one kind of shop had to be considered there would be no reason for policy to intervene in this process. Given the existence of various kinds of facility, the problem becomes a little different. Mirroring the quality differences which may arise in the public sector from large-scale provision, there may be advantages from the clustering of facilities. These might accrue either through specialisation and the provision of choice, or because shoppers are able to economise on trip-making if they need go to only one centre. In this case, they would be external economies of consumption as they are enjoyed by users, not producers. If external economies were present, then the move by one retailer to a separate location from the others would result in a lower level of overall choice, better accessibility for some users, but poorer accessibility for others. In these circumstances there would tend to be too many retailing centres, since retailers would systematically underestimate the benefit of staying in the original location by the amount of the external benefits.

In some circumstances too few could arise. For example, a 'prisoners' dilemma' problem may occur, i.e. a change in location of several retailers might be profitable because the advantages of scale in existing centres are exhausted, but individually they may not be able to bring this about. They may, as individuals, be able to find peripheral sites, but not a single site which was optimal in the sense defined earlier, i.e. struck the correct balance between access costs and the internal and external economies of concentration. Intervention may therefore be required to bring about a co-ordinated decentralisation of retailing services, when retailing is predominantly in small units, to achieve economies within the distribution process itself. Such intervention does not necessarily require a planning authority however: a large-scale private developer might be able to undertake it. But the developer for reasons examined below is not necessarily able to strike the right balance between retailing economies and access costs.

Currently there are widespread commercial pressures for extra shopping space to be added at the edge of town – or 'out of town' entirely. In these cases the developer has judged that he can attract custom despite lack of centrality and as his land and construction costs are probably lower than on a central site, his most profitable location is at the periphery. Leaving aside the issue of over-provision of space discussed in Chapter 10 and environmental issues, such as loss of visual amenity, there are three reasons why private and social interests may diverge, and hence why the developer's choice may not be correct from a social viewpoint:

(a) where there is congestion, private and social costs diverge on the road network. If congestion is beyond the optimal level, as defined in Chapter 6, because prices are not set correctly for road use, then it is likely that retailers will over-expand on sites developed first and, when choosing new sites, not select those which are best from a social or overall point of view, since the new development and those using it will not have to pay for the congestion costs they impose on others.

(b) where there are economies of scale in provision, or economies due to concentration of provision, marginal social benefits may well exceed marginal social costs, e.g. when users are diverted to the new facility, they do not take into account the losses suffered by those who remain, such as loss of variety, or increased unit costs.

(c) because a peripheral location may offer improved generalised costs of access to some groups but not to all. There may therefore be a distributional argument in favour of retaining the existing spatial pattern of provision. Equally, however, a decentralised pattern of provision will save transport costs for some.

These factors do not pull in the same direction and each requires a careful analysis. The first of these has already been referred to in earlier chapters. As the previous chapter pointed out, transport costs do not accurately reflect variations in social costs over the network. In existing town centres they are typically too low, i.e. marginal social costs exceed marginal private costs. By itself, this would suggest that existing centres would tend to over-expand. Whether this is correct or not depends on the effects likely to follow from bringing charges into line with marginal social cost. If, as is usually assumed, the divergence were greater for private than for public transport, then a correction of the divergence could create greater accessibility to the central area by inducing a switch to public transport. But if such a switch did not occur, then the implication would be that the existing centre was too large, from a transport point of view.

The second reason for divergence between private and social cost is frequently expressed in terms of damage to existing centres. Here we must distinguish between efficiency and distributional considerations. Diversion of trade will mean a loss of custom for some and a gain for others, as in the normal processes of competition. Efficiency effects may occur if new investment reduces turnover in existing centres too quickly, so that the existing capital stock cannot adjust (the analysis of Chapter 10 is relevant here). This might be a short-lived phenomenon if demand were rising rapidly in the area as a whole. It would be a long-term effect if economies of scale were lost. This would hold only if existing centres after diversion were too small to provide them or if trade did not expand quickly to make up for the losses suffered. If scale economies have already been exhausted in the existing centres, then diversion of custom will present only problems of adjustment – the significance of which will depend, as already noted, on the overall growth of business in the area.

The third effect is also largely a transport matter which can only be considered on a detailed case-by-case basis. But it is worth noting that there could be a conflict between distributional objectives. This would occur if the transport consequences were harmful to those groups dependent on public transport, while the effects of the extra retailing capacity on the prices of goods in general were favour. The possibility of this is implicit in the analysis of Chapter 10 of the impact of additional retailing space on total retailing costs. The new capacity may bring costs down, either because it embodies superior technology (in the broadest sense) or because existing space had been rationed by quantitative restriction and its price was too high. In either of these cases the effect of the new investment is to reduce costs and consequently prices throughout the retailing sector in the area affected. This gain may, therefore, have to be set against the possible losses to those who suffer from the deterioration of existing centres.

13.2 The Location of Employment

The choice of a best pattern of location for jobs can be analysed using the concepts developed in the previous section. A single employment centre requires everyone to commute to that centre. If employment decentralises, commuting costs will tend to fall. In relation to employment and transport costs alone, the object of policy would, as before, be to get the right balance between the two. Typically, however, land-use planning authorities have had environmental as well as transport objectives in mind when determining the siting of employment land uses.

In this section, therefore, we will consider the location of jobs as an example of the kind of policies which planning authorites pursue to deal with the external costs which industrial and commercial activity may impose on neighbouring residents and others. We will begin with a simple case, of a kind which can arise in devising a New Town layout, and consider the kind of policy which a number of New Towns have adopted of locating all industrial employment in one zone towards the edge of the urban area.

A plan like this is effective in achieving its main purpose, i.e. it keeps away from residential and other areas those externalities such as noise, dirt and visual disamenity which industry may be expected to produce, by reducing the area of contact between industry and other uses to a minimum. Only the character of the residential areas in the immediate vicinity of the industrial zone may be adversely affected by the presence of industry. There may be further advantages, e.g. industry may benefit from reduced transport costs by being close together, and suppliers of basic services may find it most economic to supply them at one single part of the urban area at the scale which industry may require. Most public utilities enjoy economies of scale, so this is likely to be so. But what costs may be involved in a policy of this kind?

By its very nature, a policy of simple segregation does not allow the firms involved to 'trade' any costs which may fall on them in the single location they are allowed to operate within. This location may have been carefully chosen to create the advantages mentioned above, but nevertheless some firms may find an alternative location more attractive. This might be so, for example, for a firm which employed married women whom it found difficult to recruit to its site in the industrial area because of the transport costs involved. It might be true of a firm which, although nominally industrial, had close connections with the commercial sectors, or of a firm whose main contacts were with outside firms and which, therefore, would prefer to be nearer a rail freight depot. For any or all of these reasons, firms might be prepared to pay a greater sum than their rent on the industrial site for an alternative location. If they located elsewhere, they would, of course, give rise to external costs. If the benefits to the firm exceeded the external costs it imposed, then distributional issues apart, there is advantage in it locating elsewhere. However, external costs might still be excessive from a distributional viewpoint, so the best overall position could be one in which the firm located outside the industrial zone *and* reduced environmental impact by modifying its production methods and thus reduced the nature or extent of the externalities it was responsible for.

A number of weaknesses with the simple zoning policy can easily be identified from this discussion. The first is that it provides no incentive for the reduction or the elimination of the external effects which underlie it. Although spatial segregation may reduce the impact of external costs, it does not eliminate them, unless spatial segregation goes to extreme lengths.

The second important weakness stems from the implications for transport costs of a simple zoning system in any form. Let us assume that the number of jobs and workers is fixed and does not vary with accessibility and that economies of scale or agglomeration benefits can be ignored. Using these assumptions, a layout of houses and a transport system might be devised which minimised transport costs on the journey to work. Ignoring other land uses and journey types, the difference in transport costs between this layout and the costs under the zoning solution would be a measure of the cost at which the benefits of relative freedom from environmental nuisance was being bought. Following the analysis of section 13.1, the number of employment locations should be increased to the point where the increase in environmental damage just equals the reduction in transport costs.

The third important weakness is that it rules out locational choices which, from the viewpoint of the firms involved and from the viewpoint of society as a whole, might be beneficial. The examples given above suggest why such cases might arise and it may seem that the right way to deal with them is by a case-by-case approach, which allows firms which would receive particular benefits from locations outside the industrial zones to make their case in respect of particular sites. How effective this modification of the simple policy may be depends on local circumstances. If sites can be identified where no external costs arise, then clearly the case-by-case approach can be effective. The major problem, however, stems from the nature of a quantitative control in circumstances where uses impose external costs without paying compensation for them. In the absence of a compensation mechanism the planning authority is faced with a conflict between efficiency considerations, i.e. the benefits to the urban economy from letting the firm have a particular site and distributional arguments, based on the uncompensated costs of allowing them to do so. This conflict may be removed by suitable compensation arrangements or it may be reduced by setting conditions on the use of the site concerned which limit the external effects the use may give rise to. In principle, a compensation system would be the more flexible since it would eliminate the distributional issue entirely, i.e. allow a firm to use any location where the benefits to it outweighed the costs it imposed on others.

The problem considered so far is the 'New Town' problem where a layout can be determined from the outset – problems of change have been assumed away. Within established urban areas, particularly the larger metropolitan areas, a series of issues concerning the location of jobs arise, which we will take in turn.

A first, relatively small-scale problem is that of non-conforming uses. A number of planning authorities, when they initially prepared development plans, zoned areas for residential or commercial uses which contained other sorts of uses, which were considered to be unsuitable in those areas. In some cases, such non-conforming uses were brought out and moved elsewhere, but limits of finance have meant that such policies have usually not gone very far. Recently, however, the nature of the issues involved in these policies has come to be recognised. Essentially they are those sketched out in the analysis in the preceding paragraphs which suggest that while such a policy may produce benefits, it may also impose costs, for the following reasons.

First, if firms are forced to move, then they may have to meet extra costs, such as higher rents, themselves. Second, their change of location may give rise to extra costs to users who have to travel further to obtain similar services. For example, they might be 'odd-jobbing' firms, providing services from low-value properties of a highly specialised kind or of a familiar kind but in a particularly convenient location, for many people. Third, although such activities might be considered to give rise to some external costs, they also give rise to external benefits; what is intrusive to one might simply lend variety to another, or give a feeling of community or activity. What is intrusive in a new area may not be so in an older area. Fourth, such movement may lead to longer journeys to work and possibly loss of jobs to local people. Taken together, these points suggest that in particular cases the costs of such a policy may be too high and hence that, if policy measures are available which deal with the environmental nuisance directly, more efficient policies may exist.

The problem posed by non-conforming uses links with a more general problem facing the larger metropolitan areas in most advanced countries, that of the loss of jobs in or near the urban core, particularly in manufacturing. Where areas are redeveloped, non-conforming uses may not be allowed to return or can only do so if they pay higher rents, which they may not be able to afford. This may lead to loss of jobs when the firms go out of business. The issues here are complex.

If such activities continued to exist, then this might be taken to indicate that no other private uses valued the sites concerned very highly. If a planning authority decides to replace them it must find a use, e.g. an open space, which, being a public good, would not yield a financial return, but whose social return might be considered greater than the social return under industrial use. The issue here is whether the office worker or the local resident values a pleasant view and some open space more than he does the accessibility of some specialist services and the local availability of jobs.

Suppose, however, that other private users would pay more for the sites so that when redevelopment takes place, they would be prepared to pay a higher rent to use them. This can be regarded as an improvement in the use of the land resource, since if a use does not earn its keep, there is a case for it being replaced. The particular jobs in the firms concerned may be lost but the labour involved will tend to get redeployed into other uses, even if the particular firms concerned go out of business. The price of resisting changes of this sort is an overall level of reduced efficiency in the use of land, and possibly of other resources also (i.e. if the fact that a higher rent can be paid reflects greater efficiency in the use of labour). The fact that other uses can support a higher rent of itself suggests that they do give greater benefits. This account ignores two points, first, the jobs removed by redevelopment may have created greater external benefits or fewer external costs than the new jobs. If such extra benefits did exist, they would not be reflected in the amount of rent which the firms involved were able to pay. *A priori*, however, there are no grounds for assuming that external benefits would be reduced by a change of use. They may well increase. That could only be decided in the light of the facts of a particular case. Second, it ignores distributional considerations. The jobs which are lost in a particular locality, and the resultant unemployment, may affect people in that area particularly seriously. The new uses moving in may mean that local people may have to pay more or travel further for some goods and services. But the employment effects may not simply be distributional, if the result of job loss is that the number of unemployed rises as a result, i.e. the total efficiency of the urban economy may decline. This leads us to the more general issue of job decline in the older parts of urban areas which results from many factors. Partly it is a question of out-of-date premises, partly a question of changes in the relative costs of different locations, partly it is a question of changes in the economy as a whole.

These changes may be considered within the conditions of the simple urban model and the problems which arise may be analysed in terms of divergence from them. The process going on in the economy at large and within major cities reflects changes in the structure of demand for labour. If labour and the price of labour were perfectly responsive to these changes, then the new demands for labour would bid away labour from the existing uses, and if these users felt that peripheral locations were more economic for them, they would move to them and attract labour on those sites. In these ways the overall level of efficiency of the urban economy would rise because the new employers of labour were prepared to pay more for it and the manufacturers and others changing location could produce at lower overall cost at those locations. The enjoyment of private goods would rise. In what ways might these processes be undesirable?

First, the locational decisions made by firms might not be made in full knowledge of the relative social costs. Firms do not generally have to meet in full the costs they impose on workers when they reduce their labour force. Second, these adjustment costs may in some cases be considerable and be uncompensated. Third, if the labour market is not working as perfectly as we have assumed above, then labour resources may not be redeployed immediately. These imperfections may arise: (a) from barriers to spatial mobility within the housing stock; (b) from barriers to occupational mobility; (c) from factors outside the labour market narrowly defined, e.g. social ties. Fourth, the locational decisions of the firms may be made in the light of incorrect information on the relative advantages of different sites. The relevant points here are similar to those made on urban renewal decisions in section 11.2. Because infrastructure and other services may be incorrectly priced, the advantages of new locations may be overstated. For all these reasons, we need not accept, simply because changes in location are taking place, that the private and social benefits are identical. There are *prima facie* grounds for intervention, the nature of which will depend on the factor, or factors, which suggest that the observed movements are not necessarily desirable, and on the powers which the planning authority has.

The analysis of Chapter 6 would suggest one approach, i.e. a system of taxes, subsidies and compensation payments which would bring the private and social costs into line. Whether or not such policies are appropriate depends on the precise analysis of the situation. The mere fact of unemployment would not itself be sufficient, since this might arise for reasons unconnected with a long-term divergence between the private and social costs facing firms. It may be that the divergence between private and social cost derives from speed of change. If the processes of adjustment only have a certain capacity, then very large changes in job structure may lead to severe costs for the individuals because it takes time to find other jobs, and for others indirectly affected, e.g. shopkeepers and other suppliers of services, including the public sector itself. Alternatively, the existing adjustment processes, e.g. housing mobility, may need to be improved to increase the ability of the urban economy to absorb change.

If the problem results from a serious and persistent divergence between the private costs taken into account by firms and the total social costs of their actions, then a permanent subsidy or tax policy would be justified, which would balance, following the analysis above, the benefits of increased productivity in the firms themselves, with the costs suffered by the community at large from the changes resulting from the measures taken to increase productivity. A fiscal régime of this kind may not be feasible. But while quantitative controls may be available, they are unlikely to be effective in the present context, for the reasons analysed in Chapter 10. There it was pointed out that these were only likely to bite in certain demand conditions, i.e. where pressures on particular locations were intense and the alternatives open to firms few. If this is correct, and if a fiscal régime is unavailable, then the main objective of policy must be to increase the capacity of the urban economy to adapt to the changes occurring in it. That is, if the economy cannot be centrally managed because of inadequate policy instruments, then the right course is to increase the effectiveness of the individual decision-taking units within it in reacting to the changes taking place.

13.3 Fiscal Measures and Spatial Policies: An Example

There are many examples of financial incentives being offered to encourage employment in particular parts of a national economy, both in the UK and elsewhere. These may be used in conjunction with quantitative controls: for example, manufacturing industry in the UK must obtain an industrial development certificate before it can expand production capacity outside the assisted areas, while if it does choose to expand within an assisted area, it will receive financial assistance to do so. In the urban context, quantitative controls are the rule and financial measures relatively rare. The recent report of the Panel of Enquiry on the Greater London Development Plan suggested, however, that there was a case for imposing a tax on central London employers in order to influence their locational decisions, on the grounds that there was strong *prima facie* evidence that the private costs met by employers in London were below the social costs of their being there. The implication was drawn that the reductions in central area employment already noted might be taking place at too slow a rate and ought to be encouraged by a tax which brought home to employers the full social costs of their central location.

The Panel argued that there were two major reasons why the social costs of central area locations were above the private costs. First, for virtually all transport services provided in the capital, the revenue paid by users failed to cover current operating costs. In the case of private transport it fell below social cost because of the failure to charge adequately for congestion. Second, housing in London, as elsewhere, is provided below cost, particularly in the public sector. These subsidies come from central government, hence the costs are not borne even indirectly, e.g. through local taxes, by the local population. The implication was drawn, therefore, that London employers got their labour 'on the cheap'. Put formally, the marginal private cost of labour was below its marginal social cost. They accepted that it would be difficult to remove these elements of subsidy within the sector they occurred. Hence the best way of attempting to remove the divergence between social and private cost lay in imposing a tax on employers, particularly since the bulk of transport congestion occurs at peak hours, during the journey to work.

This section does not aim to provide a full critique of this proposal, partly because that would involve a detailed examination of the precise way in which such a tax would be levied and the administrative complexities of these alternatives, and partly because circumstances have changed since the Report appeared. However, it is worthwhile looking at it in some detail to bring out some general issues which are relevant to the use of fiscal policies in general. The first point to note is that the case for imposing a tax is identical to that considered in Chapter 6. The logic of the proposal is, therefore, in line with the basic analysis of that chapter. There are three points of difficulty arising from the practical application of that analysis. These are:

(a) the problems resulting from correcting only one divergence between private and social cost when several exist;
(b) the problem of using a tax measure in conjunction with quantitative controls;
(c) the problem of being forced to remove the divergence between marginal and social cost indirectly.

Let us look at these points in turn.

In Chapter 7 it was argued that if divergences between private and social costs could be corrected by fiscal or other means, then the consequences could be left to work themselves out in the manner of the simple urban model of Chapter 3. But if there exists more than one divergence between social and private cost, then there can be no presumption that the removal of one of these will lead to an improvement in social welfare. This means that the only way in which to test whether or not an increase in welfare is likely to result is to trace through the expected effects of the policy measure concerned to see if it does in fact lead to an improvement. To take one example, in the field of transport it is generally assumed that there exist divergences between marginal and social costs on most urban roads at peak times, not only on routes leading to the centre. Furthermore, empirical observation has shown that, when jobs decentralise, a switch tends to take place in modal split, in favour of private transport. If this involves, as it frequently does, a switch to car, then the total divergence between private and social costs could increase. On the other hand, if it involves, as it may do with decentralisation of small employment units, a switch to trips on foot, then total transport costs might fall, since walking trips rarely impede others. At the present time, there can be no general presumption that the introduction of 'correct' pricing in central area transport allied with changes in the location of jobs will improve total welfare; it may, or it may not. Only empirical evidence can decide the issue.

We saw in Chapter 7 how the imposition of a tax on a given land use would reduce the bid made by users of that land use and, as a result, it would tend to reduce its share of total land take. A tax on the use of land in a specific location would alter the locational decisions concerned. Users of the land taxed in this way would tend to prefer locations elsewhere, where they could avoid the burden of the tax, although some might hang on, if the advantages to them of that location were particularly great. However, the analysis runs rather differently if we assume that quantitative controls over land supply have been in operation at the same time, restricting the amount of space which that land use has in the area concerned. As we have seen in various places, particularly Chapter 7, the effect of such a restriction will be to raise the price of land under the rationed use, creating a special scarcity rent enjoyed by the owners. If a tax is imposed on that use, then its effect will be felt on those rents, provided that the tax is not large enough to remove the special scarcity element completely. Suppose, for example, that the use concerned yielded rents £5 per annum per square foot greater than other uses; then the tax would have to exceed this amount, before that use became relatively less profitable to supply and the volume of space devoted to it tended to decrease. In practice, of course, the course of events would not be quite so simple as this. If a tax were imposed suddenly, rents would not adjust immediately, so some existing users might be forced out. But when owners renegotiated leases, they would find themselves faced with would-be tenants who would have their extra tax payments in mind, so over time rent levels would be forced down. If the tax were severe enough to lead to a reduction in space offered to the use concerned, the speed of its adjustment would clearly depend on the specificity of the space. For example, in the short run office space is unlikely to be diverted to other uses. In the longer run, if the surplus persisted, it probably would be.

The final problem is similar to that we have considered elsewhere in the case of quantitative controls. If for some reason the tax measure cannot be related directly to the externality which justifies its imposition, there are dangers that its effects will be counter-productive. For example, if the tax is based on employment per head, or on the basis of payroll, then the uses which tend to replace those forced out will be those which use more space per person. These might show rooms or exhibition areas. Following the analysis of Chapter 10, they might employ few people, but they might conceivably generate more traffic than the original uses, through the visitors attracted, many possibly at peak times. Again, this is an empirical question. The general conclusion of this brief discussion is that the problem of estimating whether or not such a tax is likely to yield a net social benefit is very similar to that of estimating the value of a quantitative control over land use. There can be no general presumption that the effects of either will be beneficial. That can only be estimated by considering the effects on the urban economy which in practice are likely to ensue.

BIBLIOGRAPHY

The economic ideas used in this book are set out in innumerable economic texts. Few of these consider cases of direct relevance to land-use planning. But they are particularly relevant to Chapter 2 as this concentrates on setting down the basic economic ideas underlying the later analysis. Some general references are given below for that chapter. With these exceptions the bibliography which follows concentrates on references which are closely related to land-use planning and to developments in analysis, such as urban rent theory, particularly relevant to it.

Chapter 1

As this chapter notes, the number of economists who have explicitly concerned themselves with land-use planning is fairly small. Foster (28), Evans (24), Stewart (75, 76) are some recent articles which discuss the significance of economic analysis to land-use planning. The books by Lichfield (45) and Lean (42) are dated and do not discuss in depth the reasons for intervention in land markets nor its likely effects. General urban economics texts such as Thompson (77), Goodall (30) and Button (12) and texts on land economics such as Listokin (48) and Andrews (2) are useful although they do not consider at length the problems with which this book is concerned. Culyer (15), although dealing with a different field may also be useful since it too starts from some basic economic principles and goes on to examine their application to a field where they have been little applied.

Chapter 2

As noted above, there are innumerable texts which set out the ideas underlying this chapter. Any selection must be fairly arbitrary. Some useful general texts are Lipsey (47), Laidler (39), Fellner (26), Henderson & Quandt (36), Leftwich (43) and Morgan (60). A more specialised reference dealing with consumer theory is Green (31). The exposition in this and subsequent chapters falls within the neo-classical orthodoxy. For an alternative view of its usefulness see Hunt & Schwartz (37).

Chapter 3

The framework presented as the simple urban model is developed in a large number of texts and articles. At a theoretical level, Evans (23) provides a clear and rigorous account and illustrates it with empirical material. Some other primarily theoretical texts are Alonso (1), Getz (29), Grether & Mieszkowski (32), Muth (61) and Wingo (78). In addition, there is a large amount of empirical work carried out within this general framework. Some examples are Averous (5), Best (9), Richardson (67) and Soot (73).

Chapter 4

The reasons for intervention in market behaviour are listed and analysed in a large number of texts. Foster (28) considers them in relation to land markets. A number of the basic ideas go back as far as Marshall (53) and Pigou (63). More recently the notion of externality and its implication for public policy has attracted a great deal of analytic attention within theoretical welfare economics and within the environmental field. Some examples of the former literature are Mishan (67, 68) and Bohm (10), and of the latter, Baumol & Oates (8), Mishan (58, 59) and Staaf & Tannian (74).

The way in which land markets may behave in the absence of planning is discussed in Madden (51) and Siegan (72).

Chapter 5

The ideas underlying this chapter are explicit in any of the texts on welfare economics already cited. This chapter avoids the issue of how individuals' preferences should be related to collective choice. Baumol (7), Mayston (55) and Sen (71) are useful references on this problem. The text of this chapter does not explore very far the distinction between efficiency and distributional effects, nor does it discuss the various texts developed within welfare economics to detect whether or not a given change is worthwhile. These can be followed up by reference to Mishan (58, 59), Pearce (62) and Dasgupta & Pearce (15).

For an alternative view to the rational model see Braybrooke & Lindblom (11) and Lindblom (46).

Chapter 6

The literature of welfare economics going back to Pigou has been concerned with the policy instrument relevant to the problems of market failure, particularly the use of taxes or subsidies to remove divergences between private and social cost. But for detailed comparison of alternative policy instruments, the literature of the applied fields is perhaps most useful. There is for example a large transport literature dealing with the case for pricing and regulatory measures – see for example (57). Equally, the environmental literature already cited is relevant.

The Land Compensation Act (40) embodies recent UK policy towards compensation for external effects, and Delafons (18) gives a useful account of the use of private covenants in the United States.

Chapter 7

Most of the analysis of this chapter develops the earlier sections and it requires few references of its own. Particularly relevant however is some of the American literature on the effects of zoning, such as Babcoke (6), Davis (17) and Reuter (68). The question of the incidence of the property tax, touched on lightly in this chapter, has attracted a large literature – see for example Grieson (33).

Chapter 8

The consumer surplus criterion described in a large number of books on cost-benefit analysis, of which two recent examples are Mishan (59) and Pearce (62) together with the collection of articles in Layard (41). Examples of standards being set regardless of their consequences are in DOE (20). Forbes (28) contains articles by Evans (24) and Lever (44) which discuss particular standards.

Chapter 9

The pricing policies to be pursued by public enterprises have attracted a large literature. Three recent general references are Millward (56), Reed (64) and Rees (66). An article by Archer (3) is particularly relevant to this chapter as it is concerned with the effects of pricing failures by suppliers of infrastructure.

Chapter 10

There is a large literature on the urban economy – see the texts on urban economics already cited. But most of this is not concerned with the effects of planning policies. However the environmental literature already referred to is highly relevant since it considers, among other things, the impact of controls and fiscal régimes on economic activity. More immediately relevant to the analysis of the chapter is Rees (65) on the urban labour market, Marriott (52) and Savage (70) on office supply and Kasper (38) on the effects of housing policies on the labour market. See DOE (20) for comments on the efficiency of planning controls in influencing the labour market. The account of plot-ratio control is based on Evans (24).

Chapter 11

There is of course a large literature on the economics of housing but not much of it is devoted to the relation between land-use control and the supply of housing. There are a number of American studies however such as Sagalyn (69) which examine the effects on housing costs of zoning regulations. Also relevant is Crouch & Weintraub (13) which examines the economics of densities higher than current US average experience and Davis (16). Elkin's study (22) of a particular large London public housing project brings out the absence of clear criteria for the determination of density. See also Lever (44), Lustig (49) and Zetter (79).

Chapter 12

The analysis on which the chapter is based is described in more detail in Harrison (34). This contains an extensive bibliography. For another general transport reference see Heggie (35).

Chapter 13

There is a large amount of literature on the problems of arrangement, much of it design or architecturally orientated. It shows little awareness of the issues discussed in this chapter. There is an economics literature concerned with the spatial arrangement of small-scale enterprises; see Davis (17). In addition, there is a literature based on a number of disciplines concerned with urban locational issues. Examples are Austin (4), Easton (22), Kasper (38), Lustig & Pack (49), Massam (54), Feldman (25) and McGlynn (50).

1 Alonso, W. *Location and Land Use*. Cambridge, Harvard University Press, 1969.
2 Andrews, R.B. (ed.) *Urban Land Use Policy: the Central City*. New York, The Free Press, 1972.
3 Archer, R.W. 'Land Speculation and Scattered Development: Failures in the Urban Fringe Land Market.' *Urban Studies*, October 1973, Vol. 10, pp. 367-72.
4 Austin, C.M. 'The Evaluation of Urban Public Facility Location: An Alternative to Benefit Cost Analysis.' *Geographical Analysis*, 1974, Vol. VI, April, pp. 136-45.
5 Averous, C.P. and Lee, D.B. (Jr.) 'Land Allocation and Transportation Pricing in a Mixed Urban Economy.' *Journal of Regional Science*, 1973, Vol. 13, August, pp. 173-85.

6 Babcoke, R.F. and Bosselman, F.P. *Exclusionary Zoning*. New York, 1973.
7 Baumol, W.J. *Welfare Economics and the Theory of the State*. 2nd ed. Cambridge, Mass., Harvard University Press, 1965.
8 Baumol, W.J. and Oates, W.E. *The Theory of Environmental Policy*. New Jersey, Englewood Cliffs, Prentice-Hall, 1975.
9 Best, R.H. *et al*. 'The Density Size Rule.' *Urban Studies*, 1974, Vol. 11, June, pp. 201-7.
10 Bohm, Peter. *Social Efficiency: A Concise Introduction to Welfare Economics*. London, Macmillan, 1973.
11 Braybrooke, David and Lindblom, Charles E. *A Strategy of Decision: Policy Evaluation as a Social Process*. London, Collier-Macmillan, 1963.
12 Button, K.J. *Urban Economics*. London, Macmillan, 1976.
13 Crouch, R.L. and Weintraub, R.E. 'Cost Benefit Analysis of a PUD (Planned Unit Development).' *Urban Land*, 1973, Vol. 32, June, pp. 3-13.
14 Culyer, A.J. *The Economics of Social Policy*. London, Martin Robertson, 1973.
15 Dasgupta, A.K. and Pearce, D.W. *Cost Benefit Analysis: Theory and Practice*. London, Macmillan, 1972.
16 Davis, O.A. 'Economic Elements in Municipal Zoning Decisions.' *Land Economics*, 1963, Vol. 39, pp. 375-86.
17 Davis, O. 'A Dynamic Hotelling-type Model.' *Environment and Planning A*, 1975, Vol. 7, pp. 153-62.
18 Delafons, J. *Land-Use Controls in the United States*, 2nd ed. Cambridge, Mass., MIT, 1961.
19 Department of the Environment. *Greater London Development Plan: Report of the Panel of Inquiry*. 2 vols. London, HMSO, 1973.
20 Department of the Environment. *The Value of Standards for the External Residential Environment*. Prepared by George Woodford, Kirstine Williams, Nancy Hill. Research Report 6, Department of the Environment, 1976.
21 Easton, R.V. 'Entropy Maximisation, and Inferred Ideal Weights in Public Facility Location.' *Environment and Planning A*, 1975, Vol. 7, pp. 191-8.
22 Elkin, S.L. *Politics and Land Use Planning: The London Experience*. London, Cambridge University Press, 1974.
23 Evans, A.W. *The Economics of Residential Location*. London, Macmillan, 1973.
24 Evans, A.W. 'Town Planning as Applied Welfare Economics.' *Urban*

Studies, Working Paper 2, Department of Social and Economic Research, University of Glasgow, n.d.
25 Feldman, S. and Gonen, A. 'The Spatiotemporal Pricing of Some Urban Public Services: Urban Ecology, Equity and Efficiency.' *Environment Planning A*, 1975, Vol. 7, pp. 315-23.
26 Fellner, W. *Emergence and Content of Modern Economic Analysis*. New York, McGraw-Hill, 1960.
27 Forbes, J. (ed.) *Studies in Social Science and Planning*. Edinburgh, Scottish Academic Press, 1974.
28 Foster C.D. *Planning and the Market*. In P. Cowan, *The Future of Planning*, London, Heinemann, 1973.
29 Getz, M. 'A Model of the Impact of Transportation Investment on Land Rents.' *Journal of Public Economics*, 1975, Vol. 4, February, pp. 57-72.
30 Goodall, B. *The Economics of Urban Areas*. Oxford, Pergamon, 1972.
31 Green, H.A. John. *Consumer Theory*. London, Penguin Books, 1971.
32 Grether, D.M., and Mieszkowski, P. 'Determinants of Real Estate Values.' *Journal of Urban Economics*, 1974, Vol. 1, April, pp. 127-46.
33 Grieson, R.E. 'The Economics of Property Taxes and Land Values: The Elasticity of Supply of Structure.' *Journal of Urban Economics*, 1974, Vol. 1, July, pp. 367-81.
34 Harrison, A.J. *Economics of Transport Appraisal*. London, Croom Helm, 1974.
35 Heggie, Ian G. *Transport Engineering Economics*. London, McGraw-Hill, 1972.
36 Henderson, J.M. and Quanot, R.E. *Micro-Economic Theory*. New York, McGraw-Hill, 1958.
37 Hunt, E.K. and Schwartz, J.G. *A Critique of Economic Theory*. Harmondsworth, Penguin, 1972.
38 Kasper, H. 'Measuring the Labour Market Costs of Housing Dislocation.' *Scottish Journal of Political Economy*, 1973, Vol. XX, June, pp. 85-106.
39 Laidler, David. *Introduction to Micro-Economics*. Oxford, Allan Publishers, 1974.
40 Land Compensation Act 1973. London, HMSO, 1973.
41 Layard, Richard (ed.) *Cost Benefit Analysis*. London, Penguin Books, 1972.
42 Lean, W. 'Economics of Land Use Planning: Urban and Regional.' London, *The Estates Gazette*, 1969.

43 Leftwich, R.H. *The Price System and Resource Allocation*. Illinois, Dryden Press, Minsdale, 1973.

44 Lever, W.F. 'Planning Standards and Residential Densities.' *Journal of the Royal Town Planning Institute*, 1971, Vol. 57, November, pp. 400-3.

45 Lichfield, N. 'Economics of Planned Development.' London, *The Estates Gazette*, 1966.

46 Lindblom, Charles E. 'The Science of Muddling Through.' *Public Administration Review*, 1959, Vol. 19, Spring, pp. 79-88.

47 Lipsey, R.G. *An Introduction to Positive Economics*. London, Weidenfeld and Nicolson, 1963, reprinted 1973.

48 Listokin, David (ed.) *Land Use Controls: Present Problems and Future Reform*. Centre for Urban Policy Research, New Jersey, Rutgers University, 1974.

49 Lustig, M. and Pack, J.R. 'A Standard for Residential Zoning Based Upon Location of Jobs.' *Journal of the American Institute of Planners*, 1974, Vol. 40, September, pp. 333-45.

50 McGlynn, N.F. *et al*. 'Operational Research in the Planning of Employment Services in Large Cities.' *Management Services in Government*, November 1974, pp. 199-209.

51 Madden, D.M. 'Houston Finds Security in a Policy of No-Zoning.' *Planning – The ASP O Magazine*, January 1973, pp. 22-7.

52 Marriott, O. *The Property Boom*. London, Hamish Hamilton, 1967.

53 Marshall, A. *Principles of Economics*. London, Macmillan, 1969.

54 Massam, B. *Location and Space in Social Administration*. London, Edward Arnold, 1975.

55 Mayston, David J. *The Idea of Social Choice*. New York, St Martin's Press, 1975.

56 Millward, Robert. *Public Expenditure Economics: An Introductory Application of Welfare Economics*. London, McGraw-Hill, 1971.

57 Ministry of Transport. *Road Pricing: Economic and Technical Possibilities*. Report of a Panel set up by the Ministry of Transport, London, HMSO, 1964.

58 Mishan, E.J. *Cost-Benefit Analysis: An Informal Introduction*. London, Allen and Unwin, 1971.

59 Mishan, E.J. *Elements of Cost-Benefit Analysis*. London, Allen and Unwin, 1972.

60 Morgan, E.V. and A.D. *The Economics of Public Policy*. Edinburgh, The University Press, 1971.

61 Muth, R.F. *Cities and Housing*. Chicago, University of Chicago Press, 1969.

62 Pearce, D.W. *Cost-Benefit Analysis*. London, Macmillan, 1971.
63 Pigou, A.C. *Economics of Welfare*. London, Macmillan, 1960.
64 Reed, P.W. *The Economics of Public Enterprise*. London, Butterworth, 1973.
65 Rees, A. and Schultz, G.P. *Workers and Wages in an Urban Labour Market*. London, University of Chicago Press, 1970.
66 Rees, R. *Public Enterprise Economics*. London, Weidenfeld and Nicolson, 1976.
67 Richardson, H.W. *et al*. 'Determinants of Urban House Prices.' *Urban Studies*, 1974, Vol. 11, June, pp. 189-200.
68 Reuter, F.H. 'Externalities in Urban Property Markets: An Empirical Test of the Zoning Ordinance of Pittsburgh.' *Journal of Law and Economics*, 1973, October, pp. 313-49.
69 Sagalyn, L.G. and Sternlieb, G. *Zoning and Housing Costs: The Impact of Land Use Controls on Housing Price*. New Brunswick Centre for Urban Policy Research, Rutgers University, 1975.
70 Savage, E. 'Some Effects of Floor-Space Ratio and Bonus Regulations on Rates of Return: A Case Study for Sydney CBD.' *Environment and Planning B*, 1974, Vol. 1, pp. 147-64.
71 Sen, A.K. *Collective Choice and Social Welfare*. London, Holden-Day, 1970.
72 Siegan, B.H. *Land Use Without Zoning*. Lexington, D.C. Heath, 1972.
73 Soot, S. 'Transportation Costs and Urban Land Rent Theory: The Milwaukee Example.' *Land Economics*, 1974, Vol. 50, May, pp. 193-6.
74 Staaf, R.J. and Tannian, F.X. (eds.) *Externalities: Theoretical Dimensions of Political Economy*. New York, Dunellen Publishing, 1973.
75 Stewart, J.M.W. 'Markets, Choice and Urban Planning.' *Town Planning Review*, 1973, Vol. 44, No. 3, pp. 203-20.
76 Stewart, J.M.W. 'Market Strategy: A Constructive Approach.' *The Planner*, 1974, Vol. 60, September/October, pp. 827-9.
77 Thompson, W.R. *A Preface to Urban Economics*, Baltimore, Johns Hopkins, 1968.
78 Wingo, Lowdon. *Transportation and Urban Land*. Washington, Resources for the Future, 1961.
79 Zetter, R. 'Planning Control and the Quality of Residential Environments.' *Journal of Planning and Environment Law*, 1974, September, pp. 515-28.

INDEX

For Product Safety Concerns and Information please contact our EU representative GPSR@taylorandfrancis.com
Taylor & Francis Verlag GmbH, Kaufingerstraße 24, 80331 München, Germany

www.ingramcontent.com/pod-product-compliance
Ingram Content Group UK Ltd.
Pitfield, Milton Keynes, MK11 3LW, UK
UKHW011000180926
475701UK00004B/487

* 9 7 8 1 1 3 8 0 8 3 8 8 2 *